Stamatia Devetzi (Ed.)

PRACTICAL ISSUES OF EUROPEAN SOCIAL SECURITY LAW

A DIALOGUE BETWEEN ACADEMIA AND PRACTITIONERS

**AN INTERDISCIPLINARY SERIES
OF THE CENTRE FOR INTERCULTURAL AND EUROPEAN STUDIES**

INTERDISZIPLINÄRE SCHRIFTENREIHE
DES CENTRUMS FÜR INTERKULTURELLE UND EUROPÄISCHE STUDIEN

CINTEUS • Fulda University of Applied Sciences • Hochschule Fulda

ISSN 1865-2255

17 Hans-Wolfgang Platzer
    Bronislaw Huberman und das Vaterland Europa
    Ein Violinvirtuose als Vordenker der europäischen
    Einigungsbewegung in den 1920er und 1930er Jahren
    ISBN 978-3-8382-1354-5

18 Aileen Heid
    Erinnerungspolitik
    Nordirlands langer Weg zum Frieden
    ISBN 978-3-8382-1351-4

19 Juliana Damm, Maren Mlynek
    Die AfD und Geflüchtete
    Was rechte Ideologie gesellschaftlich bewirkt
    ISBN 978-3-8382-1448-1

20 Julian Wessendorf
    Euroskeptizismus auf dem Vormarsch
    Positionen der politischen Rechten im
    Europaparlament
    ISBN 978-3-8382-1557-0

21 Kirsten Nazarkiewicz, Norbert Schröer (Hrsg.)
    Verständigung in pluralen Welten
    ISBN 978-3-8382-1345-3

22 Stamatia Devetzi (Ed.)
    Practical issues of European Social Security Law: A Dialogue
    between Academia and Practitioners
    ISBN 978-3-8382-1706-2

Series Editors

Volker Hinnenkamp
Gudrun Hentges
Anne Honer †
Hans-Wolfgang Platzer

Stamatia Devetzi (Ed.)

PRACTICAL ISSUES OF EUROPEAN SOCIAL SECURITY LAW

A DIALOGUE BETWEEN ACADEMIA AND PRACTITIONERS

Bibliografische Information der Deutschen Nationalbibliothek
Die Deutsche Nationalbibliothek verzeichnet diese Publikation in der Deutschen Nationalbibliografie; detaillierte bibliografische Daten sind im Internet über http://dnb.d-nb.de abrufbar.

Bibliographic information published by the Deutsche Nationalbibliothek
Die Deutsche Nationalbibliothek lists this publication in the Deutsche Nationalbibliografie; detailed bibliographic data are available in the Internet at http://dnb.d-nb.de.

ISBN-13: 978-3-8382-1706-2
© *ibidem*-Verlag, Stuttgart 2022
Alle Rechte vorbehalten

Das Werk einschließlich aller seiner Teile ist urheberrechtlich geschützt. Jede Verwertung außerhalb der engen Grenzen des Urheberrechtsgesetzes ist ohne Zustimmung des Verlages unzulässig und strafbar. Dies gilt insbesondere für Vervielfältigungen, Übersetzungen, Mikroverfilmungen und elektronische Speicherformen sowie die Einspeicherung und Verarbeitung in elektronischen Systemen.

All rights reserved. No part of this publication may be reproduced, stored in or introduced into a retrieval system, or transmitted, in any form, or by any means (electronical, mechanical, photocopying, recording or otherwise) without the prior written permission of the publisher. Any person who does any unauthorized act in relation to this publication may be liable to criminal prosecution and civil claims for damages.

Printed in the EU

Acknowledgments

In June 2021 a conference was organised in Fulda. Due to the ongoing pandemic the conference took place virtually. A small number of experienced practitioners, researchers and university teachers gathered to discuss European social security law from different perspectives.

The conference took place thanks to the financial support of DAAD (German Academic Exchange Service) and was part of a bilateral university partnership between Fulda and Thessaloniki with a research and teaching project in the field of social security coordination and migration (www.sosec.eu). We are very thankful for their generous support. We would also like to thank the authors who have contributed their chapters to this book for their commitment to the topic as well as the vivid and inspiring discussions during the conference.

The book would not have been possible without the commitment and organisational skills of the coordinator of the project, Effrosyni Bakirtzi.

A special thanks goes to our language editor, Niki Rodousakis, for her quick, thorough and careful editing of our chapters – thank you very much! We are also very grateful to our colleague, Volker Hinnenkamp, who has taken on the editorial work of making this volume ready for printing.

Fulda, March 2022   Stamatia Devetzi

Contents

1. Stamatia Devetzi
   Introduction 9

2. Eberhard Eichenhofer
   Transnational Rights in the EU – Social Security Law 19

3. Moira Kettner
   Practical Questions that Arise from the Implementation of Regulation 883/2004 on the Coordination of Social Security Systems – Perspectives from the German Ministry 37

4. Anna Rizou
   Practical Questions Arising from the Implementation of Regulation 883/2004 on the Coordination of Social Security Systems 47

5. Linda Bojanowski
   Unplanned Medical Treatment in Another Member State – Using the EHIC. Current Insights from the German Liaison Agency Health Insurance – International 59

6. Stefanie Klein
   Practical Issues in the Context of Implementing Social Security Coordination Regulation (EC) No. 883/2004 from the Perspective of the German Social Accident Insurance 71

7. Daniel Hlava
   Social Security of Posted Workers and Platform Workers – Selected Challenges 81

8. Effrosyni Bakirtzi
   Realigning the Relationship between Social Security Coordination and the Digitalisation of Work 99

9. Anna Tsetoura
   Recent Case Law on the Coordination of Social Security Systems under Regulation 883/2004 127

10. Angelos Stergiou
    Coordination as a Common Language for Social Security and as a Basis for European Solidarity 203

List of Contributors 211

1 Introduction

Stamatia Devetzi

European social security law – or social security coordination law – has been evolving for over 60 years. In fact, Regulations Nos 3 and 4 of 1958[1] concerning the social security of migrant workers were among the earliest EEC regulations.[2] These two Regulations were replaced by Regulation (EEC) 1408/71[3] and later by Reg. (EC) 883/2004.[4]

The legal basis for the coordination rules in the sphere of social security is the freedom of movement of workers, one of the founding principles of (initially) the EEC and now the EU. The purpose of social security coordination is set out in Art. 48 TFEU. Guaranteeing the right to social security when the right to freedom of movement is exercised has been one of the EU's major priorities. To achieve this, social security measures were adopted that prevent EU citizens who work and reside in a Member State other than their own from losing their acquired social security rights.

In a nutshell, social security coordination law can be described as the sum of all legal provisions, rules and principles that aim to remove social security bar-

---

[1] Regulation (EEC) 3/58, OJ 30, 16.12.1958, p. 561–596 and its implementing Regulation 4/58 of 3 December 1958, OJ 30, which entered into force on 1 January 1959.
[2] Regulations (EEC) 1 and 2 dealt with the use of language and the form of *laisser passer* to the Members of the European Parliament, respectively.
[3] Regulation (EEC) No. 1408/71 of the Council of 14 June 1971 on the application of social security schemes to employed persons and their families moving within the Community, OJ L 149, 05.07.1971, pp. 2-50.
[4] Regulation (EC) No. 883/2004 of the European Parliament and of the Council of 29 April 2004 on the coordination of social security systems, OJ L 166, 30.4.2004, p. 1–123.

riers that could prevent an individual from exercising his/her freedom of movement.[5] Coordination seeks to "deterritorialize" national social security law; it aims to "adjust social security schemes in relation to each other (...) in order to regulate transnational questions (..) and to protect the social rights of persons in case the facts of their circumstances are not limited to one State".[6] Coordination thus implies that the differences between national systems continue to remain in place in contrast to "harmonisation".

European social security law – the coordination of social security law – has been continuously evolving over the years. The purpose of coordination has shifted focus from the free movement of workers towards the free movement of *persons* – more specifically towards "persons who are or have been subject to the legislation of one or more Member States" – Art. 2 (1) Reg. 883/04.[7] The CJEU's judgements have played a key role in the development of coordination law; by ensuring a uniform interpretation of EU law in all Member States, the legal concepts the coordination mechanism is based on – and which national legislators might otherwise interpret very differently – can be consistently applied across the Union.

In recent years, new forms of employment and mobility have emerged and have rapidly spread across Europe. The concept of "migrant worker" might have been unambiguous in the 1960s to 1980s, as may have been the notion of "standard employment". Today, however, the workplace, movement between Member States as well as social security have become more "fluid": standard employment has in many cases been replaced by non-standard forms of work and new forms of self-employment. Examples include part-time work, on-demand work, platform work, bogus self-employment, etc.[8] "Fluidity" also implies changing trends in mobility: traditional long-term mobility, which implied moving from one's home Member State to another and working and living in

---

[5] Fuchs/ Cornelissen, Introduction, in: Fuchs/Cornelissen, EU Social Security Law, 2015, p. 11.
[6] Pennings, European Social Security Law, 2015, p. 7.
[7] "Nationals of a Member State, stateless persons and refugees residing in a Member State who are or have been subject to the legislation of one or more Member States, as well as the members of their families and their survivors".
[8] See, for more examples, Strban, Social Law 4.0 and the Future of Social Security Coordination in: Becker/Chesalina (Eds.), Social Law 4.0, 2021, p. 336.

that other Member State for a long(er) period of time, has been replaced or supplemented by multiple short-term movements to a different Member State.[9] Additionally, digitalisation is making it difficult to define "cross-border" work; in many cases, remote working or teleworking challenges the very idea of "crossing borders".

As regards "mobility" or mobility patterns, important aspects of coordination law that have been extensively and controversially discussed in recent years and include the posting of workers[10] and cross-border temporary work. The considerable amount of CJEU case law on these matters[11] implies that the debate on this topic continues to take place and that it remains contentious.

And last but not least: an unprecedented serious challenge – the COVID-19 pandemic – not only "forced" European Member States to take substantial steps to mitigate the economic and social impact of the health crisis; it also (initially) led to restrictions to the free movement of persons, to changes in work culture ("home office") and raised new questions about the applicable social security legislation to situations involving different Member States.

Taking these developments into account, the need to discuss the questions and challenges surrounding coordination law has emerged. Our aim was therefore to promote dialogue between practitioners and academia, focussing on issues that arise from the practical implementation of the Coordination Regulation. Many practical questions have already been addressed by existing case law: social security coordination law has always been put forward by preliminary rulings brought before the CJEU by national courts, i.e. the Court has provided answers to questions related to the implementation of the law. On the other hand, only few reports are available about how specific problems between different national social security institutions have been resolved, regardless of the cases brought before the CJEU. It is therefore crucial to examine the setting that unfolds when mobile persons' requests are contingent on the

---

[9] Strban, op cit, p. 339.
[10] For a detailed overview of discussions on postings from both a labour law and social security law perspective, see Bottero, Posting of workers in the EU - Challenges of Equality, Solidarity and Fair Competition, 2021.
[11] See the chapters of Hlava and Tsetoura in this publication.

administration of Member States' social security institutions and their interactions and collaboration. In other words, examining how the law is being applied on a "daily basis" is essential.

This study is the outcome of a conference that was organised in June 2021. It took place virtually due to the ongoing pandemic. The conference brought together several scholars who discussed European social security law from different perspectives. Our discussion focussed on current issues and the challenges coordination law faces as well as problems that arise when the law is applied by different institutions. Beyond this "practical" focus, however, we also addressed the theoretical foundations, i.e. the "character" of coordination law.[12]

The first chapter of this publication reviews the legal character of EU social security law and the development of transnational rights. *Eberhard Eichenhofer* challenges the general assumption that coordination rules should be viewed separately from substantial national social security laws. He argues that coordination law is not a mere technical mechanism for determining the international dimension of social security. If that were true, then EU legislation would be irrelevant for the establishment of any social security entitlements. This is not the case, however. On the contrary: coordination law plays an important role in shaping "transnational social security rights". These rights are understood as entitlements based on EU law and arise from rights enshrined in Member States. This is illustrated by way of several examples from the Regulation itself, highlighting the character of transnational rights as international substantive rights, such as the equalisation of facts, the delivery of services outside the competent state or the accumulation of insurance periods. *Eichenhofer* demonstrates that coordination law is more than just a technical mechanism established by EU law, which lies beyond or above the Member States' social security legislation. In fact, coordination law creates genuine European social security rights by combining EU law with Member States' social security provisions. In other words, it creates transnational substantive entitlements by transforming national entitlements into transnational European ones.

---

[12] See the chapters of Eichenhofer and Stergiou in this publication.

The next two chapters discuss the practical implementation of the coordination regulations from a ministerial perspective. Two representatives of national ministries share their views on this matter: *Moira Kettner* from the German Federal Ministry of Labour and Social Affairs, and *Anna Rizou* from the Greek Ministry of Labour and Social Affairs.

Kettner acknowledges that ministerial authorities are in continuous contact with both the relevant (national) social security institutions as well as the competent authorities in other Member States. Such continuous communication allows for profound insights into the application of coordination law. *Kettner* divides practical challenges into two categories. The first category emerges as a consequence of sudden events that require immediate action. Social security coordination during the COVID-19 pandemic falls into this category: the pandemic called for urgent action because the usual coordination procedures and standards were no longer feasible. *Kettner* argues that the exceptional architecture of the coordination regulations and the reliable cooperation between Member States proved capable to deal with this extraordinary situation, despite the fact that not all problems related to cross-border social security could be successfully resolved, as the example of financial compensation for quarantine orders shows. The second category of practical challenges for coordination law evolves over time as a result of societal or legal changes. Examples include digitalisation, the increasing heterogeneity of EU Member States, changes in traditional family patterns or age structures within the EU or the creation of new social security branches such as long-term care. To cope with all of these challenges, regular revisions of the coordination regulations are indispensable.

Rizou presents practical issues the Greek ministry and the Greek competent institutions are dealing with. One of the biggest institutions, the Electronic National Social Security Fund, faces several challenges in terms of collecting the requested information due to the massive workload, on the one hand, and understaffing, on the other. The gathering of information on portable European A1 forms, in particular, is fraught with problems, as these forms have not yet been digitised. Digitalisation efforts are underway, yet the process is slow. *Rizou* then discusses other practical issues, such as questions of medical treatment abroad or the implementation of the EESSI system, an electronic system that connects social security institutions in EU Member States.[13] The long delays in the implementation of EESSI are considered particularly problematic.

The two chapters that follow provides insights into the application of EU social security law from another practical perspective, namely from the perspective of so-called "liaison bodies",[14] which can be considered the front line in "everyday" implementation of coordination law.

The perspective of the German Liaison Agency Health Insurance is discussed in *Linda Bojanowski's* contribution. She first describes an important practical instrument of coordination law, the European Health Insurance Card (EHIC), which verifies holders' entitlement to receive unplanned cross-border medical treatment in another Member State. The EHIC is symbolic for the EU's right to free movement. *Bojanowski* describes the EHIC's legal background and criticises some of its outdated methods (for example, German healthcare providers still use photocopiers to make a copy of the EHIC). Efforts are underway in the Member States and the EU to establish an electronic EHIC. Like *Rizou*, *Bojanowski* also claims that EU social security law is currently experiencing a genuine digitalisation push through the EESSI system.

Stefanie Klein addresses practical problems and questions from the perspective of the Liaison Body of the German Social Accident Insurance. In fact, it is not only a liaison body, but also an "institution of the place of residence or place of stay", which implies that it is the "administrative front line" for coordinating national rules on accidents at work and industrial diseases under Title III Chapter 2 Reg. (EC) 883/2004. Several practical issues arise in the coordination of accidents at work at EU level. She provides some examples: the applicable legislation has proven difficult in some cases, particularly when information on the employer or place of work is missing – or when the patient her-/himself is unable to provide the necessary information. In other cases, colliding (national)

---

[13] Including the EEA states and Switzerland.
[14] A "liaison body" is defined in Art. 1 b) Reg. (EC) No. 987/09 as any (administrative) body designated by the competent authority of a Member State for one or more of the branches of social security referred to in Art. 3 Reg. (EC) No. 883/04 to respond to requests for information and assistance for the purposes of the application of Reg. (EC) No. 883/04 and Reg. (EC) No. 987/09, and which fulfils the tasks assigned to it under Title IV of Reg. (EC) No. 987/09.

interpretations of the term "accident at work" are difficult to explain to persons who have suffered an accident. The case may also be that treatment of a special benefit in kind offered by the German Accident Insurance has to be abruptly terminated and transferred to another institution, which can cause serious medical and personal problems for the respective patient. *Klein* argues that the differences between the EU Member States' social security systems are still substantial;[15] however, these systems diverge even more when it comes to accidents at work, posing a continuous challenge for the administrative application of coordination rules – but also represent a success story when benefits in kind are successfully provided.

The following two chapters deal with two challenges of coordination law that have gained momentum in recent years: the posting of workers, on the one hand, and digitalisation of work – especially the phenomenon of platform work – on the other.

Daniel Hlava's chapter reviews the special challenges the posting of workers within the EU poses for coordination law. The question which social security system applies in the case of cross-border assignments of workers arises not only in the context of posting, but also in the context of temporary work. One major issue is the far-reaching binding effect of so-called A1 certificates. *Hlava* claims that EU-wide standards for the issuance of such certificates should be established in addition to a centralised electronic certificate application procedure. The retroactivity of A1 certificates also poses practical problems. *Hlava* discusses platform work and its implications for coordination law. He provides the examples of "gigwork" and "crowdwork" to highlight the difficulties in distinguishing between an employee and a self-employed person. This is relevant for such persons' access to social security. In the case of location-independent platform work, EU coordination rules could ease the practical difficulties crowdworkers who are active in two or more Member States face when determining where they are carrying out the substantial part of their employment or self-employment activity.

---

[15] In addition to the three EEA states and Switzerland.

Effrosyni Bakirtzi presents an overview of the impact of digitalisation on the world of work and explores the challenges it has created for the EU coordination system. She discusses two cases: the first case involves frontier and cross-border workers; the second case examines the situation of cross-border platform workers whose legal status is often unclear. She describes the extraordinary situation caused by the COVID-19 pandemic for the first case, namely cross-border and frontier workers, the pandemic's implications for their social security rights and the solutions found at EU level as well as in selected EU countries. Despite the extraordinary conditions triggered by the coronavirus, no substantial changes with regard to the applicable legislation were observed, partially because many countries relied on Art. 16 of Reg. 883/04. However, it will be interesting to observe whether the post-COVID era will bring permanent changes to the work organisation of such workers. The second case, namely cross-border platform work, is more complicated from a legal perspective. *Bakirtzi* first defines platform work and then discusses the divide between employee and self-employment status: distinct classifications of platform workers in different Member States might raise issues with regard to the coordination of social security systems. Another problem is the potentially marginal nature of platform work and its impact on the applicable legislation. She argues that in times of virtual mobility and transitions in working arrangements, the regulation on labour mobility and social security coordination must be aligned to close the gaps in social protection.

The CJEU is often confronted with questions regarding the practical problems of coordination law. *Anna Tsetoura's* chapter provides an overview of the CJEU's recent case law on the coordination of social security systems. Her research covers a 5-year period. She presents selected cases that address a wide range of issues from social security benefits (old-age, sickness, invalidity, family and unemployment benefits) to special non-contributory benefits, social security contributions and applicable legislation, including postings of workers and third-country nationals under Regulation 883/2004. She provides for a comprehensive assessment of these cases based on comparisons with previous cases brought before the Court. *Tsetoura* further argues that the Court's rulings offer efficient protection of social security rights that apply objective criteria which neither undermine the functionality of the coordination mechanism nor the financial balance of social security systems. However, the "problematic" situations that arise in connection with the posting of workers, as well as with certain phenomena of artificial arrangements are reflected in some judgements. Ultimately, the Court appears to be balancing the requirements of States' planning as far as their social security systems are concerned and the social security protection provided to those who make use of the freedom of movement.

In the final chapter, *Angelos Stergiou* describes coordination as a common language for social security and as a basis for European solidarity. As long as no common concept of social security exists in the EU, coordination seems to be playing the role of developing a common language between Member States. This is achieved, for example, by the development of common definitions: it is crucial for the legal concepts on which the coordination mechanism is based to be uniformly interpreted and applied across the EU. Moreover, coordination can – or should – also represent a common basis for European solidarity. According to *Stergiou*, coordination should not be limited to a purely technical role. On the contrary, it should become a mechanism for organising citizens' mutual solidarity based on an appropriate articulation of national social security systems to facilitate the free movement of European citizens. However, an extensive promotion of European citizenship has not yet occurred – especially because the borders are closed for those who do not have sufficient resources, ensuring that national welfare systems are not overburdened. He concludes that the more the idea of Europe recedes, the more coordination is entangled with national interests; the more the idea of Europe is promoted, the more coordination develops in a positive way.

References

Becker, Ulrich/Chesalina, Olga (eds), Social Law 4.0, New Approaches for Ensuring and Financing Social Security in the Digital Age, Baden-Baden, 2021.

Bottero, Matteo, Posting of Workers in EU Law: Challenges of Equality, Solidarity and Fair Competition, Alphen aan den Rijn, 2021.

Fuchs, Maximilian/Cornelissen, Rob, EU Social Security Law, Baden-Baden, 2015.

Pennings, Frans, European Social Security Law, Antwerp, 2015.

Strban, Grega, Social Law 4.9 and the Future of Social Security Coordination, in Becker, Ulrich/Chesalina, Olga (eds), Social Law 4.0, New Approaches for Ensuring and Financing Social Security in the Digital Age, Baden-Baden, 2021, pp. 335-361.

2 Transnational Rights in the EU – Social Security Law

Eberhard Eichenhofer

1 What are the aims of the coordination of social security law?

Social security law plays a crucial role in EU law. The European Economic Community's (EEC) first legal act of general application was ratified in Regulations Nos. 3/4 of 1958 and dealt with the coordination of social security law. Was this the hallmark of an emerging European social security policy? Most observers might disagree, but this starting point was truly more than just a symbolic gesture or mere window dressing for the emerging common or single market.

This first EEC legislation replaced regulations that had previously been established by international treaties. EEC coordination law introduced multilateral rules – originally agreed in bilateral agreements – and generalised provisions for more than just two states. Coordination law is widely understood as a technical mechanism for determining the international dimension of social security. Based on this assumption, it is not farfetched to conclude that these rules do not have a substantial impact on Member States' social security laws. According to doctrine, coordination rules are a class of their own and remain separate from substantial social security laws. While the former generally aim to establish applicable law, the latter are considered to be substantive law. This doctrine continues to prevail in the discourse on coordination law, which most scholars interpret as being a more technical and highly sophisticated, but second-rank legislation in terms of substance. The question about the function of coordination law is important, however, as it provides insights into the role of EU legislation in social security policy. If the assumption of the merely technical character of coordination law is correct, then EU legislation is irrelevant for the establishment of any social security entitlements.

This view misrepresents the function of coordination law and its significance for individual social security rights. A deeper look into specific social security coordination rules reveals the substantive and substantial function of social security coordination rules. The following section sheds light on the crucial role the coordination of EU social security law plays in shaping "transnational social security rights".

"Transnational social security rights" are understood as entitlements that are based on international or EU law and that arise from rights enshrined in the State. Such rights are not self-evident and contradict the traditional understanding of international and European law.

Traditionally, in a world subdivided into separate states, every individual is entitled to the rights provided for by the legal system of his or her State – namely the state they reside in or that they are most closely connected with. However, this assumption is contradicted by the fact that an individual can be subject to the rights of several states. This view is underpinned by the traditional perspective of the conflict of laws, namely the law on the applicable legislation, which is derived from the theory of Savigny and has thus been inherited from the 19th century. Rights are conceived as an individual's unilateral entitlements vis-à-vis public bodies.

The conflict of laws should therefore be exclusively limited to the determination of the law that is applicable to cross-border situations. According to this assumption, every person unequivocally belongs to the legal system of a State; international law is therefore tasked with identifying the respective competent state. Against this background, the assumption of transnational legal claims is far from the orthodox vision that each legal entitlement is created by a specific State, because all transnational entitlements can be assigned to more than one legal order. They therefore represent a specific category in substantive law by virtue of combining international and various national provisions, which in turn generate new entitlements that are embedded in both national and international law.

This is illustrated by way of several examples from European social security law (Chapters 2 and 3). Finally, transnational social security rights are defined in more detail conceptually, systematically and in terms of their consequences (Chapter 4).

2 EU social security law

2.1 The conflict of laws and coordination rules in EU social security law

EU social security law is enshrined in Regulation (EC) No. 883/2004. It comprises provisions on the conflict of laws and on the coordination of benefits and obligations. First, it standardises the law applicable to cross-border situations in the Member States (Arts 11-16 of Regulation (EC) No. 883/2004), thereby ensuring a uniform application of social security law among all Member States; above all, it ensures that the social security law of only one Member State is applied in cross-border situations (Art. 11(1) of Regulation (EC) No. 883/2004). European social security law, moreover, comprises a vast number of coordination provisions, in particular in Arts 17-90 of Regulation (EC) No. 883/2004, many of which contribute significantly to the formation of transnational legal rights.[1] EU standards regularly take precedence over similar provisions in Member State's respective laws.[2]

2.2 Characteristics and peculiarities of EU choice of law rules

EU conflict of laws rules are unilateral rules, because the international scope of application of the respective competent State follows from these, even if the answer about the applicable law for all Member States is provided in general terms in Arts 11-16 of Regulation (EC) No. 883/2004.[3] "Unilateral" conflict of

---

[1] Devetzi, 2000, p. 39 et sequ.
[2] Compare the rules established under German law in §§ 3-6 SGB IV.
[3] Heinz-Dietrich Steinmeyer in Ruland/Becker/Axer, 2018, § 33 para. 24; Astrid Wallrabenstein in Schlachter/Heinig, 2016, § 22 para. 32 et sequ.

laws rules do not imply that the EU assigns the international scope of application of its laws to all States in the same manner. The EU's conflict of laws rules in social security are one-sided because the question of the applicable law does not arise as a question of legal relevance for the institutions and courts applying social security law in their respective States, because they either apply their own national law or none at all. They, therefore, do not have to answer the question of the application of other States' laws to which the conflict of laws rules would provide an answer, and which could also be referred back or forward.[4]

The necessary one-sidedness of the conflict of laws rules in social security law can be explained by their public law character. Public laws generally unilaterally regulate the relationship of individuals to a particular State. By contrast, private law conflict of laws rules are more generalised because the State applying the law is not necessarily involved in the private law relationship to be adjudicated and is therefore faced with a choice of law issue in terms of the decision's substantive fairness, e.g. whether compensation for dismissal shall be paid in a cross-border employment relationship if the law chosen by the parties provides for this option while the law applicable to the State of employment provides for protection against dismissal.

Such choice of law issues arise in both private international law and in international labour law, but not in international social security law. This discrepancy can be explained by the fact that the term 'application of law' means two different things in public and in private law. In private law, it entails the assessment of cross-border living conditions in accordance with the standards of the law closest to the subject matter. The civil courts appointed for this purpose are faced with the choice of law based on the general conflict of laws rules. Civil courts decide the choice of law issue against the background of internationally similar rights drawing on the criterion of proximity, i.e. by invoking the national law that is "closest" to the facts to be decided.

Unilateral conflict of laws rules and the unilateralism of public law, on the other hand, one-sidedly shape the relationships between individuals and the bearer

---

[4] Eichenhofer, 1987, p. 220 et sequ.; ibid.,2022, para 138 et sequ; Neumeyer, Internationales Verwaltungsrecht (International Administrative Law), Vol. IV (1936), p. 79.

of public power through the unilateral use of State power. This is the essence of "subject theory" (*Subjekttheorie* in German), the leading theory of demarcation between public and private law today. It recognises that public law unilaterally confers special rights to public bodies and authorities. State agencies and authorities are established by a State, and its laws comprehensively justify their actions because they are exercising State power. The execution of a State's public law therefore necessarily rests on its agencies and authorities, i.e. the rights and competent addressees cannot be separated from one another. If the State confers unilateral powers on its authorities, they alone can exercise them, whereas the authorities of other states cannot.

Public authorities thus only have to determine whether they are competent or not; they do not have to decide with binding force which of several foreign authorities *might* be competent and empowered to act. That is, public authorities – unlike civil courts – are not faced with choice of law questions.

Procedural and substantive laws on social security are harmonised within a Member State; judicial reviews by domestic courts are limited to the actions of the domestic administration. National courts do not have to deal with questions of international jurisdiction on the assertion of claims against external institutions. Administrative action and administrative judicial reviews take place under one and the same law of a given State.

2.3 Domestic public law often takes arrangements under foreign public law into consideration

This does not mean that a State's public law does not recognise foreign public law at all. On the contrary, transnational claims are an expression of the fundamental recognition of foreign public laws' legal positions within the framework of domestic public law.

Article 84 of Regulation (EC) No. 883/2004 allows social security institutions in the debtor's state of residence to enforce claims for contributions or repayments from other Member States' social security institutions. The State enforcing the claim for payment based on foreign social security law by way of administrative assistance does not apply the law of this other State; it applies its own administrative enforcement law to enforce claims based on foreign social security law. Such norms establish transnational legal claims.[5]

An EU law provision links claims for contributions or repayments under the law of another Member State to the enforcement powers of the State providing assistance. Any foreign claim can be enforced domestically across borders since Art. 84 of Regulation (EC) No. 883/2004 has introduced this possibility as a transnational norm.

3 Transnational rights as international substantive rights – illustrated by various regulatory examples

Transnational social security rights derive from substantive norms that apply to international situations. In addition to the unilateral conflict of laws rules, EU social security law primarily features transnational rules on coordination.

Coordination rules are international law rules that relate the legal relationships of several competent States to one another and ensure that they have a cross-border effect. Conflict of laws and coordination rules facilitate and create transnational social security rights. They are enshrined in Arts 4 to 7 of Regulation (EC) No. 883/2004, and are differentiated according to type of benefit in Arts 17-70 of Regulation (EC) No. 883/2004. The most important coordination rules are equal treatment (Art. 4 of Regulation (EC) No. 883/2004), the assimilation of facts (Art. 5 of Regulation (EC) No. 883/2004), accumulation periods (Art. 6 of Regulation (EC) No. 883/2004), the export of cash benefits (Art. 7 of Regulation (EC) No. 883/2004), benefit assistance (Arts 17-20 of Regulation (EC) No. 883/2004) and the elimination of double entitlement. In addition, the favourability principle has been developed in case law to resolve conflicts between EU law and Member States' autonomous social security laws.

---

[5] Neumeyer, Internationales Verwaltungsrecht, Vol. IV (1936), p. 169 ff. speaks of "Überwirkung": cross-border effect; Schuler, 1988, p. 236 et sequ.; Eichenhofer, 1987, p. 226 et sequ.

3.1 Multiple employment

Persons who have multiple employment contracts are employed in different countries for more than a one-month period and thus become subject to compulsory insurance in each State. As no individual may be subject to the social security legislation of several States at the same time (Art. 11 of Regulation (EC) No. 883/2004), the issue of accumulation of entitlements must be resolved.

This is achieved by the norm established in Article 13 of Regulation (EC) No. 883/2004. It covers gainful activities carried out in several Member States and stipulates that the resultant income is to be aggregated in both States (Art. 13(5) of Regulation (EC) No. 883/2004). Furthermore, the overall activity is to be assigned to the law of the State in which the activity has its economic centre of gravity (Art. 13(1) of Regulation (EC) No. 883/2004). The overall activity, which is subject to the rights of two Member States, is thus formulated as a transnational claim on the basis of an international law norm and is subject to the contribution law of the Member State to which the overall activity is economically closest.[6]

3.2 Equalisation of facts

The principle of equality of facts has been developed in case law to complement the specific equality requirements that exist in EU law. The principle is more than a gap-filler and -closer. Case law extends this requirement to a number of elements of entitlement in numerous judgements. The European Court of Justice (CJEU) has recognised the equality of facts with reference to periods of insurance,[7] unemployment,[8] criminal imprisonment,[9] gainful employment,[10]

---

[6] Devetzi, in Hauck/Noftz, EU-SozialR, 2020, K Art.13 Rn. 5 et sequ.
[7] CJEU 15.12.2011 C-257/10 (Bergström), ECLI:EU:C:2011:839; 10.02.2006-C-137/04 (Rockler), ECLI:EU:C:2006:10.
[8] CJEU 09.07.1975 C-20/75 (D'Amico), ECLI:EU:C:1975:101; 22.02.1990-C-228/88, E-CLI: EU:C:1990:85.
[9] CJEU 28.06.1978 C-1/78 (Kenny), ECLI:EU:C:1978:140.
[10] CJEU 07.06.1988 C-20/88 (Roviello), ECLI:EU:C:1988:283; 09.12.1993-C-45/92, C-46/92 (Lepore and Scamuffa), ECLI:EU:C:1993:921; -18.12.2014-C-523/13 (Larcher) E-CLI: EU:C:2014:2458.

income,[11] inclusion in the education system,[12] activity in the public service,[13] residence,[14] including that of spouses[15] or children,[16] military service,[17] raising children,[18] accidents at work,[19] receipt of social benefits,[20] and care of a child with a disability.[21] It has thus developed its effect in all sub-areas of social security law to which Regulation (EC) No. 883/2004 applies.

An equalisation which is de facto denied is often interpreted as a violation of the beneficiary's freedom of movement;[22] an individual who makes use of his or her right of freedom of movement stands to lose other rights. Hence, a higher parental allowance is also due if it is payable following a sickness benefit payment, and if this particular payment was provided for under the law of another Member State other than that of the State liable to pay the benefit.[23]

Article 14 of Regulation (EC) No. 883/2004 extends the right of voluntary insurance to individuals residing outside the competent State, thereby extending the power to take out voluntary insurance for periods of employment or insurance in states other than that in which voluntary insurance is paid.[24] Similarly, any

---

[11] CJEU 07.07.1988-C-154/87 (Wolf), ECLI:EU:C:1988:379; 04.10.1991-C-349/87 (Paraschi), ECLI:EU:C:1991:372.
[12] CJEU 21.09.1991-C-27/91 (Le Manoir), ECLI:EU:C:1991:441; 12.09.1996-C-278/94 (Kommission./.Belgien), ECLI:EU:C:1996:22;15.09.2005 C-258/14 (Ionannides), ECLI:EU:C:2005:2009.
[13] CJEU 16.12.1993-C-28/92 (Leguaye-Neelsen), ECLI:EU:C:1993:942.
[14] CJEU 05.02.2002-C-277/19 (Kaske), ECLI:EU:C:2002:74;18.07.2006-C-406/04 (de Cuyper), ECLI:EU:C:2006:491.
[15] CJEU 05.12.1995-C 321/93 (Martinez), ECLI:EU:C:1995:301; 18.01.2007-C-332/05 (Celozzi), ECLI:EU:C:2007:35.
[16] CJEU 12.06.1997 C-266/95 (Garcia), ECLI:EU:C:1997:292.
[17] CJEU 13.03.1997-C-131/95 (Mora Romero), ECLI:EU:C:1997:317.
[18] CJEU 3.11.2002-C135/99 (Elsen), ECLI:EU:C:2002:647; 07.02.2002-C-28/00 (Knauer), ECLI:EU:C:2002:82; 21.02.2008-C-507/06, ECLI:EU:C:2008:110; 19.07.2012-C-522/10 (Reichelt Albert), ECLI:EU:C:2012.475.
[19] CJEU 07.03. 1991-C-10/90 (Masgio), ECLI:EU:C:1991:107; 15.12.2011-C-257/10 (Bergström), ECLI:EU:C:2011:839; 21.01.2016 C-453/15 (Kauer); ECLI:EU:C:2016:37; 07.04. 2016 C-84/15 (ONem), ECLI:EU:C:2016:220.
[20] CJEU 28.04.2004-C-373/02 (Ötztürk), ECLI:EU:C:2004:232; 15.12.2011-C-257/10 (Bergström), ECLI:EU:C:2011:839; 07.02.2002-C-28/00 (Knauer), ECLI:EU:C:2002:82; 21.
[21] CJEU 12.03.2020-C-769/18 (Caisse d'assurance retraite et de la santé au travail d'Alsace Moselle), ECLI:EU:C:2020:203.
[22] CJEU 03.03.2011-C-440/09 (Tomaszewska), ECLI:EU:C:2011:114.
[23] CJEU 15.12.2011 C-257/10 (Bergström), ECLI:EU:C:2011:839; 16.02.2006-C-137/04 (Rockler), ECLI:EU:C:2006:10.
[24] CJEU 12.02.2015 -C-114/13 (Bouman), ECLI:EU:C2015:81.

child-rearing periods in another state are to be treated the same way as those in the competent State for the purpose of calculating the entire child-rearing period.[25]

If a qualifying period required for receipt of a reduced earning capacity pension is interrupted by illness, maternity leave or a period of unemployment in a state outside of the competent State, it will be taken into account.[26] If the previously held professional position is of relevance to determine an individual's disability pension, any career advancements made in foreign employment are to be equated with equal positions in the home State.[27]

The provision included in a pension insurance scheme that entitlement to an invalidity pension ceases if a work accident occurs must also be applied if that work accident is compensable under the law of another Member State.[28] Similarly, if entitlement to a pension benefit ceases if the insured person has been ordered to serve a criminal sentence, any prison sentence imposed under the law of a State other than that liable to pay benefits must be treated equally.[29] If the increased early retirement pension – which provides for a raise in the minimum pension – depends on a specific pension amount, Article 5(a) of Regulation (EC) No. 883/2004 stipulates that pension rights acquired under the law of other Member States must be treated equally in the calculation of the increased early retirement pension.[30]

The harmonisation of facts reinforces many individual provisions of international social security law because it is a rule of equivalence. It thus extends the effects of the law of one State to the facts that arise under the law of other States, thereby expanding the latter. The equal treatment of facts does not imply that the respective State usurps powers, rather it extends the effects of its norms to international situations to close gaps in protection, thus creating transnational claims to secure equal treatment.

---

[25] CJEU 07.02.2002 -C-28/00 (Knauer), ECLI:EU:C:2002:82.
[26] Devetzi in Hauck/Noftz, EU-SozR, Art. 14 Rn.4 ff.
[27] CJEU 04.10.1991-C-349/87 (Paraschi), ECLI:EU:C:1991:372.
[28] CJEU 18.04.2002 C-290/00 (Duchon), ECLI:EU:C:2002:234.
[29] CJEU 28.06.1978 C-1/78 (Kenny), ECLI:EU:C:1978:140.
[30] CJEU 05.12.2019 C-398/18 (Bocero/Torriconi), ECLI:EU:C:2019:1050.

3.3 Delivery of service outside the competent State

Arts 17-21 of Regulation (EC) No. 883/2004 specify rules on cross-border medical benefits related to health insurance and maternity healthcare. Arts 36, 40 of Regulation (EC) No. 883/2004 regulate the provision of assistance within the scope of occupational accident insurance. The European Health Insurance Card (EHIC) was created to ensure cross-border benefits in the event of illness and sickness during pregnancy and maternity leave. These rules are of relevance for insured persons seeking medical treatment outside the competent State (of employment), in their State of residence or in another state. Arts 17-20 of Regulation (EC) No. 883/2004 give such entitlements to insured persons who reside in another Member State as well as to cross-border commuters; they are thereby granted any immediately necessary entitlements to healthcare in their State of residence.[31]

Furthermore, according to Art. 20 of Regulation (EC) No. 883/2004, insured persons may seek treatment in another Member State with prior approval from the competent State, if the treatment due under the law of the competent State is not available or cannot be provided in time.[32] This entitlement does not arise, however, if the respective treatment is in fact available in the competent State but is provided at a higher standard in another Member State.[33] The aforementioned EU standards link legal relationships of the individual's State of employment with his or her State of residence or his or her State of employment and medical treatment, and establish transnational claims to medical treatment. The issue of cross-border benefits is settled in accordance with Art. 36 of Regulation (EC) No. 883/2004.

Entitlement to benefits based on the law of the State of employment is effectuated in the legal forms provided for in the State of residence or State in which treatment is sought. If the law of the state of employment follows the principle of benefits in kind, but the law of the State of residence or treatment follows that of reimbursement, the benefit is to be provided according to the law of the

---

[31] CJEU 16.05.2006-C-372/04 (Watts), ECLI:EU:C:2006:325; 12.04.2005 C-145/03 (Keller), ECLI:EU:C:2005:211.
[32] CJEU 23.10.2003-C-56/01 (Inizian), ECLI: EU:C:2003:578; 12.04.2005 C-145/03 (Keller), ECLI:EU:C:2005:211.
[33] CJEU 09.10.2014-C-268/13 (Petru), ECLI:EU:C:2014:2271.

State of treatment, and not according to the law of the competent state. This means that the treatment received is to be paid on the spot instead of relying on an internal settlement between the service provider and the health insurance fund.

3.4 Accumulation of insurance periods

The benefits system of a State's social security law is generally based on facts that have been established and realised under its law. Social security facts are periods of employment or of insurance that must have been accumulated in accordance with the State's law for entitlement to rights. Equivalent facts that are realised under the social security law of other States, on the other hand, can (and should be) regulated by these States. The international order among States' social insurance systems is therefore intricately linked to the mutual recognition of their systems.

EU coordination law and social security agreements are based on this general assumption. It follows that an international insurance history must necessarily be shaped by international legal regulations in such a way that the insurance relationships established under different States' laws remain effective and are linked with one another.

EU law relates insurance rights of different States to one another, connects them and develops transnational claims from them. These regulations ensure that the rights established in different States are preserved and that their effects evolve together. To this end, social security agreements and EU law contain principles and regulatory procedures such as the unification of conflict of laws rules, the equality of facts, accumulation of periods of employment and insurance, and rules on the export of cash benefits and assistance with benefits in kind, which are based on equality of residence. These rules of international law supplement the legal regulations of the participating States' social insurance systems.

Based on the relationship between international and state pension insurance laws that apply in an international social insurance process,[34] a transnational

---

[34] Eichenhofer, 2022 (8. Aufl.), Rn. 287f.

entitlement to a pension ultimately arises from elements of the participating States' applicable pension laws in conjunction with international law standards. These arise from the periods completed under the different rights of Member States, the rights that accrue therefrom and their accumulation under EU law. The periods of accumulation in different Member States is limited to entitlement to benefits and does not extend the scope and amount of a cash benefit. The amount of cash benefits is in principle determined by the law of the State under which this right was acquired. International law determines whether an insurance responsibility remains cumulative in the event of a benefit becoming payable or whether it is transferred to the insurance of another State – the State of the individual's last employment before the insured event of unemployment or occupational disease occurred (Art. 36, 62 of Regulation (EC) No. 883/2004). Transnational claims in all conceivable forms are based on the rights provided by different Member States, the relationships of which are the subject of an international law norm. This norm determines whether the insurance burden is borne pro rata temporis or unilaterally concentrated in one institution.

3.5 Division of family benefits among several beneficiaries

A child usually has two parents, i.e. both parents are (or can be) entitled to family benefits. If both parents and the child are covered by the law of their State of residence, the latter must resolve the competition of entitlements between the parents in accordance with the principle of the one-time equalisation of burdens: only one child benefit can be claimed for each child! Pursuant to section 64(2) sentence 2 of the German Income Tax Act, this conflict is resolved by the parents' decision: they must, by mutual agreement, determine the parent entitled to the child benefit. This rule does not apply in international cases, however, because in such cases, the beneficiaries for one and the same child arise from different rights. To implement the principle of the one-time equalisation of burdens in such cross-border cases as well, an international legal solution is necessary. This was created in Art. 68 of Regulation (EC) No. 883/2004.

Article 68 of Regulation (EC) No. 883/20054 regulates this situation of competition. The provision creates a transnational entitlement to family benefits for parents entitled to such benefits for one and the same child under different laws. This is achieved by establishing a priority rule between the competing claims under different laws. To resolve the competition, the first principle (Article 68(1) of Regulation (EC) No 883/2004) is that the State of employment takes precedence over the State of residence.

If one parent is employed in State A and the other is a resident of State B, the family benefit provided in State A takes precedence over that provided in State B. If the parents' entitlement results from the fact that both work in different States, the State of employment of the parent in which the child resides takes precedence – this is the second principle. If the amount of the family benefit paid by the lower-ranking State exceeds that of the higher-ranking State, the latter must pay the difference in the benefit amount – this is the third principle (Art. 68 (2) of Regulation (EC) No. 883/2004). The parents are thereby guaranteed the highest possible amount of family benefit from both States, double payment is avoided and finally, the State of employment is given priority over the State of residence. The benefits the parents are entitled to follows from a norm of EU law which links the right to family benefits provided by different Member States, relates them to each other and – through its own transnational rules and prioritisation – optimises the entitlements of beneficiaries and specifies different States' benefit obligations in a fair relationship to one another.

3.6 Favourability in EU social security law

Transnational legal claims also result from the resolution of conflict situations between EU law and Member States' autonomous social laws.[35] Such situations are characterised by the fact that an EU regulation may deny a right which a Member State's applicable autonomous social law specifically provides for; for example, a child benefit for residents, whereas EU law regulates child benefits for employees. What happens when a parent resides in State A, which provides for a child benefit for all residents, but is employed in State B, which does not provide for such a benefit in view of the child's age?[36]

---

[35] Initiated by case law: CJEU 21.101975 -C-24/75 (Petroni), ECLI:EU:C:1975:129.
[36] CJEU 20.052008 C-352/06 (Bosmann); ECLI:EU:C:2008:209.

The primacy of application of EU law (Art. 3 TFEU) would require the State of residence's autonomous law to give way to the law of the individual's State of employment. This, however, would also imply that EU law is depriving the beneficiary of social rights he or she would otherwise be entitled to. Faced with this consequence, the case law of the CJEU ensures that EU law does not eliminate any existing social security rights, and in all cases confers the rights a beneficiary is entitled to. [37]

In this particular situation of conflict, EU law withdraws its claim of validity in the interest of material favourability for those entitled to it. The claim that arises thereby must also be understood as a transnational claim, just as it is derived from the given Member State's autonomous law. This only applies because competing EU law is not to be applied for reasons of substantive favourability.

4 Concluding observations

The coordination of European social security law is more than a technical mechanism established by EU law rules that are beyond or above the Member States' social security legislation. European coordination law thereby creates substantive European social legislation. It has captivated legal scholars, not only due to its very sophisticated formal structure, but also because of its obvious social benefits for the respective addressees: migrants, frontier workers, tourists, ERASMUS students, who are all supported and protected on this very basis. Apart from its advantageous and socially benevolent side, coordination law symbolises a category of social rights, which is unknown to and has not yet been explored by conventional legal thinking. This is a very unfortunate shortcoming, as it exposes the intellectual backwardness of conventional legal doctrines on the coordination of EU social security law!

EU coordination law creates genuine European social security rights by combining EU law with Member States' social security provisions. When we talk about accumulation periods and transnational assistance in the event of an occupational accident or health insurance, it becomes very obvious that the question arises due to the simple fact that the individual has acquired different

---

[37] CJEU 12.06.2012 -C-611/10, C-612/10 (Hudzinski and Wawrzyniak), ECLI:EU:C:2012:339; 23.04.2015, C-382/13 (Franzen), ECLI:EU:C:2015:261.

social rights under different social legislations. This raises the question whether social protection emerges from international employment based on legal positions acquired under different national laws. The protection of unemployment insurance for frontier workers is another issue that arises within the scope of coordination of EU social security law, particularly when it comes to determining an entitlement for benefits of the residents of one State who were previously active in another Member State. When evaluating these provisions, one reflects upon social security entitlements that emerge from the law of a variety of competent States in relation to EU law and the social security laws of various Member States.

Accumulation periods refer to coverage under the law of the competent State and the EU law's commitment to include any accumulation periods covered under another Member State's law. Two calculations apply in this regard – 1) the customary practice of the calculating State, and 2) that of the State in which the international career was pursued. The payable amounts are to be identified and the higher amount is to be paid to the beneficiary – the result is preferential treatment in substance! When we reflect on transnational assistance in kind, any entitlement to care under the law of the competent State covered by an EU law provision becomes relevant in respect of the services provided within the scope of other Member States' health care or occupational accident care schemes, as well as the rules established in EU law to compensate the service providers for services rendered to beneficiaries under EU law. When unemployment insurance protection is determined for frontier workers, EU law provides for protection under the law of the worker's State of residence when he or she performs work in another Member State. The State of residence provides protection, but the State of former employment profited from the worker's contributions, and is therefore liable to compensate the State of residence's system for the expenditures in favour of the unemployed former frontier worker.

These constructions are established by EU law, i.e. these social security entitlements would not exist without EU law. Insofar, such transnational social security rights are genuine constructions of EU law because they cannot be substituted by national law. These examples do not only illustrate the very existence of genuinely substantive EU law on social security rights, but also help us understand the underlying construction of genuine EU social security rights based on the coordination of social security law deriving from Member States' social security legislation.

These rights are not only enshrined in EU law; the different Member States' social security laws are also interrelated with one another. All of these rights taken together ensure protection for migrant workers and are embedded in the legislation of the competent State. Because of EU law, the competent State provides for entitlements that would otherwise not be available: accumulation periods, mutual transnational assistance and protection in case of unemployment without previous coverage under the competent State's unemployment insurance law. That is, because of EU law, entitlements arise under the law of the competent State, which the latter does not in fact provide for.

The requirement under EU law to aggregate accumulation periods gives rise to pensions that are not provided for by the competent State, i.e. benefits that are partially based on insurance coverage under the law of another Member State. The right to healthcare – enshrined in the law of the competent State – is limited to treatment provided by service providers in that particular State. EU law expands service providers' range of services to include those that are provided for in other Member States. If EU law protects frontier workers under the law of their State of residence for work performed in other Member States, it entitles that worker to rights that are only provided for by EU law and not by the law of the State of residence.

EU coordination law is not only about determining the applicable law. This is only one of its components; the emphasis lies on substantive law aspects. The choice of law rules (Arts 11-16 of Reg. 883/2004) are only one component of coordination law, whereas another component is far more important – a component that I describe as the conversion of national law entitlements into internationally effective ones.

This second factor is decisive for coordination. It creates transnational substantive entitlements by transforming national entitlements into transnational European ones.

The conventional saying that the EU "only'" coordinates Member States' social security systems is hence a misrepresentation – with far-reaching intellectual consequences, as it fundamentally neglects the fact that the EU in fact creates new substantive transnational social security provisions through coordination law, which are embedded in both EU and the Member States' social security laws!

References

Devetzi, Stamatia, Die Kollisionsnormen des Europäischen Sozialrechts, Berlin, 2000.

Eichenhofer, Eberhard, Internationales Sozialrecht und Internationales Privatrecht Baden-Baden, 1987.

Eichenhofer, Eberhard, Sozialrecht der EU, Berlin, 2022 (8th edition).

Hauck, Karl/Noftz, Wolfgang, EU-Sozialrecht, Berlin, 2020.

Neumeyer, Karl, Internationales Verwaltungsrecht, Vol. IV, Berlin, 1936.

Ruland, Franz/Becker, Ulrich/Axer, Peter (eds), Sozialrechtshandbuch 2018, (5th edition).

Schlachter, Monika/Heinig, Michael, Europäisches Arbeits- und Sozialrecht, Baden-Baden, 2016.

Schuler, Rolf, Das Internationale Sozialrecht der Bundesrepublik Deutschland, Baden-Baden, 1988.

3 Practical Questions that Arise from the Implementation of Regulation 883/2004 on the Coordination of Social Security Systems – Perspectives from the German Ministry

Moira Kettner

1 Introduction

One question the reader of the title of this article may ask before even beginning to read is: "Is a sentence containing the words "practical" or "practice" and "ministerial" not a contradiction in itself?" Such a question is, of course, slightly provocative. But on the other hand, it is also obvious that working in a "competent authority" within the meaning of Article 1 lit m) of Regulation (EC) No. 883/2004 at ministerial level is different from working for social security providers and/or liaison offices that directly apply the regulation in individual cases, e.g. issuing Portable Documents, having direct access to the System of "Electronic Exchange of Social Security Information" (EESSI), etc.

It must also be acknowledged, however, that a competent ministerial authority is in continuous contact with both the relevant national social security institutions as well as the competent authorities in other Member States. Such continuous communication provides for profound insights into the application of Regulations (EC) No. 883/2004 and (EC) No. 987/2009 (hereinafter: regulations) in practice. At the same time, the ministerial distance from "work in the field" makes it possible to distinguish whether a given practical challenge is a unique case requiring a unique solution or whether it is of a more general nature and should thus be approached in a more general way. The more general the challenge and its possible solution are, the more likely it is that a ministry will get involved.

Practical questions that arise from the implementation of the regulations can be as copious and diverse as in unique cases. Nonetheless, the more 'general' challenges mentioned above can be further divided into two sub-groups:

One group of challenges arises as a consequence of sudden events outside the day-to-day routine. They are not "unique" because they affect more than just a few individual cases – and require immediate and urgent action. Social security coordination in times of the COVID-19 pandemic indisputably falls into this category.

The second group of challenges does not arise as suddenly but develop over time within the scope of structural, societal or legal changes. Digitisation is such a structural change, for example, as is increasing heterogeneity of EU Member States, changes in traditional family patterns or age structures within the EU, the creation of new policy fields or social security issues such as long-term care. Such developments do not unfold overnight or within a few weeks like the pandemic did. They can take years, sometimes even decades, to develop. At a certain point, however, they become a practical challenge for coordination. This is the reason why a regular revision of the regulations is essential.

2 Social security coordination during the COVID-19 pandemic

While the pandemic is not yet over, we are fortunately far from the chaotic situation we faced when it first hit Europe in early 2020, and when the conditions were far more severe than they are today.

Examples of how social security coordination was affected at the time include, among many others: (i) institutions' day-to-day work routines were hampered, including the speed of issuance of Portable Documents, postal services (which were restricted), or the use of electronic signatures; (ii) direct contact between citizens and institutions was limited because institutions were either closed or working under restricted public hours; (iii) non-urgent medical examinations were cancelled, therefore medical checks necessary for continued entitlement to an invalidity pension could not always be conducted on time; (iv) frontier workers became unemployed and were precluded from moving back to their Member State of residence to claim unemployment benefits there due to quarantine measures or COVID-19-related lack of transport means; (v) partially/intermittently unemployed cross-border/frontier workers met all conditions to be entitled to the corresponding benefit, except that they might not have been fully available in the Member State of employment due to COVID-19-related border restrictions; (vi) unemployed persons exporting their unemployment benefits could not register on time with the unemployment services of the Member State of destination due to COVID-19-related restricted opening/operating hours; (vii) unemployed persons who had exported their unemployment benefits for the maximum period of time were precluded from returning to the Member State granting the benefits in time due to quarantine measures/ COVID-19-related border restrictions/ COVID-19-related lack of transport means; (viii) persons in need of medical treatment remained outside the competent Member State, but had no or an outdated European Health Insurance Card (EHIC); (ix) planned medical care in another Member State could not be provided within the period described in the PD S2 due to the COVID-19 pandemic, and (x) frontier workers were requested to work from home because remote working contributed to "flattening the curve". What the consequences with a view to applicable legislation were was unclear to many. Was a PD A1 or a derogation agreement needed? Would the applicable legislation change?[1]

In became very clear, very fast within the Administrative Commission for the Coordination of Social Security Systems (AC) in early 2020 that the pandemic required immediate action because the usual coordination routines and standards were no longer reliable due to the extraordinary situation – this had a profound impact on a considerable number of citizens. Clearly, citizens could not be punished for not being in a position to follow the usual administrative procedures because of the pandemic, and that the related challenges were not to be

---

[1] For a detailed overview on teleworking and the applicable legislation in the context of the pandemic, see European Labour Authority (2021), Impact of teleworking during the COVID-19 pandemic on the applicable social security: Overview of measures and/or actions taken in the EU Member States to facilitate a flexible approach to the applicable social security of teleworking cross-border workers.

addressed at the legislative level, but that a quick uniform (administrative) approach by Member States and their institutions would be preferable.

What did delegations to the AC do? The French and German delegations volunteered to act as so-called "leading delegations" within the AC. Within the scope of the AC, they collected the problems Member States, institutions and citizens were experiencing with a view to coordination and the pandemic. They reviewed the regulations and corresponding case law to find solutions to the challenges identified, which were already included in the regulations and their inherent flexibility – where necessary and appropriate, the notion of *force majeure* was also considered. This compilation of challenges/solutions was then presented to the AC for endorsement[2] (additionally, a formal AC decision was passed to extend deadlines in reimbursement procedures[3]).

The general principles of the guidance note included the following points:

- *Force majeure was to be considered on a case-by-case basis, but was not to be the starting point for each individual case.* When competent institutions assessed cases linked to the COVID-19 pandemic, the usual procedures were to be followed. If the normal procedures could not be applied, however, reference to *force majeure* increased the room for manoeuvre.

- *Compatibility with national legislation*: Member States were not required to follow any recommendation that was not compatible with their applicable national laws, especially as regards data protection and data security legislation.

- Where possible, the use of the Electronic Exchange of Social Security Information *(EESSI) for communication (instead of postal mail)* was recommended.

---

[2] The guidance note has not been published. It was endorsed at the 362nd meeting of the AC on 17 June 2020 and – due to the ongoing pandemic – again at the 365th and 367th meetings of the AC.

[3] Administrative Commission for the Coordination of Social Security Systems Decision No. H9 of 17 June 2020 regarding the postponement of deadlines mentioned in Articles 67 and 70 of Regulation (EC) No. 987/2009 of the European Parliament and of the Council as well as in Decision No. S9 due to the COVID-19 pandemic, OJ C 259, 7.8.2020, p. 9, *and* its extension Decision No. H11 of 9 December 2020 regarding the postponement of deadlines mentioned in Articles 67 and 70 of Regulation (EC) No. 987/2009 as well as in Decision No. S9 due to the COVID-19 pandemic, OJ C 170, 6.5.2021, p. 4–5.

- *Use of supporting evidence other than official documents provided for in the Regulations*: It was recommended to accept supporting evidence for claims submitted by individuals if the official document could not be provided by the respective institution within a reasonable period of time – provided that this was legally possible under the national legislation of the competent Member State.

However, the note did not provide solutions to all problems related to cross-border social security. For example, financial compensation for quarantine orders was covered by sickness insurance in some Member States while it was considered a matter of State liability outside the social security system in others. The corresponding gaps in compensation for persons in cross-border situations were thus unsatisfactory, but could not be resolved within the framework of social security coordination.

Overall, however, the exceptional architecture of the coordination regulations as well as the reliable cooperation between Member States proved – once again – to be capable to deal with such an extraordinary practical challenge as the pandemic.

3   Revising the coordination regulations

The coordination regulations can generally be considered a toolbox: social security coordination is relevant in and for a multitude of individual cases – but no matter how "unique" an individual situation may be, a tool can usually be found in that "toolbox" to deal with the given situation. This may not come as a surprise, considering the fact that the current regulations are the result of decades of experience.

Yet the world around us is constantly evolving. Life and social security in the EU in 2021 are not what they used to be over 60 years ago when the first coordination regulations were passed. Even over the past 17 years – since Regulation (EC) No. 883/2004 was passed – or over the past nine years – when the Regulation was last amended – considerable changes have taken place in society and in the lives of many citizens, including changes in labour mobility within the EU, in national as well as in EU legislation. Hence, just like a good toolbox at home needs to be updated every now and then, the coordination regulations also need to be regularly revised.

The following practical questions about the implementation of the status quo coordination can be good reasons to revise the regulations' provisions:

How can different, sometimes contradictory interests be balanced fairly? One key challenge in the coordination of social security systems has always been to balance the interests of the stakeholders involved: it is important for the rules to allow citizens the greatest possible degree of mobility, to be tailored to the multitude of individual cases, but nevertheless to be simple, straightforward and transparent. Member States and the respective service providers additionally want fair burden sharing between the Member States and a reasonable administrative burden when processing individual cases (e.g. data exchange, reimbursement procedures). The attempt to balance all of these interests – some of which are directly contradictory – can sometimes be compared to the search for an "egg-laying woolly lizard".

How can the heterogeneity of EU Member States be duly respected and taken into consideration? As the EC/EU has grown to now 27 Member States, the abovementioned balance of interests has become more complex: the social security systems of the EU-27 are more heterogeneous in their entirety than the EEC-6 60 years ago. At the same time, living conditions, the cost of living, wages and benefit levels are quite varied.

When and how can coordination regulations take modernised and new social security policies into account? Social, employment or family policies in many Member States are now based on a different basic understanding than was the case in the past: often, the welfare aspect has receded into the background and benefits are more closely linked to "counter-demands" (e.g. active job search, promotion of female employment). When benefits are exported to other Member States it is (more) difficult to ensure that the corresponding "counter-demands" are equally implemented. Moreover, demographic change has led to the introduction of a new formal social security branch in some Member States with long-term care insurance, while other Member States have incorporated long-term care benefits into their sickness benefit schemes.

To what extent must or should the regulations contain references to relationships with other EU legal acts (and/or ECJ jurisdiction)? Numerous EU legal acts have points of contact with the national coordination of social security systems. The regulations must therefore not only be coherent and manageable in and by themselves, they must also function in relation to other regulations and directives. How these legal acts relate to each other must be clearly defined. For better comprehensibility of the regulations, it is useful to explicitly mention ECJ case law, which has influenced the interpretation/application of the regulations' previous version, not only with a view to rare "unique" case constellations.

The current revision has been ongoing for nearly five years.[4] Negotiations on the precise wordings of the chapters in question have been and continue to be lively and controversial, both within the Council and European Parliament as well as within the framework of the informal trilogue that was launched in early 2019.[5] However, the principle aims of the revision of the relevant chapters may be less controversial and can be easily subsumed under the abstract categories mentioned above:

Equal treatment: the reformulation of the principle of equality in Article 4 of Regulation (EC) No. 883/2004 aims to establish the relationship of this regulation with another EU legal act, namely the Free Movement Directive 2004/38/EC[6], in accordance with the case law of the ECJ in cases C-140/12

---

[4] Cf. Proposal for a Regulation of the European Parliament and of the Council amending Regulation (EC) No. 883/2004 on the coordination of social security systems and Regulation (EC) No. 987/2009 laying down the procedure for implementing Regulation (EC) No. 883/2004 (text with relevance for the EEA and Switzerland) of 13 December 2016, COM/2016/0815 final - 2016/0397 (COD).

[5] Trilogue parties reached a provisional agreement in March 2019, which is accessible at https://data.consilium.europa.eu/doc/document/ST-7698-2019-ADD-1-REV-1/en/pdf. However, this provisional agreement did not obtain the necessary majority in Council.

[6] Directive 2004/38/EC of the European Parliament and of the Council of 29 April 2004 on the right of citizens of the Union and their family members to move and reside freely within the territory of the Member States amending Regulation (EEC) No. 1612/68 and repealing Directives 64/221/EEC, 68/360/EEC, 72/194/EEC, 73/148/EEC, 75/34/EEC, 75/35/EEC, 90/364/EEC, 90/365/EEC and 93/96/EEC, OJ L 158, 30.4.2004, pp. 77-123.

Brey[7], C-333/13 Dano[8], C-67/14 Alimanovic[9], C-199/14 Garcia-Nieto[10] and C-308/14 Commission v the United Kingdom[11], and thus refers to the abovementioned question "relationship with other EU legal acts and ECJ jurisdiction".

Applicable legislation: the revision of these provisions primarily aims to better incorporate the Member States' interests by improving the prevention of unfair (posting) practices and abuse. What is remarkable about the revision of this particular chapter is that there is no impact assessment. This means that there is a lack of objective information on the extent of unfair practices and abuse under current law, as well as of an assessment of which legitimate interests should take a back seat in the interest of fighting abuse and to what extent. In fact, against this background, it is hardly surprising that applicable legislation is one of the two chapters for which no compromise has yet been found in the trilogue negotiations.

Long-term care benefits: the goal of revising the provisions on long-term care has a simple explanation: this relatively new branch of social security is to be given more visibility in the regulations without fundamentally changing the coordination that already exists and works well (cf. above question "modernised and new policies").

Unemployment benefits: the revision of this chapter is based on at least two of the challenges mentioned above, including the difficult aim of balancing interests – which might also be a reason why the trilogue partners are still struggling to find a compromise on this issue as well. Unemployment benefits vary widely across Member States, not only in terms of benefit levels and duration, but also in terms of the associated scope of "counter-demands" or placement services. This heterogeneity makes it even more difficult to develop general provisions that "fairly" take into account or balance the legitimate interests of all those involved (even the question of what is "fair" in this context is likely to lead to very different answers - depending on who is asked).

---

[7] CJEU of 19 December 1993 – C-140/12 (Brey), ECLI:EU:C:2013:565.
[8] CJEU of 11 November 2014, C-333/13 (Dano), ECLI:EU:C:2014:2358.
[9] CJEU of 15 September 2015 – C-67/14 (Alimanovic), ECLI:EU:C:2015:597.
[10] CJEU of 25 February 2016 – C-299/14 (Garcia-Nieto), ECLI:EU:C:2016:114.
[11] CJEU of 14 June 2016 – C-308/14 (Commission v United Kingdom), ECLI:EU:C:2016: 436.

Family benefits: these amendments take the changed image of the family unit into account. In addition to "classic" family benefits such as child benefits, a new family benefit category has been added in many Member States in recent years, serving to replace the income of parent(s) who temporarily stay at home to care for their child (the traditional image of the single-earner family no longer corresponds to reality nor to political will). With the revision, the coordination of family benefits shall explicitly and accurately take these different categories (as well as the corresponding case law of the ECJ) into account.

4 Conclusion

It is clear from the above that – from a ministerial point of view – practical issues relating to the application of the regulations are primarily issues that are of relevance beyond a specific individual case. Even in extreme situations such as the pandemic, it is clear that the flexibility already built into the regulations and the cooperation between the Member States which is built on trust are good prerequisites for addressing these issues.

To ensure a consistently high quality of the coordination regulations, a regular revision of the regulations is essential. In connection with the current revision, it is proving particularly complex to strike a balance between different interests in individual areas.

4 Practical Questions Arising from the Implementation of Regulation 883/2004 on the Coordination of Social Security Systems

Anna Rizou

1 Introduction

Social security coordination rules concern cross-border situations, i.e. they apply to situations involving the laws of more than one Member State. According to Article 48 TFEU, the adoption of coordination rules at European Union (EU) level is necessary to exercise the right of free movement. Without coordination rules, free movement might be restricted and the movement of persons would be less likely if it resulted in the loss of social security rights acquired in another Member State. It is therefore essential for the rules of coordination to be in line with the evolving legal and social frameworks within which they operate and to facilitate the exercise of citizens' rights, while ensuring legal clarity and a fair and equitable distribution of financial burdens between the institutions of the Member States involved.

1.1 European Regulations 883/04[1] and 987/09[2]

From 1 May 2010, Regulation (EU) No. 465/2012 revised the system of coordination of social security rules established in Regulations (EC) No. 883/2004

---

[1] Regulation (EC) No. 883/2004 as in force.
[2] Regulation (EC) No. 987/2009 as in force.

and (EC) No. 987/09. Subsequent discussions and evaluations within the Administrative Committee for the Coordination of Social Security Systems revealed the need to continue the reform process, particularly in the areas of long-term care, unemployment and family benefits.

1.2 Proposal[3] for a Regulation of the European Parliament and of the Council amending Regulation (EC) No. 883/2004 on the coordination of social security systems and Regulation (EC) No. 987/2009 establishing the procedure for implementing Regulation (EC) No. 883/2004

On 13 December 2016, the European Commission submitted its proposal to amend Regulation (EC) No. 883/2004 on the coordination of social security systems and Regulation (EC) No. 987/2009 establishing the procedure for implementing Regulation (EC) No. 883/2004. The proposal's general objective is to continue reforming EU social security coordination rules by making them more transparent and fairer, and by improving their enforceability, contributing to the facilitation of the free movement of persons within the EU. The proposal focused on six areas: (i) access by economically inactive mobile citizens to certain social benefits; (ii) applicable legislation for posted and sent workers and persons working in two or more Member States; (iii) long-term care benefits; (iv) family benefits; (v) unemployment benefits, and (vi) miscellaneous amendments.

Important landmarks have been reached so far, and 16 trialogues have taken place. At the last trialogue, a preliminary political agreement was reached but was rejected in Coreper. The Council has continued negotiations with the European Parliament with a view to reaching a compromise on three outstanding issues, namely: In the chapter on Applicable Legislation:

1) The obligation of prior notification and exemptions from this obligation;

---

[3] European Commission, COM (2016) 815 Final,2016/0397/13.12.2016 (COD) Proposal for a REGULATION OF THE EUROPEAN PARLIAMENT AND OF THE COUNCIL amending Regulation (EC) No. 883/04 on the coordination of social security systems and Regulation (EC) No. 987/2009 laying down the procedure for implementing Regulation (EC) No. 883/2004.

2) Method to determine the location of the registered office or place of business in case of activity in two or more Member States.

In the chapter on Unemployment Benefits:

3) Rules on unemployment benefits for cross-border and frontier workers as well as on the duration of the export of entitlements for workers in cross-border situations.

1.3 Future negotiations[4]

The EU rules on social security coordination contribute directly to the free movement of workers and concern legislation on a number of issues, such as sickness; maternity and equivalent paternity benefits; old-age pensions; pre-retirement and invalidity benefits; survivors' benefits and death grants; unemployment benefits; family benefits; benefits in case of accidents at work and occupational diseases. In practice, the majority of issues have already been provisionally agreed upon between the co-legislators. The three outstanding issues mentioned above remain under discussion. An amendment is of utmost importance for improving the free movement of workers, a fundamental EU right.

2 Practical Issues

2.1 Implementation of European legislation on the coordination of social security systems in the Member States by the Greek competent authority and competent institutions

In applying the European Regulations for the coordination of social security systems since January 1981 for employees and since July 1982 for self-employed persons, Greece has accumulated extensive administrative and implementation experience. The Greek competent authority is the Ministry of Labour and Social Affairs. The competent institutions are the Electronic National Social Security Fund (e-EFKA), which is responsible for all pension benefits, sickness allowance and death grants; the National Health Provision Organisation

---

[4] Council of the European Union, Presidency paper No. 9969/21/6/2021.

(EOPYY), which is in charge of sickness benefits in kind, as well as the Manpower Employment Organisation (OAED) for unemployment and family benefits.

2.2 Implementation process of Article 16 of Reg. 883 / 04

In terms of implementation of Article 16 of K883 / 04, the Ministry of Labour and Social Affairs is the competent authority for concluding the relevant Exemption Agreement. According to the provisions of Article 13 para. 3 of Regulation (EC) 883/2004, which entered into force on 01 May 2010, individuals who are regularly employed in one Member State and self-employed in another are subject to the legislation of the Member State in which they are regularly employed. For an insured worker to be exempt from the obligation to pay double contributions for the duration of his or her posting to another EU company, his or her employer must submit a relevant request to the competent authority of the company the worker is posted to. The procedure entails communication between the two designated competent authorities. After submission of the relevant application, the competent authority of the country of origin (the country in which the employee wants to remain insured) sends a proposal for exemption from social security legislation to the competent authority of the host Member State for the specified period. If the competent authority of the host Member State agrees, it sends a letter to the competent authority of the Member State of origin confirming the agreement between the two Member States and the completion of the exemption procedure, thereby exempting the respective person from any contributions due in the host Member State for the period referred to in the Exemption Agreement.

2.3 The exemption procedure under Article 16: now completed electronically through the European Electronic Data Interchange System (EESSI)

All years of insurance accumulated in any EU Member State must be taken into account to establish a worker's pension rights (principle of including all periods of insurance). Thus, in case of a pension claim, the competent institution of the Member State shall take the insurance periods covered by the legislation of another Member State into account as if they were periods accumulated under its own legislation, and each institution shall provide a partial benefit depending on the insurance period accumulated by the worker in the respective Member State. Any problems related to the granting of exemptions must be discussed between the Member States' competent authorities, and if any fraud or errors are detected, the exemption agreement must be corrected or, if necessary, revoked.

2.4 Practical issues the National Social Security Fund (e-EFKA)[5] is facing

Available information on e-EFKA[6] is limited due to its massive workload and understaffing. e-EFKA continues to face challenges in collecting the requested information and data due to the lengthy and difficult transitional period of reorganisation and transformation into a single social security institution. The gathering of information on portable European A1 forms is fraught with difficulties, as these forms are not digitised. Digitalisation efforts are underway; however, the process is slow and the focus has recently shifted to the implementation of the European Electronic Insurance Data Exchange System (EESSI).

e-EFKA maintains not only a separate register of pensioners who reside in Greece but also of those who receive a pension from another Member State. Communication between the competent institutions mostly takes place electronically, for example, to determine which country's legislation is applicable in case of uncertainty about an individual's employment status (employed or self-employed). The competent institutions are also tasked with the prevention of fraud or errors in social security, especially in the case of posted workers, i.e.

---

[5] Law 4387/16, Government Gazette A´85 / 12.5.2016 "Unified Social Security System Reform of the insurance pension system Adjustments for income tax and gambling and other provisions."

[6] The Unified Social Insurance Institution (EFKA) was renamed Electronic National Social Security Institution (e-EFKA) by Law 4670/20 (Government Gazette 43 / t.AI 28/02/20) of 1 March 2020, and was integrated into the Unified Fund for Auxiliary Insurance and Lump Sum Benefits (E.T.E.A.E.Π.), which is the largest administrative and organisational integration of pension and lump-sum insurance institutions of Greece.

the exchange of information, cross-checking of data with the labour inspectorate, tax offices and other auditing authorities to verify the authenticity of printed documents in an effective way. To fight fraud and errors in the payment of pensions, for example, a bilateral administrative cooperation agreement has been concluded between e-EFKA and the German competent institution to exchange data on deaths.

The changes induced by the COVID-19 pandemic in e-EFKA's work and its European and transnational cooperation partners in the field of social security coordination primarily entail the extension of invalidity pensions for a given period without prior review by the Disability Certification Centre (KEPA). The Centre is in charge of determining the degree of disability of persons insured by an insurance bodies, including the State, as well as uninsured persons. It sets the rate of disability pensions as well as any benefits disabled persons are entitled to. It furthermore coordinates life certificates for e-EFKA pensioners residing in the EU/ EEA / Switzerland and DSKA countries (third countries with which bilateral agreements on social security have been concluded) [extension of pensions].

2.5 Practical issues the National Organisation for the Provision of Health Services (EOPYY[7]) is facing

In Greece, prior authorisation from the national health insurance institution is required when seeking medical treatment in another Member State. Authorisation to receive medical treatment in another Member State depends on whether the individual has exercised his or her right to scheduled cross-border healthcare under the Social Security Regulations (EC) 883/2004 or Directive 2011/24 / EU. As a general rule, prior approval is necessary when planning to seek medical treatment in another Member State or in case of special treatment/ surgeries that either require specialised expertise in terms of medical equipment or staff, or if treatment in the Member State of origin is more costly. Prior authorisation is required for both closed (inpatient) and open (outpatient) care/ hospitalisation. A request for prior authorisation for medical treatment in

---

[7] Articles 17 and 19 of Law 3918/2011 "Structural changes in the health system and other provisions" Government Gazette 31 / A /2.3.2011 - Establishment and name of a national organisation of health services (EOPYY).

another Member State must be submitted to the Greek health insurance institution. If the individual's request is approved, the institution issues a European form (S2), which must be presented to the healthcare provider in the other Member State as proof of coverage for the treatment by the Greek social security system.

According to Directive 2011/24 / EU, there is no requirement for prior approval from the national health insurance institution when seeking medical treatment in another Member State. However, EU legislation gives Member States the option to introduce such an obligation to obtain approval in advance for certain types of care. In Greece, an obligation for prior authorisation applies to (i) any medical treatment that includes at least one overnight stay in the hospital; (ii) medical treatment that requires highly specialised and expensive medical infrastructure or equipment; (iii) treatment for a condition that poses a risk to the safety of the patient or of the general population, and (iv) medical treatment provided by a healthcare provider which, as the case may be, could raise serious and specific concerns about the quality and safety of healthcare.

2.6 Consequences for the institution when a negative decision on prior authorisation is issued after medical treatment has already been provided

Administrative memos on the provision of scheduled medical treatment are usually issued before hospitalisation, except in cases of requests for ex post authorisation submitted upon the patient's return to Greece. However, if the competent institution's binding decision is negative, the request is rejected and the costs for the treatment are not reimbursed by the health insurance institution.

2.7 Review of the insurance status of a person claiming necessary medical benefits in kind who does not possess a European Health Insurance Card

For the provision of necessary medical benefits in kind during temporary residence of an insured person in Greece who does not possess a European

Health Insurance Card (EKAA[8]), the healthcare provider or the National Organisation for Healthcare Provision (EOPYY) has the possibility to request the issuance and direct submission of the respective certificate (Certificate of Temporary Replacement – PPA) by the European insurance institution, especially in case of hospitalisation. The medical services provided by the State structures of another Member State or by a private provider must otherwise be paid privately with the possibility of reimbursement upon submission of a request to the competent insurance institution under the relevant provisions of Reg. (EC) 987/2009. In case the insured person seeks treatment from a private healthcare provider, he or she will have to pay out of pocket and, in accordance with Greek national legislation, will not be reimbursed. The insured person has the possibility to apply to his or her health insurance provider for a review of reimbursement of medical costs for treatment sought in another EU Member State in accordance with Directive 2011/24 / EU on cross-border healthcare.

3 EESSI[9]

The Electronic Exchange of Social Security Information (EESSI) is an IT system that connects social security institutions in EU Member States and facilitates electronic data exchange between 32 countries: the 28 European Union (EU) Member States (MS) and the three European Economic Area (EEA) countries, Norway, Iceland, Liechtenstein and Switzerland.[10] The EESSI is based

---

[8] Decision No. S1 of 12 June 2009 concerning the European Health Insurance Card (relevant text in the EEA and EC/Switzerland Agreement) OJ C 106, 24.4.2010, pp. 23-25. Decision No. S2 of 12 June 2009 concerning the technical specifications of the European Health Insurance Card (relevant text in the EEA and EC/Switzerland Agreement) (2010/C 106/09).

[9] Decision E1 concerning the practical arrangements for the transitional period of data exchange via electronic means referred to in Article 4 of Regulation (EC) No. 987/2009 of the European Parliament and of the Council. Entry into force: 1 May 2010.

[10] Decision E2 concerning the establishment of a change management procedure applicable to details of the bodies defined in Article 1 of Regulation (EC) No. 883/2004 of the European Parliament and of the Council listed in the electronic directory, which is an inherent part of EESSI. Entry into force: 1 September 2010.

on Regulation (EC) No. 883/2004 on the coordination of social security systems[11] (the Basic Regulation) and Regulation (EC) No. 987/2009 of the European Parliament and of the Council of 16 September 2009 laying down the procedure for implementing Regulation (EC) No. 883/2004 of 29 April 2004 on the coordination of social security systems[12] (the Implementing Regulation).

Scope of EESSI is the territory of the EU, EEA and Switzerland. The rules apply to nationals of Member States, stateless persons and refugees residing in a Member State, who are or have been subject to the legislation of one or more Member States, as well as to members of their families and descendants. Data exchange takes place between the competent authorities in all Member States in areas governed by the Regulations on Social Security Coordination, namely (i) sickness, maternity and equivalent paternity benefits; (ii) old-age pensions, pre-retirement and invalidity benefits; (iii) survivors' benefits and death grants; (iv) unemployment benefits; (v) family benefits, and (vi) benefits in respect of accidents at work and occupational diseases.

The purpose of EESSI is to strengthen the protection of citizens' rights by facilitating electronic exchange of information to support social security coordination between the Member States' competent authorities. Hard copies currently being used for communication between competent administrations are to be superseded by EESSI.

IT-based exchanges in EESSI (i) facilitate and speed up decision-making for the calculation and payment of social security benefits; (ii) allow for more efficient verification of data; (iii) provide for a more flexible and user-friendly interface between different systems; and (iv) provide an accurate collection of statistical data on European exchanges.

---

[11] Decision E3 concerning the transitional period as defined in Article 95 of Regulation (EC) No. 987/2009 of the European Parliament and of the Council. Entry into force: 1 February 2012.

[12] Decision E4 of 13 March 2014 concerning the transitional period as defined in Article 95 of Regulation (EC) No. 987/2009 of the European Parliament and of the Council. The relevant text for the EEA and EC/Switzerland Agreement OJ C 152, 20.5.2014.

3.1 Problems and challenges for Greece – Delays at national level

The Ministry of Labour and Social Affairs is the competent authority for any issues relating to the European coordination of social security. Within the scope of its responsibilities, the Ministry exercises control over and supervises the Greek social security institutions in matters of application of provisions of the European Regulations for the Coordination of Social Security Systems 883/2004 and 987/2009 as well as in matters of implementation of the European measures within the scope of these Regulations.

3.2 The timeline of Decision E7[13] of the Administrative Commission

According to the European Commission, in March 2021, 45 of the 99 operational scenarios ("business use cases" - BUCs) met the 80 per cent threshold as agreed in Decision E7 according to which the Member States must implement the "Reference Implementation for a National Application" (RINA) within six months for each social security institution ("FCAs"). Due to the large number of BUCs, all Greek social security institutions are affected and for this reason, the stakes are high as there are long delays in the implementation of EESSI/RINA in the three major institutions, e-EFKA, OAED and EOPYY, but also in "small institutions"[14],[15] These delays, primarily concentrated in e-EFKA, have resulted from the reorganisation of the institution, which was upgraded to a national social security institution. The reasons for the delays include the adoption of new organisational structures following the mergers of numerous services and branches, the time-consuming legal procedures of announcing public tenders, as well as the COVID-19 pandemic, but also the fact that European issues are not currently considered a priority of the institutions' administrations.

---

[13] Administrative Commission for the Coordination of Social Security Systems Decision No. E7 of 27 June 2019 concerning practical arrangements for cooperation and data exchange until the Electronic Exchange of Social Security Information (EESSI) is fully implemented in Member States (relevant text to the EEA and to the EC/Switzerland Agreement) 2020/C 73/04 PUB/2020/20.

[14] "Small institutions" are characterised by a very small volume of exchanges in EESSI, and no significant impact on their overall operation is anticipated. The small institutions are health insurance institutions outside of e-EFKA, which certify their insurance capacity and issue European Health Insurance Cards to those covered by them.

[15] Article 53 of Law 4387/16 which provides for the inclusion of bodies, branches, sectors and accounts in e-EFKA.

3.4 Current developments

The Ministry of Labour and Social Affairs is in the process of developing the business scenarios assigned to it (exchange of 6 BUCS for the exceptions of Article 16 of EP 883/04, and some horizontal scenarios). e-EFKA adopted a temporary solution for the implementation of a "light" RINA by the end of May 2021 to meet the deadlines of Decision E7. A Government Cloud is being developed. The entire process in EOPYY has been delayed for three months due to appeals and in the best case without any further delays, the contract will be concluded and implementation carried out within five months. In short, by the end of September 2021, the project could have been completed if all institutions involved had taken immediate action without delay.

5 Unplanned Medical Treatment in Another Member State – Using the EHIC
Current Insights from the German Liaison Agency Health Insurance – International*

Linda Bojanowski

1 Introduction

The European Health Insurance Card (EHIC) verifies the holder's entitlement to receive unplanned State-provided cross-border medical treatment in another European Union Member State as well as in Iceland, Liechtenstein, Norway (EEA States), Switzerland and the United Kingdom based on Regulation (EC) No. 883/2004[1]. It confirms the EHIC holders' entitlement to medical treatment during his or her temporary stay in an EU/EAA State, Switzerland or the United Kingdom. During their stay in Germany, individuals with an EHIC, who are covered by statutory health insurance in their country of origin, can claim healthcare services directly from a German healthcare provider. All individuals covered by statutory health insurance in one of the States mentioned above has the right to an EHIC. The EHIC entitles individuals (e.g. tourists, posted workers or students) to necessary medical benefits in kind so their stay in another State does not need to be prematurely terminated. The EHIC covers medical

---

* Note: The following content does not reflect a generally agreed opinion of the German Liaison Agency Health Insurance – International. It merely reflects views based on research carried out by Linda Bojanowski.
[1] Regulation (EC) No. 883/2004 of the European Parliament and of the Council of 29 April 2004 on the coordination of social security systems.

treatments that cannot be postponed until the insured person's return to his or her home country. In other words, the EHIC is symbolic for the EU's right to free movement. It ensures that a planned stay in another State can continue as intended despite the need for unforeseen medical treatment. According to data from 2019, around 250 million EHICs have been issued. That is, over half of entitled citizens are in possession of an EHIC.[2]

The EHIC was gradually introduced from 1 June 2004 until 31 December 2005. EHICs have been issued since 1 January 2006, and are accepted in all of the above-mentioned countries.[3] Previously, entitlement to coverage was demonstrated by means of the form "E 111", whereby the letter "E" did not stand for "electronic"; it simply indicated that the form was an official EU document.

The EHIC cannot be used for planned medical treatments in another State.[4] If an insured person wants to seek medical treatment in another State, he or she must request a Portable Document S2 prior to travelling to the State of treatment. When an individual moves his or her habitual residence to another State, the Portable Document S1 verifies his or her entitlement to medical treatment in that respective State.

2 Legal background in brief

Article 19 Reg. (EC) No. 883/2004 stipulates that an insured person and any member of his or her family residing in a State other than the competent Member State shall be entitled to benefits in kind that become necessary on medical grounds during their stay. "Stay" in this regard refers to "temporary residence" in accordance with Article 1 lit. k Reg. (EC) No. 883/2004. Based on the so-called "insured person fiction", individuals insured abroad shall be treated in Germany on the same terms as persons insured under German legislation. This implies that they are entitled to all legally prescribed benefits in kind under

---

[2] De Wispelaere/De Smedt/Pacolet, Cross-border healthcare in the EU under social security coordination – Reference year 2019, p. 11, 13.
[3] European Commission/Employment, Social Affairs & Inclusion, Moving and working in Europe, https://ec.europa.eu/social/main.jsp?catId=857&langId=en&intPageId=1304.
[4] See Article 1 Decision No. S1 of the AC.

German law, including medical and dental treatment, hospitalisation and medicines.[5] Any reduction to benefits in kind derives from the fact that the competent State remains responsible for the provision of cash benefits (Article 21 Reg. (EC) No. 883/2004). Article 35 Reg. (EC) No. 883/2004 stipulates that the costs of the benefits in kind provided on an interim basis by the relevant institution in the host State (i.e. in the State of stay) shall be reimbursed by the competent institution in the State of origin.

According to Article 25 Reg. (EC) No. 987/2009[6], to access these entitlements, the insured person must present the EHIC – which indicates entitlement to benefits in kind – issued by the competent institution in his or her Member State of origin to the healthcare provider in the host Member State. In case of exceptional circumstances, e.g. if an insured person's EHIC has been stolen or lost, the competent institution shall issue a Provisional Replacement Certificate (PRC) with a limited period of validity (Article 5 Decision No. S1 of the Administrative Commission for the coordination of social security systems (AC)).[7] The format of the PRC is identical in all Member States and contains the same data as the EHIC.

The design and specifications of the EHIC were determined by the AC. All of the EHIC's technical specifications were established in Decision No. S2 of the AC.[8] The Decision covers all of the relevant specifications of the EHIC, such as data to be included, its size and colour. Moreover, it contains a pictorial example of the EHIC. When the Decision was concluded in 2009, it was already planned for the EHIC to be an electronic medium. Institutions would then be able to store the card's data in electronic form, for example on a microchip or magnetic strip. To date, it seems that no participating State is issuing EHICs

---

[5] In Germany, all legally determined benefits are laid down in the Social Code Book V (SGB V).
[6] Regulation (EC) No. 987/2009 of the European Parliament and of the Council of 16 September 2009 laying down the procedure for implementing Regulation (EC) No. 883/2004 on the coordination of social security systems.
[7] Decision No. S1 of 12 June 2009 concerning the European Health Insurance Card.
[8] Decision No. S2 of 12 June 2009 concerning the technical specifications of the European Health Insurance Card.

with this electronic option. The currently available equipment of healthcare providers in Germany would not be able to read the electronic data included in the EHIC, because the necessary technical means do not exist.

3 Process of EHIC use in Germany

Each State participating in the EHIC system shall ensure that the card can be used in a host State's national structures. Individuals who hold an EHIC and who are covered by the statutory health insurance of another EU Member State or Iceland, Liechtenstein, Norway, Switzerland and the United Kingdom can claim benefits in kind from a German healthcare provider directly during their temporary stay in Germany. However, only medical treatment provided by a contracted doctor, i.e. a practitioner who has concluded a contract with a German statutory health insurance fund, is covered by the EHIC. These include German doctors and dentists who are registered with the statutory health insurance in Germany and are referred to as "Kassenarzt" (statutory health insurance physician), "Vertragsarzt" (registered contract physician) or doctors who accept "Alle Kassen" ("all health insurance funds").[9] Germany is one of the few countries with a dual health insurance system (i.e. statutory and private).

Since no healthcare insurer is currently issuing electronic EHICs, German healthcare providers must make a copy of the EHIC using a photocopier, a very outdated method in view of today's digital age. Moreover, the EHIC holder has to fill in and sign a so-called "Patient's Declaration". This Patient's Declaration is a German construction that is available in several languages. The form includes, among others, information on the duration of the individual's stay in Germany and confirms that the patient has not entered the country for the purpose of seeking medical treatment. Furthermore, the patient must select the German statutory health insurance fund that shall deal with the reimbursement of costs (the so-called 'assisting health insurance fund'). There are currently

---

[9] For more information, see GKV-Spitzenverband, DVKA, Going to Germany with your European Health Insurance Card (EHIC), https://www.dvka.de/media/dokumente/merkblaetter/urlaub_in_deutschland_1/EHIC_Dt_englisch.pdf.

103 statutory health insurances in Germany.[10] The individual is bound to the selected health insurance fund for the duration of the respective treatment. The Patient's Declaration form also states that the patient must provide proof of identity (national ID or passport). If no proof of identity can be presented, the doctor is entitled (and in fact obligated) to charge the costs for treatment privately. These costs are determined in accordance with the scale of fees for doctors in Germany.

The use of the EHIC in Germany is laid down in the agreement on the use of the EHIC of 1 July 2004, which was concluded between the National Association of Statutory Health Insurance Physicians ("Kassenärztliche Bundesvereinigung") and the National Association of Statutory Health Insurance Funds ("GKV-Spitzenverband").[11]

There is no regulation in the EU that requires healthcare providers to verify the identity of persons requesting medical treatment based on an EHIC. According to Reg. (EC) Nos 883/2004 and 987/2009, it suffices to present an EHIC. Luxembourg, like Germany, also checks the ID of EHIC holders in accordance with the concluded national contract. The European Court of Justice has decided that Member States themselves shall lay down the rules at national level on the procedure for granting benefits, as long as these are in line with European requirements.[12]

One of the main motivations for verifying patients' identity is the prevention of misuse of the EHIC. The aim is to prevent individuals, who have lost the entitlement to benefits provided for under the legislation of a given Member State, from taking advantage of benefits based on their EHIC in another State. Reimbursement cannot be denied by the issuing institution as long as a valid EHIC can be presented (Article 2 para. 2 Decision No. S2 of the AC). An EHIC is valid as long as the validity period printed on the card has not expired. An EHIC's validity period can range from several months to a maximum of ten

---

[10] A list of all statutory health insurance funds in Germany is available here: https://www.gkv-spitzenverband.de/service/krankenkassenliste/krankenkassen.jsp.
[11] Vereinbarung zur Anwendung der europäischen Krankenversicherungskarte vom 1. Juli 2004 in der Fassung vom 1. Oktober 2018 zwischen der Kassenärztlichen Bundesvereinigung, K. d. ö. R., Berlin und dem GKV-Spitzenverband, K. d. ö. R., Berlin.
[12] CJEU, 16 May 2006, C-372/04, ECLI:EU:C:2006:325.

years. There is no standardised rule on the duration of an EHIC's validity. Hence, an EHIC's period of validity is determined by the issuing institution.[13] In Germany, it can range between several months to several years, whereby a validity period of five years is most common. Usually, the EHIC's period of validity corresponds to the validity of the individual's national health insurance card, because the EHIC is printed on its backside. It is therefore reasonable to assume that all persons covered by statutory insurance in Germany are also in possession of an EHIC.[14]

The date of validity printed on the EHIC does not, however, indicate whether the cardholder's health insurance coverage status has changed since the issuance of the EHIC. A real-time validity check of the EHIC would therefore be desirable, which would be possible if an electronic EHIC were available.

4 Electronic EHIC

Efforts are underway in the Member States and at EU level to establish an electronic EHIC. An electronic EHIC should be downloadable via a secure platform and the holder should be able to present his or her EHIC to the healthcare provider using an electronic device, such as a tablet or smartphone. It should furthermore be possible to check the validity of the EHIC in real time. Moreover, an electronic version of the EHIC would be more sustainable.

The European Commission presented its Action Plan of the European Pillar of Social Rights in March 2021.[15] This Plan includes the introduction of the European Social Security Pass (ESSPASS). ESSPASS aims to make it easier and faster to access information about the scope of an individual's social protection across borders. The possibilities and options for such a pass will be tested in a pilot project. The previous proposal of introducing a European national insurance number has been abandoned. The pilot project consists of two phases.

---

[13] See Art. 3 Decision No. S1 of the AC.
[14] De Wispelaere/De Smedt/Pacolet, Cross-border healthcare in the EU under social security coordination – Reference year 2019, p. 14.
[15] European Commission, The European Pillar of Social Rights Action Plan, 2021.

The first one focusses on the digitalisation of the Portable Document A1 procedure, which entails determining the applicable law. The second phase involves the digitalisation of the EHIC.[16]

Several Member States have highlighted the importance of introducing an electronic version of the EHIC for their social security institutions, healthcare providers and insured persons, and are encouraging coordinated action to explore possible approaches to digitalisation of the EHIC. This process indisputably requires coordination so each Member State can embed the necessary technical and administrative steps for digitalisation into their national processes. For German health insurers, for example, the introduction of an electronic EHIC means that the national health insurance card will have to be modified because the physical EHIC is currently printed on its backside. In addition, all healthcare providers will have to be equipped with the necessary technical devices. The realisation of an electronic EHIC will thus require an extended period of implementation. An interim solution could be the parallel use of a physical and an electronic version of the EHIC.

The issuance of the EHIC in an electronic format was already envisaged in the implementation of the Single Digital Gateway Regulation[17], which aims to make a number of administrative procedures – such as applying for an EHIC – fully available online for cross-border users by December 2023.

EU social security legislation is currently experiencing a genuine digitalisation push through the Electronic Exchange of Social Security Information (EESSI) system. Electronic data exchange was already envisaged when Reg. (EC) Nos 883/2004 and 987/2009 entered into force (Article 2 Reg. (EC) No. 987/2009). Its actual implementation, however, has taken quite some time and EESSI is still not fully operational. The aim is for all communication between social insurance institutions to take place electronically through EESSI. Communication between these institutions is accelerated through the EESSI: data exchange using postal services ("E" documents) is clearly far more time-consuming.

---

[16] European Commission, The European Pillar of Social Rights Action Plan, 2021, p. 30.
[17] Regulation (EU) 2018/1724 of the European Parliament and of the Council of 2 October 2018 establishing a single digital gateway to provide access to information, to procedures and to assistance and problem-solving services and amending Regulation (EU) No. 1024/2012.

The "special feature" of Reg. (EC) Nos 883/2004 and 987/2009 is that the participating institutions can contact each other directly. There is no need for contact via foreign offices, diplomatic representatives or even liaison bodies. All institutions can engage in direct cross-border contact and do not have to take the route via the liaison offices, with the exception of the reimbursement process, which generally always runs via liaison bodies in a bundled procedure (Article 66 para. 2 Reg. (EC) No. 987/09).

Within EESSI, institutions contact each other via specified business use cases (BUCs). A BUC is a business process that includes a sequence of steps required to complete a given case in a specific social security scheme. Within each BUC, different structured electronic documents (SEDs) are designated for use in communication. The Administrative Commission is responsible for defining the structure, content and procedures in detail (Article 4 Reg. (EC) No. 987/09).

If a patient is unable to present an EHIC/PRC, an entitlement certificate can be requested directly from the competent institution using the SEDs intended for this purpose (the document "Application for a certificate of entitlement – temporary stay" and "Certificate of entitlement – temporary stay"). The insured person can also contact his or her health insurance provider and request a PRC directly. In the best case, he or she avoids having to pay his or her treatment costs out of pocket. These administrative steps could become obsolete with the introduction of an electronic EHIC, which could be verified at any time using a digital platform.

5 The new Global Health Insurance Card

The United Kingdom's withdrawal from the EU on 31 January 2020 has a significant impact on the use of EHICs in cross-border situations between an EU Member State and the United Kingdom. The Withdrawal Agreement concluded between the EU and the United Kingdom[18] entered into force on 1 February 2020. It provided for full application of the coordination regulations for social

---

[18] Agreement on the withdrawal of the United Kingdom of Great Britain and Northern Ireland from the European Union and the European Atomic Energy Community.

security for a transitional period until 31 December 2020 and, in case of a continuous cross-border relationship between the United Kingdom and a given EU Member State, beyond that date. It can therefore be understood as a "set of protection of the status quo". In addition, it regulates issues that arise after the end of the transitional period but which have their origin before that date. It intends to protect existing and future entitlements and to ensure that these can be accessed and benefits received even at a later date in accordance with the terms of Reg. (EC) Nos 883/2004 and 987/2009.

The competent institutions in the United Kingdom, e.g. the DHSC Overseas Healthcare Team[19], began issuing new EHICs in February 2020, which no longer bear the EU logo. This design is based on the samples of EHICs issued in Switzerland and Liechtenstein. It does not mean, however, that all previously issued EHICs with the EU logo lost validity after February 2020. Institutions began issuing the so-called "Citizens' Rights" EHIC for some time after the Withdrawal Agreement entered into force. The name derives from the relevant chapter (Part Two) on the coordination of social security systems in the Withdrawal Agreement, which is entitled "Citizens' Rights". To be eligible for a Citizens' Rights EHIC, the individual must be covered by Article 30 of the Withdrawal Agreement – the full social security coordination rules enshrined in Reg. (EC) Nos 883/2004 and 987/2009 apply in accordance with Article 31 of the Withdrawal Agreement.

A special regulation applies to students from the United Kingdom who moved to an EU/EEA Member State or Switzerland to participate in a temporary study programme before 1 January 2021. Under the terms of the Withdrawal Agreement, these students can continue to use their EHIC to receive benefits in kind in their country of study. According to the Withdrawal Agreement, however, they are no longer entitled to such benefits if they move to another EU/EEA Member State or to Switzerland in the course of their studies. Such students are eligible for a special Citizens' Rights EHIC, which is limited by means of a country code for use in the respective country of study.

---

[19] Which institution(s) in which State issue EHICs can be checked here: https://ec.europa.eu/social/social-security-directory/pai/pai-search-institution/language/en.

Ultimately, before the end of 2020, the United Kingdom and the EU concluded a new agreement, the Trade and Cooperation Agreement.[20] It contains a protocol for the coordination of social security systems and entered into force on 1 January 2021 (provisionally until 30 April 2021). It applies to situations that arose on or after 1 January 2021, which did not have any cross-border links between an EU Member State and the United Kingdom. It contains rules for the coordination of social security systems which essentially correspond to the provisions of Regulations (EC) Nos 883/2004 and 987/2009, with a few exceptions.

The Withdrawal Agreement and the Trade and Cooperation Agreement ensured seamless protection in cross-border social security situations. In the course of negotiations on the Trade and Cooperation Agreement, a new Global Health Insurance Card (GHIC) was introduced, which provides for continued access to benefits during a temporary stay in another country. It has the same structure and contains the same information as existing EHICs. It is important to note that the Trade and Cooperation Agreement has a different territorial scope than the Withdrawal Agreement or Reg. (EC) Nos 883/2004 and 987/2009. It does not apply to EEA States and Switzerland, i.e. the GHIC cannot be used in those States. The GHIC is currently only valid in the EU-27.[21]

Within the scope of the Trade and Cooperation Agreement, the competent institutions in the United Kingdom request Member States' healthcare providers to cover students who have been issued a special Citizens' Rights EHICs, which confirms their entitlement to healthcare in all EU Member States. The healthcare of students with a Citizens' Rights EHIC is thus covered in all Member States, with the exception of EEA Member States and Switzerland, i.e. even though healthcare was initially to be limited by means of a country code. The restriction to healthcare coverage in one country became obsolete with the rights created by the Trade and Cooperation Agreement. Lastly, the United Kingdom began issuing another "special" GHIC specifically for residents of

---

[20] The Trade and Cooperation Agreement between the European Union and the European Atomic Energy Community, on the one hand, and the United Kingdom of Great Britain and Northern Ireland, on the other.

[21] More information on the GHIC from the UK government: https://www.gov.uk/global-health-insurance-card and from the NHS: https://www.nhs.uk/using-the-nhs/healthcare-abroad/apply-for-a-free-uk-global-health-insurance-card-ghic/.

Northern Ireland. This GHIC has a neutral design, i.e. it does not display the British flag.

These developments clearly show how important it is to keep abreast of the latest developments. The United Kingdom currently issues six different EHICs/GHICs which must all be accepted by healthcare providers in EU Member States. Reliable exchange of information is therefore indispensable. In the best case, all healthcare providers in all States involved should be included to ensure that citizens' entitlements can be granted as smoothly as possible.

6 Conclusion

It is worth taking a closer look at the administrative processes behind the legal framework of the EHIC. This paper sheds light on the movement and innovative will behind the EHIC. The digitalisation of the EHIC will continue to be a priority in the near future. At the same time, the EHIC system is a valued and well-functioning system that is even adopted in new agreements. The Trade and Cooperation Agreement, which was adopted during the Brexit negotiations, has integrated the concept of the EHIC and transferred it to the new GHIC. The EHIC is a document that promotes the free movement of persons. It is symbolic of a "European Social Union".[22] It is furthermore remarkable that this concept was integrated into the GHIC – even though the right of free movement ended with the withdrawal of the United Kingdom from the EU. This demonstrates the independent role the EHIC has established for itself in the meantime.

---

[22] De Wispelaere/De Smedt/Pacolet, Cross-border healthcare in the EU under social security coordination – Reference year 2019, S. 11.

References

De Wispelaere, Frederic/De Smedt, Lynn/Pacolet, Jozef, Cross-border healthcare in the EU under social security coordination – Reference year 2019, 2020, https://ec.europa.eu/social/BlobServlet?docId=23780&langId=en.

European Commission (Publication Office of the European Union), The European Pillar of Social Rights Action Plan, 2021.

European Commission/Employment, Social Affairs & Inclusion, Moving & working in Europe, https://ec.europa.eu/social/main.jsp?catId=857&langId=en&intPageId=1304.

6 Practical Issues in the Context of Implementing Social Security Coordination Regulation (EC) No. 883/2004 from the Perspective of the German Social Accident Insurance

Stefanie Klein

1 Introduction

The Liaison Body of the German Social Accident Insurance DGUV e.V., DVUA (Deutsche Verbindungsstelle Unfallversicherung – Ausland) is an integral part of the Federal Association of the German Social Accident Insurance. According to the statutory provision of § 139a Social Code VII (SGB VII – social code for accidents at work and industrial diseases) it covers two different functions in the context of Reg. (EC) No. 883/04, namely (i) the functions of a liaison body, on the one hand, and (ii) those of an institution of the place of residence or stay, Art. 1 r) Reg. (EC) No. 883/04, on the other. A liaison body is defined in Art. 1 b) Reg. (EC) No. 987/09 as any body designated by the competent authority of a Member State for one or more of the branches of social security referred to in Art. 3 Reg. (EC) No. 883/04 to respond to requests for information and assistance for the purposes of the application of Reg. (EC) No. 883/04 and Reg. (EC) No. 987/09, and which has to fulfil the tasks assigned to it under Title IV of Reg. (EC) No. 987/09. An institution of the place of residence and an institution of the place of stay refers, respectively, to the institution that has competence to provide benefits in the place of the respective person's residence and to the institution with competence to provide benefits in the respective person's place of stay in accordance with that institution's legislation or, where no such institution exists, in accordance with the legislation of the institution designated by the competent authority of the respective Member State (see Art. 1 r) Reg. (EC) No. 883/04). Incorporating both functions in one administrative body, the tasks carried out by DGUV e.V., DVUA can be considered administrative front line work in terms of coordinating national rules on accidents at work and industrial diseases under Title III Chapter 2 Reg. (EC) No. 883/04.

This article presents examples of practical issues DGUV e.V., DVUA deals with in its daily administrative procedures. The body's main playing field includes:

- Clarification of the legislation applicable to the respective individual,
- provision of benefits in kind in Germany to individuals insured in another Member State,
- cooperation between institutions, mainly institutions in Germany and other Member States that deal with accidents at work and industrial diseases,
- reimbursement between institutions for accidents at work or industrial diseases that are provided in another Member State (and vice versa), and
- general consultation on all issues related to all actors involved, such as partner institutions in Germany and other Member States, persons who have suffered either an accident or are suffering from an industrial disease, employers based in Germany and in other Member States, etc.

The majority of tasks the DVUA deals with in Germany are cases involving workers to whom another Member State's social security law applies, and who suffer an accident at work. Accidents occur during the performance of work or self-employed activity in Germany. The competent social security institutions[1] for these individuals are based in another Member State.

In cases of accidents at work, the competent institutions are responsible for investigating the obligation of insurance against certain risks in their respective country and of reviewing the obligation for contributions to be paid for risks covered by their national laws. In addition, they determine whether the facts of

---

[1] Art. 1 q) Reg. (EC) No. 883/04.

an incident can be defined as an "accident at work" in accordance with their national laws.

Only when these three prerequisites are met:

1. The law of another Member State applies,

2. the individual is covered against the risk of accidents at work, and

3. the facts of the respective incident define it as an accident at work under the national law of the other Member State

will benefits in kind be provided by DVUA as the institution of the respective individual's place of residence or stay in Germany. The provision of benefits is in line with the legal rules of Germany's Social Code VII for benefits in kind (paragraphs 26 – 44 Sozialgesetzbuch VII). The actual costs for the provision of benefits in kind for an accident at work that has occurred in one Member State are reimbursed by the competent institution in the other Member State via the liaison body (Art. 35 Reg. (EC) No. 883/04, Art. 62 Reg. (EC) No. 987/09).

During the administrative implementation process to coordinate accidents at work at the EU level, several practical issues that pose challenges to the administrative bodies arise. This article addresses some of these challenges.

2 First practical problem: clarification of applicable legislation

The first information DVUA usually receives about a presumable accident at work for which it might have competence is a so-called "D-Arztbericht", a medical report by an accident insurance consultant, namely a physician in Germany who, inter alia, is specialised in accident injuries and is officially acknowledged as such by the German Social Accident Insurance. After receiving this initial information, DVUA must clarify whether the facts and data provided about the accident as well as about the injured person, the employer, the place of performance of work and the health insurer are sufficient to investigate the case further and whether another Member State's legislation might be applicable to the injured person. One challenge in this first step of fact checking is the information provided in the report (see example below).

Durchgangsarztbericht – UV-Träger –						Lfd. Nr. ▮
Unfallversicherungsträger				Eingetroffen am 09.05.2019	Uhrzeit 10.00	
Name der versicherten Person ▮	Vorname ▮		Geburtsdatum ▮	Krankenkasse unbekannt	Familienversichert [X] Nein [ ] Ja: keine Kopie an Kasse	Name des Mitglieds
Vollständige Anschrift ▮				Bei Pflegeunfall Pflegekasse der pflegebedürftigen Person		
Beschäftigt als		Seit		Telefon-Nr.	Staatsangehörigkeit	Geschlecht
Unfallbetrieb (Name, Anschrift und Telefon-Nr. des Arbeitgebers, der Kita, der (Hoch-)Schule, der pflegebedürftigen Person)						
1 Unfalltag 09.08.2019	Uhrzeit 08.00	Unfallort		Beginn der Arbeitszeit Uhr	Ende der Arbeitszeit Uhr	
2 Angaben der versicherten Person zum Unfallhergang und zur Tätigkeit, bei der der Unfall eingetreten ist Laut Aufnahmebericht (fremdanamnetisch durch den begleitenden Notarzt) auf der Frankfurter Messe in einem Hochspannungsraum Kontakt mit einem Starkstromkabel (10 kV), ob es zu einem Stromdurchfluss kam oder einem Lichtbogen ist unklar. Nach Aufwachen auf der Intensivstation (22.08.2019) Befragung des Patienten: Er sei von einem Freund auf das Messegelände "eingeschleust" worden im Kofferraum.						

In this example, the notice under "health insurance" (Krankenkasse) is "unknown" (unbekannt). The individual's occupation (Beschäftigt als) is not noted, neither is the work start date (Seit). The nationality of the person is not provided (Staatsangehörigkeit) and neither is any information on the injured person's employer (Unfallbetrieb). Moreover, the brief description of the facts of the accident state that the seriously burned patient had first arrived at the Frankfurt trade fair in the boot of a car. His friend had smuggled him in, and while the individual was conducting some electrical work in a high-voltage electrical room, he was electrocuted by a high-voltage cable. The accident took place on 9 August 2019 and the patient woke up in the intensive care unit of a hospital on 22 August 2019.

This example vividly illustrates the problems DVUA might face during the first step of reviewing the information made available about a given case:

- The information in the report is incomplete or misleading,
- even basic details to be able to adequately assess the applicable legislation, such as the place of occupation/the employer, are missing,
- the patient is not able to provide necessary information,
- in some cases, for example when an individual is smuggled onto given premises to perform work, the employer, purchaser, partner or friends involved are difficult to contact because of the legal limbo associated with clandestine employment.

Language barriers at German service providers or in the oral and written communications from DVUA to the injured person are a constant companion, a challenge DVUA tries to meet halfway by offering communication in foreign languages. One must bear in mind that individuals who suffer an accident at work in a foreign country or who suffer severe injury may find themselves in a personal and medical crisis situation which may not make communication or even the ability to act possible, even more so in an unfamiliar environment with different structures, services, competences and persons.

3 Second practical problem: provision of benefits in kind in Germany by the German Social Accident Insurance as the institution of place of residence and the institution of place of stay, Art. 1 r) Reg. (EC) No. 883/04

As mentioned in the introduction, the competent institution is in charge of determining whether the facts and circumstances of an accident in another Member State meet the requirements to be qualified an accident at work.

If this is the case, the institution of the place of residence or of stay shall provide the person involved with benefits in kind.

The legal criteria in the national laws of the 27 EU Member States to determine whether an accident qualifies as an accident at work vary. The criteria listed in paragraph 8 SGB VII and the German jurisdiction referring to it simply do not apply. They only serve as a preliminary classification or working tool to determine whether a case should be further investigated and to involve DVUA if the case can be considered a probable accident at work. The final decision on Reg. (EC) No. 883/04 shall be taken by the competent institution.

For example, the German approach to consider a commuting accident as an accident at work does not reflect a common understanding of the EU's national laws. This results in a variety of colliding understandings of the term "accident at work", which are difficult to explain to the injured person. The necessity for additional consultation in such cases is usually not necessary in Germany due to the availability of wide-ranging and generous services and the country's approach to generally recognising and treating accidents at work with all appropriate means.[2] In other countries, however, the qualification of accidents as accidents at work or the availability of services may be restricted, thus limiting the provision of benefits to people who are accustomed to Germany's standards.

4 Third practical issue: continuation of – once acknowledged – provision of benefits in kind

Art. 36 Reg. (EC) No. 883/04 specifies that a person who has suffered an accident at work or an occupational disease and who resides or is staying in a Member State other than the competent Member State shall be entitled to the special benefits in kind of the scheme covering accidents at work and occupational diseases, which are provided on behalf of the competent institution, by the institution of the place of residence or stay in accordance with the legislation being applied, as though the respective individual were insured under the said legislation. Art. 35 para. 1 Reg. (EC) No. 987/09 stipulates that where the competent institution disputes the application of the legislation on accidents at work or occupational diseases under Article 36 Reg. (EC) No. 883/04, it shall without delay inform the institution of the place of residence or stay that has provided the benefits in kind which will then be considered sickness insurance benefits.

The coordination rules for accidents at work include a provision for the competent institution to set time limits for the institution of residence or of stay to provide benefits in kind. If the competent institution disputes the application of the legislation on accidents at work – without providing details on the legal reasoning for a limitation in its national law – the institution in the place of stay which has thus far provided benefits must respect these findings. Art. 35 Reg. (EC) No. 987/09 requires an immediate halt to the provision of benefits in kind, i.e. the services covered by SGB VII and a transfer of the case to the German Health Insurance as the institution of residence or stay. Any treatment, e.g. in case of an intensive and time consuming rehabilitation programme in a specialised rehabilitation clinic in Germany[3], comes to an abrupt end when

---

[2] Para. 1 II SGB VII: mit allen geeigneten Mitteln (with all appropriate means).
[3] BG Kliniken (bg-kliniken.de)

DVUA is informed by the competent institution of the dispute of the application of the legislation on accidents at work. This is rarely in the interest of the service provider or patient, nor does it reflect the general approach of the German Accident insurance to promote rehabilitation using all appropriate means and the reintegration into the labour market, which clearly deviates from health insurances' approach of implementing means of necessity[4].

When treatment, i.e. a special benefit in kind under the German Accident Insurance, has to be terminated abruptly and transferred to another institution, the patient faces an array of medical and personal problems. Such cases also raise administrative questions for the competent institution and may sometimes entail additional financial and planning challenges for the service provider.

5 Fourth practical issue: "benefits of participation" as "special benefits in kind"?

One legal issue the DVUA deals with in theoretical and practical terms is whether certain benefits for participating[5] in the German Statutory Accident Insurance are to be considered as "special benefits in kind of the scheme covering accidents at work" (Art. 36 para. 2 Reg. (EC) No. 883/04).

Art. 36 Reg. (EC) No. 883/04 stipulates as a general rule of the coordination of benefits in kind that a person, who has suffered an accident at work, shall be entitled to the special benefits in kind of the scheme provided by the institution of the place of residence or stay, as though he/she were insured under the said legislation.

The legal definition of "benefits in kind" in Art. 1 va) ii) Reg. (EC) No. 883/04, for the purposes of Title III, Chapter 2 (accidents at work and occupational diseases), codifies all benefits in kind relating to accidents at work and occupational diseases as defined in point (i) above and provided for under the Member States' accidents at work and occupational diseases schemes; whereas Art. 1 va) i) Reg. (EC) No. 883/04, for the purposes of Title III, Chapter 1 (sickness, maternity and equivalent paternity benefits) determines benefits in kind provided for under the legislation of a Member State, which intend to

---

[4] Para. 12 SGB V.
[5] Leistungen zur Teilhabe (benefits for participation).

supply, make available, pay directly or reimburse the cost of medical care and products and services ancillary to such care. This includes long-term care benefits in kind.

The German Social Accident Insurance provides for many special benefits. These benefits are either tailored to treat special serious injuries that occur, in particular, in an occupational context, or to adapt to changed living conditions in the long run as a result of lasting consequences of an accident at work. One of these special benefits is the "benefit for participation" which entails the remodelling of the patient's home (apartment or house) to adapt his or her living quarters to specific physical needs that have arisen as a result of the accident at work.[6]

A woman was insured in Spain when she suffered an accident at work while residing in Germany. DVUA as the institution of the woman's place of residence provided for the remodelling of her home in line with Germany's national provisions.[7] The actual costs for the adaptation of her home amounted to approximately EUR 11.000. The competent institution in Spain, however, rejected the application to cover those costs. It did not consider the remodelling of a home necessitated by an individual's physical needs following an accident at work to be a benefit in kind under Art. 36 para. 2, Art. 1 va ii) Reg. (EC) No. 883/04. The Spanish institution argued that the remodelling of a patient's home did not fall within the scope of the legal definition of benefits in kind that can be considered medical care and products and services ancillary to that care. The German interpretation goes beyond the wording and meaning of the legal definition provided for in Art. 1 va ii) Reg. (EC) No. 883/04. DVUA argued that the legal concept of delegation to all legal provisions of benefits in kind in the Member State of the respective institution of residence with the notion of *special benefits in kind* in case of accidents at work in accordance with Art. 36 para. 2 Reg. (EC) No. 883/04 overrules the restrictive reading of the legal definition in Art. 1 va) ii) Reg. (EC) No. 883/04. Art. 36 para. 2 was to be interpreted in the light of an overall concept of a complete legal delegation to the benefits in kind envisaged in the national law of the Member State of

---

[6] Wohnungshilfe (accommodation assistance).
[7] wohn.pdf (dguv.de) (10.3.2022).

residence. An injured person must be treated and receive all benefits in kind provided under the German scheme of accidents at work, as if he or she were insured under Germany's legislation (Art. 36 Reg. (EC) No. 883/04). The concept of mutual provision of benefits in kind and equal treatment leaves no space for choosing between the 'best of both worlds', i.e. between the countries involved, nor for limiting certain benefits in kind whilst those same benefits in kind would be provided to a person insured in Germany.

6 Other practical issues

Additionally, the ongoing practical challenges related to the reimbursement procedures of the actual costs and the objections of other Member States to acknowledge benefits in kind provided and paid for by DVUA as the respective institution of residence or stay shall be briefly mentioned. This concerns the internal procedures between DVUA and its partners.

7 Conclusion

The differences in social security systems and in the approaches of the 27 EU Member States (and the three additional states of the European Economic Area and Switzerland) are wide-ranging; the systems deviate at an even narrower level in terms of dealing with accidents at work. This represents an ongoing challenge for DVUA in its double function as a liaison body and the institution of the place of residence and stay when applying the coordination rules. Nonetheless, DVUA's administrative application of coordination rules – based on the general German understanding of rehabilitation applying all appropriate means to all injured persons – continues to face challenges, but is often a story of success if it reaches the stage of being able to provide benefits in kind. Guaranteeing the freedom of movement and bolstering the European spirit of one union continues to be crucial these days, especially for individuals in need who find themselves in an unfortunate situation such as an accident at work.

7 Social Security of Posted Workers and Platform Workers – Selected Challenges

Daniel Hlava

The coordination of social security systems raises a multitude of practical questions. This article deals with two selected challenges of EU coordination law. One is the well-known problem of the posting of workers which the amendment of the coordination regulation seeks to improve. In this context, the Court of Justice of the European Union (CJEU) has repeatedly dealt with questions related to the effects of A1 certificates in the past. This article reviews the difficulties that continue to arise in this regard. The second challenge this article examines is an issue that has gained momentum in recent years, namely how to deal with platform work. Questions about the coordination of social security law arise in this regard, in particular where non-local services are provided via an online platform that is based abroad.

1 Coordination of social security systems and the posting of workers[1]

1.1 The problem of the strict binding nature of A1 certificates

To coordinate the EU Member States' different national social security systems, the Coordination Regulation lays down the general principle that a worker who performs work in another Member State is subject to the social

---

[1] The statements in this section are partly based on the article by Hlava, AuR 2019, p. 84 et seqq.

security rules of that respective Member State (Article 11(3)(a) of Regulation No. 883/2004).

However, various exceptions to this principle apply. If a worker is temporarily posted (up to 24 months) to another Member State to perform work for another company on behalf of his or her employer, he or she continues to be subject to the social security system of his or her Member State of origin (Article 12(1) of Regulation No. 883/2004). An application can be submitted to the competent institution in the State of origin for the issuance of an A1 certificate (Portable Document A1 – PD A1) to confirm the continuation of social security protection in that State.

In 2019, approx. 3 million employees were posted to another Member State to perform work.[2] According to available data, a total of 505,737 Portable Documents (PDs) A1 were issued in 2019 for workers to perform work in Germany. At the same time, Germany was also the country that posted the highest number of workers to other EU Member States. Posted workers from Germany are sent primarily to Austria (262,296 PDs A1) and to France (214,164 PDs A1).[3]

A PD A1 establishes a presumption that the worker is covered by the social security system in his or her State of origin and is binding for the host Member State's social security agencies (Article 5(1) Regulation No. 987/2009)[4] to avoid double or multiple insurance payments.[5] As already confirmed by the CJEU, A1 certificates are strictly binding unless they have been cancelled by the issuing institution. Hence, according to the judgement in *A-Rosa Flussschiff*, host Member States' social security agencies are bound by an A1 certificate, even if Regulation No. 883/2004 is not applicable to the workers concerned.[6] Only if the A1 certificate is proven to have been fraudulently obtained can a court in the host Member State – on condition that the issuing institution

---

[2] Fries-Tersch et al., Annual report on intra-EU labour mobility 2020, p. 20.
[3] De Wispelaere et al., Posting of workers – Report on A1 Portable Documents issued in 2019, p. 11.
[4] CJEU of 30 March 2000 – C-178/97 (Banks and others), ECLI:EU:C:2000:169, para. 40.
[5] Cf. CJEU of 26 January 2006 – C-2/05 (Herbosch Kiere), ECLI:EU:C:2006:69, para. 21; Heuschmid/Schierle in Preis/Sagan (eds), Europäisches Arbeitsrecht, § 5 para. 37.
[6] CJEU of 27 April 2017 – C-620/15 (A-Rosa Flussschiff), ECLI:EU:C:2017:309, para. 52; cf. Reinhard, ZESAR 2018, p. 179.

does not review the certificate within a reasonable period of time – discount it.[7] This very limited exception is only available to courts during proceedings to establish the obligation to pay social security contributions. A national social security agency cannot discount an existing A1 certificate.[8]

1.2 The impracticable procedure to nullify A1 certificates

If a social insurance agency has doubts about the validity of an A1 certificate or about the information it includes, it can contact the issuing institution (Article 5(2), (3) of Implementing Regulation No. 987/2009). In accordance with the general principle of cooperation in good faith between Member States, which stipulates that Member States shall assist each other in meeting their obligations under Union law (cf. Article 4(3) TEU), if requested, the issuing institution must conduct a review of the A1 certificate. If the institutions involved fail to reach an agreement, the matter can be referred to the Administrative Commission, which shall mediate between the different positions (Article 5(4) of Regulation (EC) No. 987/2009).

The Administrative Commission consists of one government representative of each EU Member State; the EU Commission participates in an advisory capacity. The Administrative Commission is tasked with resolving administrative and interpretative questions related to the Coordination Regulation and the Implementing Regulation (Articles 71 et seq. of Regulation (EC) No. 883/2004). Due to its mediation function, the Administrative Commission's decisions merely have the status of an "opinion".[9] According to the CJEU's case law, the Administrative Commission cannot adopt legally binding decisions.[10] Its decisions therefore have no effect on the legal force of A1 certificates. If the issuing institution does not comply with the Administrative Commission's opinion, the host Member State's only option is to initiate infringement proceedings before the

---

[7] CJEU of 6 February 2018 – C-359/16 (Altun and others), ECLI:EU:C:2018:63, paras. 54 et seq.
[8] CJEU of 11 July 2018 – C-356/15 (Commission v Belgium), ECLI:EU:C:2018:555, para. 105.
[9] CJEU of 6 September 2018 – C-527/16 (Alpenrind and others), ECLI:EU:C:2018:669, para. 63; cf. Hlava, AuR 2019, p. 84 et seqq.
[10] Cf. CJEU of 5 December 1967 – 19/67 (van der Vecht); CJEU of 22 January 2014 – C-270/12 (United Kingdom v Parliament and Council), ECLI:EU:C:2014:18, para. 63.

CJEU against the State of origin. The judges will then review the question of the applicable law.[11]

Figure 1: *Overview of the dialogue and mediation process*

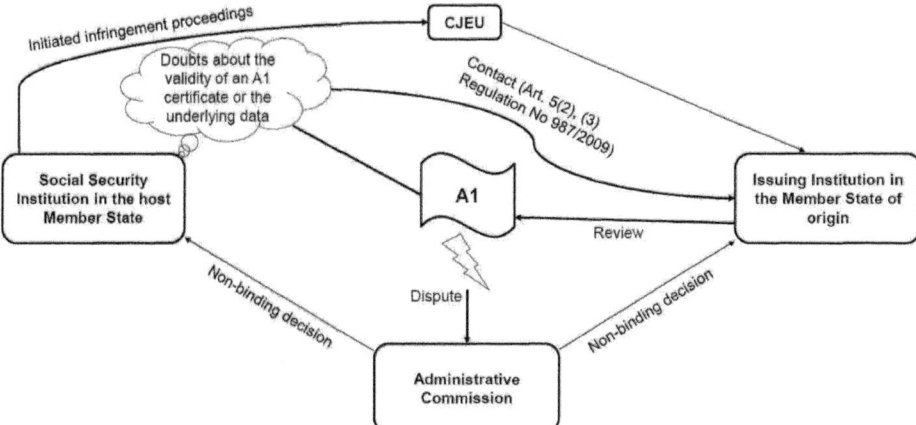

Several factors relating to the nullification procedure of A1 certificates warrant criticism. The lack of the procedural outcome's legal effect and the protracted process are major weaknesses, i.e. the procedure is not a practicable solution.[12] This situation is exacerbated by the fact that postings usually only last for a few months,[13] while the validation procedure of the A1 certificate usually takes far longer. By the time a decision is issued, workers have usually already returned to their States of origin, making it much more difficult – also for those workers – to enforce the law.

The European Commission aims to address this issue by introducing a legal amendment.[14] According to the proposal currently under discussion, the issuing institution would be required to review the A1 certificate at the request of an institution of the host Member State and, if necessary, correct or revoke it

---

[11] CJEU of 6 September 2018 – C-527/16 (Alpenrind and others), ECLI:EU:C:2018:669, para. 61; CJEU of 27 April 2017 – C-620/15 (A-Rosa Flussschiff), ECLI:EU:C:2017:309, para. 46.
[12] Cf. Hlava/Kraemer, Arbeitnehmerrechte grenzüberschreitend sichern, in WSI Report Nr. 67, p. 29.
[13] The total unweighted average duration per PD A1 is 139 days: De Wispelaere et al., Posting of workers – Report on A1 Portable Documents issued in 2019, p. 34.
[14] COM(2016) 815 final.

within 25 working days. If the certificate is found to be fraudulent, its revocation shall have retroactive effect. The documents on which this decision is based shall be forwarded to the requesting institution within 25 working days (or within two working days in case of proven urgency). However, no legal consequences in case of non-compliance with these requirements are yet foreseen.[15]

There is currently a political debate about the European Parliament's request for A1 certificate applications to be submitted prior to the relevant posting.[16] Opponents of this proposal assert that this would create unnecessary bureaucracy. However, in view of the objective to end the abusive use of A1 certificates, a document verifying that an application for an A1 certificate has been submitted in the State of origin should be sufficient. This is not unnecessary bureaucracy.[17] Because the Council of the EU called for exemptions from this requirement for individuals who travel for business or for short-term postings, the European Commission has submitted a proposal to allow for an exemption for employment in another EU Member State for a maximum of 24 hours. This, however, also entails potential for abuse, as there is no obligation to provide any evidence of the date of entry into the host Member State.[18]

A few suggestions to resolve these problems can be made: legal policy considerations on whether failure to review an A1 certificate within the proposed deadline should result in the loss of its strictly binding effect should be put forward.[19] Decisions of the Administrative Commission should have the force of law, which can be overturned by the CJEU. However, due to the far-reaching binding effect of A1 certificates, the requirements of such certificates should be

---

[15] Criticising this: German Trade Union Confederation (Deutscher Gewerkschaftsbund) – DGB, Stellungnahme zur Koordinierung der Systeme der Sozialen Sicherheit, 15 March 2017, p. 18.
[16] Hochscheidt/Nazarek, Soziale Rechte ohne Grenzen? – Die ewige Reform der EU-Koordinierung der sozialen Sicherheit; cf. Hlava et al., SozSich 2021, pp. 109 et seq.
[17] Hochscheidt/Nazarek, Soziale Rechte ohne Grenzen?
[18] Hochscheidt/Nazarek, Soziale Rechte ohne Grenzen? More on the discussions and compromise proposals in the trialogue of 7 December 2020, cf. Agence Europe, Interinstitutional negotiations on coordinating social security systems will resume under the Portuguese Presidency of the EU Council, Europe Daily Bulletin No. 12618, 9/12/2020, agenceurope.eu/en/bulletin/article/12618/24; this is also summarised in Hlava et al., SozSich 2021, pp. 109 et seq.
[19] Hlava/Kraemer, Arbeitnehmerrechte grenzüberschreitend sichern, in WSI Report Nr. 67, p. 29.

harmonised and EU-wide standards for their issuance should be established.[20] A 2020 study by Eurofound highlights that the procedures differ considerably in the different Member States.[21] In addition, a centralised electronic certificate application procedure should be considered – a European electronic register would considerably simplify the application procedure as well as the monitoring possibilities.[22]

1.3 The problem of the retroactivity of A1 certificates

The already mentioned retroactivity of A1 certificates[23] causes another practical problem. According to the CJEU's case law, the retroactive binding effect even supersedes a conflicting decision that has already been issued on the host Member State's social security obligation.[24] The CJEU justifies this by stating that a decision on compulsory insurance is not comparable to an A1 certificate.[25]

This practice should be viewed with scepticism. It might represent an incentive for companies posting workers to only apply for A1 certificates retrospectively when requested by authorities to do so.[26] This could increase the risk of illicit work, especially because controls by the authorities are inadequate.[27] If a social security obligation established in the host Member State can be de facto cancelled retroactively by an A1 certificate issued at a later point by another Member State, the result is legal uncertainty. At any rate, if a social security obligation in the host Member State has been confirmed in court proceedings, it would be problematic if a document of another Member State's authority (as part of the executive) automatically takes precedence with retroactive effect

---

[20] Hlava/Kraemer, Arbeitnehmerrechte grenzüberschreitend sichern, in WSI Report Nr. 67, p. 29.
[21] Eurofound: Improving the monitoring of posted workers in the EU.
[22] Motion of the Bundestag parliamentary group BÜNDNIS 90/ DIE GRÜNEN, Bundestagsdrucksache 19/24433, p. 4; Hlava/Kraemer, Arbeitnehmerrechte grenzüberschreitend sichern, in WSI Report Nr. 67, p. 29.
[23] CJEU of 30 March 2000 – C-178/97 (Banks and others), ECLI:EU:C:2000:169, para. 54.
[24] CJEU of 6 September 2018 – C-527/16 (Alpenrind and others), ECLI:EU:C:2018:669.
[25] CJEU of 6 September 2018 – C-527/16 (Alpenrind and others), ECLI:EU:C:2018:669, para. 75.
[26] Hlava, AuR 2019, p. 84 et seqq.
[27] Hlava/Kraemer, Arbeitnehmerrechte grenzüberschreitend sichern, in WSI Report Nr. 67, pp. 28 et seq.

over the court's final decision. The underlying objective of Article 5(1) of Regulation (EC) No. 987/2009 to avoid double insurance does not justify this far-reaching effect.[28]

1.4 The problem of social security coordination in the case of temporary agency workers

The question which social security system applies in the case of a cross-border assignment of workers arises not only in the context of the posting of workers, but also in the case of cross-border assignments of temporary workers. There were concerns that temporary work agencies might engage in so-called "forum shopping" by establishing headquarters in a Member State with (low) social security contributions that are more favourable for the company. Whether this is permissible essentially depends on whether the temporary work agency "normally carries out its activities" in the Member State in which it is established (Article 12(1) of Regulation (EC) No. 883/2004), since only then are its employees covered by that State's social security system.

In this regard, the Grand Chamber of the CJEU ruled in the TEAM POWER EUROPE case in 2021 that Article 14(2) of Regulation (EC) No. 987/2009 must be interpreted as meaning that a temporary work agency established in a Member State must – to be considered as "normally carrying out its activities" in that Member State within the meaning of Article 12(1) of Regulation (EC) No. 883/2004 – perform a significant share of its activity of assigning temporary agency workers to user undertakings established and performing activities in the territory of that Member State.[29] The ruling leaves open the question about the percentage of turnover the temporary employment agency must generate from assignments in its country of origin. As a rough guideline, according to the Practical Guide of the Administrative Commission, "e.g. turnover of approximately 25% of total turnover in the posting State could be a sufficient indicator, but cases where turnover is under 25% would warrant greater scrutiny".[30]

---

[28] Hlava, AuR 2019, p. 84 et seqq.
[29] CJEU of 3 June 2021 – C-784/19 (TEAM POWER EUROPE), ECLI:EU:C:2021:427.
[30] Administrative Commission: Practical guide on the applicable, p. 9; cf. Niksova, HSI-Report 2/2021, p. 9.

It should be noted that the CJEU's decision only refers to cases in which a temporary worker is posted to one other Member State. If the temporary worker is employed in several Member States, Article 13(1)(b)(i) of Regulation No. 883/2004 might be of relevance. It regulates multiple employment and determines whether the social security system of the Member State in which the temporary work agency is established is applicable. The problem in this regard is that the provision does not require (as Article 12(1) of Regulation No. 883/2004 does) for the employer to "normally carry out its activities there". There is therefore a risk that temporary work agencies will use the option of employment in at least one other Member State to circumvent the provision of Article 12 (1) of Regulation No. 883/2004.[31] EU legislators should intervene here and include the same condition in Article 13(1)(b)(i) of Regulation No. 883/2004.[32]

2 Social security of platform workers

2.1 Platform work and the coordination law – a brief introduction

Another issue to be considered is social security in the platform economy. What do we actually mean when we speak of platform work? It refers to work that is assigned via a virtual platform that can be located anywhere in the world. "Gig-work" is described as location-based work, where employees are assigned work via a platform and physically perform that work on site, e.g. food delivery services or taxi services such as Uber. Platform work can also entail location-independent services that can be performed from anywhere in the world via the internet (so-called "crowdwork"). The range of crowdwork-related tasks is very wide, from microtasks, such as writing captions, to highly skilled tasks, such as creating product designs. The platforms have very different business models; some platforms function purely as intermediaries for work, while others establish detailed specifications for the provision of services by their crowdworkers.[33]

---

[31] Niksova, HSI-Report 2/2021, p. 10.
[32] Niksova, HSI-Report 2/2021, p. 12.
[33] More details on the delimitation of different platforms and the definition of terms, cf. Leimeister et al., Crowd Worker in Deutschland; Berg et al., Digital labour platforms and the future of work.

But what do these new forms of work imply for the coordination of social security law? Most social security systems are employment-based. This notion is traditionally based on a physical concept of work. Work is performed on site in an establishment and the location determines the applicable social security system. EU coordination rules follow the lex loci laboris principle and use it as the basis for determining the competent State in case of cross-border activities.[34] The rise of new forms of work and specifically work via digital platforms, some of which are based in different Member States, can complicate the coordination of national social security systems, as geographical stability between the worker, his or her employer and the Member State are no longer a given in all cases.[35]

The case of gigwork should be more straightforward, as services are provided physically on site by the platform worker in the same State. The social security rules of this State therefore apply (Article 11(3)(a) Regulation No. 883/2004). The domicile of both the employer and the gigworker is irrelevant in this regard. Purely digital platform work such as crowdwork, on the other hand, may be carried out in two or more Member States. Article 13(1)(a) of Regulation No. 883/2004 – according to which the employee is subject to the legislation of the Member State of residence if he or she carries out a substantial part of his or her activity there – applies to crowdwork that can be classified as dependent employment. The same applies to crowdworkers who – and this is likely to be the case for the majority of workers[36] – pursue a self-employed activity that might be covered by Article 13(2)(a) of Coordination Regulation (EC) No. 883/2004. Yet how can we measure whether a substantial part of an individual's employment or self-employment activity is carried out in a specific Member State? According to Article 14(8) of Regulation (EC) No. 987/2009, an activity is substantial if it accounts for at least 25 per cent of the individual's total working time or income. Ultimately, it depends on an overall assessment of the circumstances.

---

[34] Schoukens, Building Up and Implementing the European Standards for Platform Workers, in Becker/Chesalina (eds), Social Law 4.0, pp. 317 et seq.
[35] Strban, Social Law 4.0 and the Future of Social Security Coordination, in Becker/Chesalina (eds), Social Law 4.0, pp. 346 et seqq.
[36] Cf. Leimeister et al., Crowd Worker in Deutschland, p. 40.

The Coordination Regulation does not contain a definition of "employee" or "self-employed person". Instead, it refers to national law.[37] In principle, the Member State on whose territory the crowdworker performs his or her activity is responsible for determining the nature of that activity. A crowdworker who carries out similar activities in two Member States may thus be classified as an employee in one State and as a self-employed person in the other, with the result that the Member State of employment is competent for that individual's social security in accordance with Article 13(3) of Regulation (EC) 883/2004.[38]

The following two labour law rulings illustrate the complexities that arise when the question whether a platform worker is an employee or a self-employed person under national law is of relevance for access to social security, and consequently also for the coordination of social security systems.

2.2 Gigwork – The example of Uber

We use the example of Uber to take a closer look at the gigwork economy. Uber's business model in a nutshell is bringing passengers and drivers together via a platform or app. It is similar to a taxi service, but the drivers are not formally employed by Uber and use their own cars to transport passengers. The company considers itself to be an intermediary for orders only, and not an employer. The processing of orders takes place via Uber.

In a 2016 ruling, the London Employment Tribunal[39] dealt with the question whether an Uber driver should be considered an employee under British law and should thus be entitled to minimum wage and paid annual leave. The Tribunal decided that it "is not real to regard Uber as working for the drivers and the only sensible interpretation is that the relationship is the other way around. Uber runs a transportation business. The drivers provide the skilled labour through which the organisation delivers its services and earns its profits".[40] Para. 92 of the judgement lists the 13 most important arguments that led the

---

[37] Strban, Social Law 4.0 and the Future of Social Security Coordination, in Becker/ Chesalina (eds), Social Law 4.0, p. 344 with further proofs.
[38] Strban, Social Law 4.0 and the Future of Social Security Coordination, in Becker/ Chesalina (eds), Social Law 4.0, pp. 346 et seq.
[39] London Employment Tribunal of 28 October 2016 – 2202550/2015.
[40] London Employment Tribunal of 28 October 2016 – 2202550/2015, para. 92.

court to decide that Uber drivers are indeed employees under British law. It demonstrated Uber's control over the drivers and that the service, e.g. the rating system, is similar to a disciplinary system, where drivers with a bad ranking are excluded from the platform. Drivers must accept rides, otherwise they will be deactivated; Uber sets the fare and there are several specifications for the drivers, e.g. choice of vehicle, choice of music and other forms of how to perform the work, which Uber controls.

The decision of the London Employment Tribunal was recently upheld by the Supreme Court.[41] However, it remains to be seen whether this approach will be followed by other European states and whether Uber drivers will be included in social security systems as employees.

2.3 Crowdworkers as employees?

In German law, an employee is defined as follows according to Section 611a German Civil Code (Bürgerliches Gesetzbuch – BGB): "The employment contract obliges the employee to perform work in the service of another in personal dependence and under instructions from a third party."[42] The understanding of who is a worker and thus subject to social insurance is similar. Section 7 of the Social Code Book IV (Sozialgesetzbuch – SGB IV) states: "Employment is non-self-employed work, in particular in an employment relationship. Indications for employment are work according to instructions and integration into the work organisation of the employer." This implies that every worker is also an employee in terms of social security law. However, the concept of employee can have an even broader scope of application.[43]

---

[41] Supreme Court of 19 February 2021 – uksc-2019-0029 (Uber BV and others v Aslam and others).
[42] Furthermore, Section 611a German Civil Code states in more detail: "The right to issue instructions may concern the content, performance, time and place of work. A person is bound by instructions if he or she is not essentially free to organise his or her work and determine his or her working hours. The degree of personal dependence also depends on the nature of the respective activity. In order to determine whether a contract of employment exists, an overall assessment of all circumstances must be made. If the actual implementation of the contractual relationship shows that it is an employment relationship, the designation in the contract is irrelevant".
[43] Brose, SozSich 2019, pp. 330, 331.

The question whether crowdworkers can be employees is controversial.[44] The German Federal Labour Court handed down a sensational ruling at the end of 2020.[45] A company had offered "microjobs" via an online platform based on a basic agreement and general terms and conditions. A crowdworker had been working for the platform for a long time, completing around 3,000 orders within 11 months. His tasks included visiting petrol stations and supermarkets, photographing the presentation of goods and forwarding the photos to the platform via an app. The higher the number of orders he completed, the higher his ranking on the platform. A higher ranking thus meant that he could carry out more and better-paid orders via the platform. Suddenly, his account was blocked without explanation and he could no longer pursue his gainful employment. He filed a complaint before the court claiming he was an employee of the platform.

One crucial question that arose in this case was whether the crowdworker was bound by instructions and was personally dependent on the platform, although he was not contractually bound to do so. The Federal Labour Court reviewed the facts of the individual case and came to the following conclusion:

> "Actual constraints due to an organisational structure created by the principal can also be suitable to induce the employee to behave in the desired way without concrete instructions having to be issued. (...) In order to assume an employment relationship, the principal must rather have taken organisational measures by which the employee – even if not directly instructed, but indirectly guided – is urged to continuously accept work assignments and to personally complete them within a certain time frame according to precise specifications. In this way, personal dependence within the meaning of Section 611a BGB can also be given by the incentive system of a platform. (...) However, a de facto planning security as in the case of the use of one's own staff can result from the fact that the employee is encouraged via the app provided by the client to continuously accept a certain order quota according to detailed specifications of the crowdsourcing company."[46]

In its review, the Court addressed employees' gaming instinct for the first time, which was deliberately used by the platform to run an incentives and control

---

[44] Fundamentally cf. Däubler/Klebe, NZA 2015, pp. 1032 et seqq.
[45] In the law on protection against dismissal: German Federal Labour Court of 1. December 2020 – 9 AZR 102/20.
[46] German Federal Labour Court of 1 December 2020 – 9 AZR 102/20, para. 36.

system (gamification). It stated that the platform "stimulated the 'gaming instinct' of users [i.e. crowdworkers] by offering them points for experience and the associated benefits with the aim of inducing them to regularly engage in activities"[47]. Among other arguments, the Federal Labour Court concluded that the crowdworker in this case was to be considered an employee.

Because there are so many different activities and platforms, whether a crowdworker should be considered an employee depends on the facts of each individual case. This ruling, however, introduces new standards on how such cases are to be assessed.[48] The crowdworker in this case was furthermore also recognised to be a worker in terms of social security.

2.4 Developments at European level and further proposals under discussion

Due to the difficulty of classifying the status of platform workers, many proposals are under discussion on how to improve their social protection. One of them is the European Agenda for the collaborative economy by which the European Parliament aims "to ensure fair working conditions and adequate legal and social protection for all workers in the collaborative economy, regardless of their status".[49]

The planned Digital Services Act[50] contains a number of regulations for the platform economy. It does not directly address platform workers' working conditions, but it does, for example, improve the transparency of platforms.

In June 2021, the European Commission launched the second phase of consultations with the social partners on possible measures to address the challenges related to the working conditions of platform work.[51] What types of proposals will result from these negotiations and which are in fact implemented remains to be seen.

---

[47] German Federal Labour Court of 1 December 2020 – 9 AZR 102/20, para. 50.
[48] Cf. also Wenckebach, SR 2020, pp. 165 et seqq.
[49] European Parliament resolution of 15 June 2017 on a European Agenda for the collaborative economy (2017/2003(INI)), para. 39.
[50] Cf. European Commission, The Digital Services Act: ensuring a safe and accountable online environment.
[51] Consultation Document of 15 June 2021, C(2021) 4230 final.

Many other proposals are under discussion in Member States. For example, calls have been made to include all working persons in social security systems, regardless of their status, at least in relation to solo self-employed persons.[52] Enzo Weber has developed the concept of "Digital Social Security" according to which platform operators should provide social security for platform workers and transfer a contribution to a payment system supervised by the ILO or World Bank, from which the workers' contributions should be paid into the workers' national social security systems.[53] Numerous other proposals have been discussed.[54]

A 2019 survey of platform workers in Germany also highlights the need for improvements in access to social security. According to the survey, the lack of social security is the greatest disadvantage of platform work in general.[55] Social protection gaps exist for platform workers around the world. An ILO survey of crowdworkers in 2017, for example, found that only 61.3 per cent of respondents had health insurance, 35 per cent had a pension/retirement plan and 37 per cent were covered by other forms of social insurance (only 16.1 per cent were insured against unemployment).[56]

3 Summary

These two examples illustrate that the coordination of social security systems faces old and new challenges. EU legislators must make legal adjustments to the social security of posted workers and temporary agency workers to find solutions that establish legal certainty, on the one hand, and that are practicable, on the other. Several proposals have been under political discussion for some time.

In the case of location-independent platform work, EU coordination rules could ease the practical difficulties crowdworkers who are active in two or more Member States face when determining where they are carrying out a substantial

---

[52] On the proposals with further references, Eichenhofer, In welchem Staat unterliegen grenzüberschreitend Plattformarbeitende der Sozialversicherungspflicht?, p. 6.
[53] Weber, Digital Social Security.
[54] Cf. e.g. Gruber-Risak, Soziale Sicherung von Plattformarbeitenden.
[55] Baethge et al., Plattformarbeit in Deutschland, p. 26 (Fig. 18).
[56] Cf. Berg et al., Digital labour platforms and the future of work, pp. 60 et seq.

part of their employment or self-employment activity. The issue of platform workers' social security protection still raises questions because of their often unclear status. Further impulses from Brussels can be expected in this regard in the future. As the 2020 ruling of the German Federal Labour Court shows, the traditional concept of employee can also encompass newer forms of work such as crowdwork and thus include persons in need of protection who do not perform traditional activities within a specific social security system.

References

Administrative Commission, Practical guide on the applicable legislation in the European Union (EU), the European Economic Area (EEA) and in Switzerland, 2013, https://ec.europa.eu/social/main.jsp?catId=868&langId=en (28/7/2021).

Baethge, Catherine Bettina; Boberach, Michael; Hoffmann, Anke; Wintermann, Ole, Plattformarbeit in Deutschland – Freie und flexible Arbeit ohne soziale Sicherung, 2019, https://www.bertelsmann-stiftung.de/fileadmin/files/BSt/Publikationen/GrauePublikationen/Plattform_07lay.pdf (27/7/2021).

Berg, Janine; Furrer, Marianne; Harmon, Ellie; Rani, Uma; Silberman, M Six, Digital labour platforms and the future of work – Towards decent work in the online world, Geneva, ILO, 2018.

Brose, Wiebke, Sozialrechtlicher Beschäftigtenbegriff und digitale Arbeit – Sozialversicherungsrechtliche Einordnungsschwierigkeiten von Crowdwork, Soziale Sicherheit (SozSich) 2019, issue 8-9, pp. 330-336.

Däubler, Wolfgang; Klebe, Thomas, Crowdwork: Die neue Form der Arbeit – Arbeitgeber auf der Flucht?, Neue Zeitschrift für Arbeitsrecht (NZA) 2015, issue 17, pp. 1032-1041.

De Wispelaere, Frederic; De Smedt, Lynn; Pacolet, Jozef, Posting of workers – Report on A1 Portable Documents issued in 2019, European Union 2021, doi: 10.2767/487681.

DGB, Stellungnahme zur Koordinierung der Systeme der Sozialen Sicherheit, 15 March 2017, https://www.dgb.de/themen/++co++b87a1712-145b-11e7-a447-5254 00e5a74a (27/7/2021).

Eichenhofer, Eberhard, In welchem Staat unterliegen grenzüberschreitend Plattformarbeitende der Sozialversicherungspflicht?, https://www.deutsche-rentenversicherung.de/SharedDocs/Untertitel/eichenhofer_lang_textversion.html;jsessionid=D5761 DEBE9EB315A636737BAC100AA5F.delivery2-1-replication (27/7/2021).

Eurofound, Improving the monitoring of posted workers in the EU, Luxembourg 2020, doi: 10.2806/3528.

European Commission, The Digital Services Act: ensuring a safe and accountable online environment, https://ec.europa.eu/info/strategy/priorities-2019-2024/europe-fit-digital-age/digital-services-act-ensuring-safe-and-accountable-online-environment_en (27/7/2021).

Fries-Tersch, Elena; Jones, Matthew; Siöland, Linus, Annual report on intra-EU labour mobility 2020, European Union, 2021, doi: 10.2767/075264.

Gruber-Risak, Martin, Soziale Sicherung von Plattformarbeitenden – Expertise für den Dritten Gleichstellungsbericht der Bundesregierung, 2020, https://www.drittergleichstellungsbericht.de/de/article/242.soziale-sicherung-von-plattformarbeitenden.html (28/7/2021).

Hlava, Daniel, Anwendbares Sozialversicherungssystem bei Arbeitnehmerentsendung – Anm. zu EuGH vom 06.09.2018 – C-527/16 (Alpenrind u.a.), Arbeit und Recht (AuR) 2019, issue 2, pp. 84-86.

Hlava, Daniel; Höller, Johannes; Klengel, Ernesto, Sozialpolitik im Fokus der deutschen Ratspräsidentschaft im 2. Halbjahr 2021, Soziale Sicherheit (SozSich) 2021, issue 3, pp. 109-111.

Hlava, Daniel; Kraemer, Birgit, Arbeitnehmerrechte grenzüberschreitend sichern, in AG Soziales Europa der Hans-Böckler-Stiftung (ed), #zukunftsozialeseuropa – Das Europäische Wirtschafts- und Sozialmodell stärken, WSI Report No. 67, 2021, pp. 26-31, https://www.boeckler.de/pdf/ p_wsi_report_67_2021.pdf (27/7/2021).

Hochscheidt, Lukas; Nazarek, Robert, Soziale Rechte ohne Grenzen? – Die ewige Reform der EU-Koordinierung der sozialen Sicherheit, 2 December 2020, www.dgb.de/themen/++co++33c1b23e-3494-11eb-baf0-001a4a160123 (27/7/2021).

Leimeister, Jan Marco; Durward, David; Zogaj, Shkodran, Crowd Worker in Deutschland – Eine empirische Studie zum Arbeitsumfeld auf externen Crowdsourcing-Plattformen, HBS-Study No. 323, 2016, https://www.boeckler.de/pdf/p_study_hbs_323.pdf (27/7/2021).

Niksova, Diana, Anwendbares Sozialversicherungsrecht bei grenzüberschreitender Arbeitnehmerüberlassung – Anmerkung zu EuGH v. 03.06.2021 – C-784/19 – Team Power Europe, in HSI-Report 2021, issue 2, https://www.hugo-sinzheimer-institut.de/faust-detail.htm?sync_id=HBS-008066 (28/7/2021).

Preis, Ulrich; Sagan, Adam (eds), Europäisches Arbeitsrecht, 2nd edition, Cologne 2019.

Reinhard, Hans-Joachim, Wanderarbeitnehmer / Bescheinigung 101 – Anmerkung zum Urteil des EuGH vom 27.4.2017, Rs. C-620/15 (A-Rosa Flussschiff GmbH/. Union de recouvrement des cotisations de sécurité sociale et d'allocations familiales d'Alsace (Urssaf), Rechtsnachfolgerin der Urssaf du Bas-Rhin, Sozialversicherungsanstalt des Kantons Graubünden), ZESAR 2018, issue 4, pp. 177-180.

Schoukens, Paul, Building Up and Implementing the European Standards for Platform Workers, in Becker, Ulrich; Chesalina, Olga (eds), Social Law 4.0 – New Approaches for Ensuring and Financing Social Security in the Digital Age, Baden-Baden 2021, pp. 309-334.

Strban, Grega, Social Law 4.0 and the Future of Social Security Coordination, in Becker, Ulrich; Chesalina, Olga (eds), Social Law 4.0 – New Approaches for Ensuring and Financing Social Security in the Digital Age, Baden-Baden 2021, pp. 335-361.

Weber, Enzo, Digital Social Security – Outline of a concept for the 21st century, in Working Paper Forschungsförderung No. 138, 2019, https://www.boeckler.de/pdf/p_fofoe_WP_138_2019.pdf (27/7/2021).

Wenckebach, Johanna, BAG: Crowdwork ante portas! Von persönlicher Abhängigkeit in der digitalen Arbeitswelt, Soziales Recht (SR) 2020, issue 5, pp. 165-175.

8 Realigning the Relationship between Social Security Coordination and the Digitalisation of Work

Effrosyni Bakirtzi

1 Introduction

The very first European Regulations on social security for migrant workers were adopted in 1958.[1] They were replaced by Regulation 1408/71[2], and later simplified by Regulation 883/2004.[3] European social security coordination law has been evolving for over 60 years.[4] The landscape of the modern workplace has transformed considerably since initial attempts to coordinate Member States' national social security systems were undertaken. Due to the progressively increasing need for flexibility, both for the employer and employee, new forms of employment emerged and spread quickly across Europe.[5] The relevance of

---

[1] Regulation 3/58 of 25 September 1958, OJ 30 and its implementing Regulation 4/58 of 3 December 1958, Official Journal 30, which entered into force on 1 January 1959.
[2] Regulation (EEC) No. 1408/71 of the Council of 14 June 1971 on the application of social security schemes to employed persons and their families moving within the Community, Official Journal L 149, 05/07/1971, pp. 2-50.
[3] Regulation (EC) No. 883/2004 of the European Parliament and of the Council of 29 April 2004 on the coordination of social security systems, Official Journal L 166, 30/04/2004, pp. 1–123.
[4] On the historical context of the EU and the coordination of social security, see Jaan Paju, The European Union and Social Security Law, Oxford/Portland, Oregon, 2017p. 15 et seq.
[5] These new forms of employment were extensively examined during the years 2013 and 2014 in a research project carried out by the European Foundation for the Improvement of Living and Working Conditions, the results of which have been published in Eurofound, New Forms of Employment, Publications Office of the European Union, Luxembourg, 2015. On the methodology used for this research project, see Irene Mandl, Overview of

these new forms of employment has been gradually increasing and are transforming the labour market. This transformation is driven by the digitalisation of work in several spheres.

The present chapter provides an overview of the impact of digitalisation on the world of work and explores the challenges this phenomenon has created for the European social security coordination system. Two distinct cases are considered. The first case involves frontier and cross-border workers, particularly in view of the extraordinary situation caused by the COVID-19 pandemic. The second case explores cross-border platform workers whose position in the social security coordination system is unclear due to their uncertain legal status and their fluid work modalities. The final section of the chapter focusses on the enforcement of EU rules in social security coordination followed by some concluding remarks.

2 Digitalisation of work and the transformations of the employment relationship

The new forms of employment are classified into two distinct groups: (i) new models of employment relationships between the employer and employee or the client and worker, and (ii) new work patterns, i.e. different ways of performing work. These types of employment do not correspond to the 'standard' employment relationship, namely full-time and open-ended employment contracts in the premises of the employer, which was the prevailing form of work when the first regulation was adopted. In addition to these new forms of employment, such as fixed-term, part-time, temporary agency, on-call, zero hours work and freelance contracts, which quickly emerged due to the labour market transformations triggered by and in the aftermath of the economic crisis, we must also consider the effects of the digitalisation of work.

These new forms of work have continued to evolve as a result of the increasing digitalisation of work, which is evident in several aspects of both work organisation and employment relationships. The use of digital tools facilitate remote

---

New Forms of Employment, in Bernd Waas, New Forms of Employment in Europe, Bulletin of Comparative Labour Relations, Alphen aan den Rijn, 2016, pp. 7-22.

working, i.e. performing work outside the employer's premises in a non-conventional workplace under teleworking or mobile working arrangements. Moreover, these new forms of employment are drifting away from the traditional employer-employee relationship towards multiple/a network of employers who hire employees for ad hoc assignments or who share employees, or even use voucher-based work.[6] Such contractual relationships may not always fall within the scope of the application of labour law as the workers might be classified as freelancers or self-employed contractors. In addition, the high mobility of such workers, not only in view of their unconventional workplaces but also because of contractual transitions and the performance of work in two or more EU countries, may lead to conflicts of law as regards the applicable national rules. International private law solutions based on currently applicable national labour law[7] and the social security coordination law may not suffice to address the issues arising from the digitalisation of work.

3 The challenges digitalisation poses for social security coordination

The challenges digitalisation raises for social security coordination have thus far only been dealt with within the context of the practical application of the Social Security Coordination Regulations with the introduction of the Electronic Exchange of Social Security Information (EESSI)[8] and the potential of introducing a European Social Security Pass (including the portable documents A1

---

[6] Voucher-based work refers to an employment relationship and payment that is grounded on a voucher instead of an employment contract. Voucher systems are usually a means to fight undeclared or informal work and they are mostly used in the agriculture and household services sectors. See Eurofound (2015), New forms of employment, Publications Office of the European Union, Luxembourg, p. 82et seq.

[7] The applicable legislation to individual employment contracts of workers who make use of their right to free movement arises from the freedom of the parties to the employment relationship to choose the applicable labour law in accordance with Article 8(1) in combination with Article 3 of Regulation (EC) No. 593/2008 of the European Parliament and of the Council of 17 June 2008 on the law applicable to contractual obligations (Rome I), OJ L 177, 4.7.2008, pp. 6-16. If there is no agreement, the applicable law is determined in conformity with Articles 8(2) to (4) of the Regulation.

[8] A fully operational EESSI in mid-2022 will facilitate the transnational coordination of social security systems according to Franz Terwey, Sozialversicherung als digitale Netzstruktur innerhalb der EU, Vom Online-Management zum plattformgestützten Universaldienst, ZESAR, Vol. 1, 2022, p. 5, https://doi.org/10.37307/j.1868-7938.2022.01.04.

and the European Health Insurance Cards) by 2023.⁹ Both of these initiatives envisage administrative procedures to facilitate a quick transfer of information between national authorities, access to documents and distance services to citizens who exercise their right to move freely within the European Union (hereafter EU).

Nevertheless, substantial issues may become an obstacle to the implementation and application of the social security coordination rules and consequently to the free movement of persons within the EU. These substantial law issues relate to the legal concepts and work constellations that have emerged due to the transformation of the world of work in the era of digitalisation. The EU rules on labour mobility cannot be detached from the EU rules on social security coordination. Therefore, the gaps identified with regard to labour mobility, such as the absence of an EU definition of worker,¹⁰ may extend to and have an impact on the application of the social security coordination regulation.

The effects of globalisation pose challenges for the legal protection of labour and social security of highly mobile individuals, workers with multiple employers, those who perform work in several countries and digital nomads. This contribution does not look beyond EU borders, however. Investigating the phenomenon of digital work at the global level is a complex task and requires extensive research and comparative legal work to arrive at reliable and substantive results.

---

[9] According to the European Pillar of Social Rights Action Plan, Publications Office of the European Union, Luxembourg, 2021, p. 30.

[10] On the prospective development of an EU definition of worker, see Study of the European Economic and Social Committee, The definition of worker in the platform economy: Exploring workers' risks and regulatory solutions, 2021 (accessible at: https://www.eesc.europa.eu/sites/default/files/files/qe-05-21-286-en-n_0.pdf). On a purposive approach to the definition of the concept of "worker", see Martin Risak and Thomas Dullinger, The concept of "worker" in EU law: Status quo and potential for change, ETUI Report 140, 2018. On the tendency to expand the concept of employee in the case law of the CJEU, Felipe Temming, Systemverschiebungen durch den unionsrechtlichen Arbeitnehmerbegriff – Entwicklungen, Herausforderungen und Perspektiven, Soziales Recht, Ausgabe 4, 2016, pp. 158-168.

4 The relevance of digitalisation of work for the coordination of social security systems

4.1 The case of frontier and cross-border workers

Frontier workers[11] are defined in Article 1(f) of Regulation 883/2004[12] as individuals pursuing an activity as employed or self-employed persons in a Member State but reside in another Member State to which, as a general rule, they return daily or at least once a week.[13]

The social security rights of frontier and cross-border workers are similar although the activity of frontier workers is performed in one Member State while they reside in another. The activity of cross-border workers, on the other hand, is performed in two or more Member States.

4.1.1 The impact of the COVID-19 pandemic on labour mobility across borders

Although the trend of increased mobility has been observed in the EU in recent years, it was reversed after the outbreak of the COVID-19 pandemic. Physical mobility was reduced and workers' mobility was further hampered by travel restrictions and national lockdowns and other emergency measures introduced to contain the spread of the virus. The free movement of persons within the EU faced unprecedented challenges. Many people were reluctant to search for new work opportunities in other countries or were not able to move to another country for work due to travel restrictions. Soon demand for seasonal or care

---

[11] For a clarification of the notion, see Dr. Albrecht Otting in: Hauck/Noftz, EU-Sozialrecht, Artikel 1 Definitionen, Berlin, 2015.

[12] This legislation also applies to Iceland, Liechtenstein and Norway through the European Economic Area Agreement, as well as to Switzerland through a bilateral agreement.

[13] The differentiation of frontier from cross-border workers is of less relevance in social security coordination law compared to tax law. In bilateral double-taxation agreements, the definition of frontier worker is more restrictive and in certain cases excludes cross-border workers by the introduction of a spatial criterion. See European Parliament, Directorate General for Research, WORKING PAPER, Social Affairs Series – W 16A – Frontier Workers in the European Union, available at: https://www.europarl.europa.eu/workingpapers/soci/w16/summary_en.htm. In the present chapter, the terms cross-border and frontier worker is used interchangeably.

workers could not be met in countries whose labour supply depended heavily on migrant workers.

The working conditions of cross-border and frontier workers in the EU have changed since the outbreak of the pandemic. In addition to restrictions to the free movement of persons as a result of the introduction of border controls, another measure introduced with the purpose of limiting social interaction was the extensive use of teleworking or mobile working with the assistance of (new) digital technologies. In some countries, teleworking became mandatory, where possible, while it remained optional or was partially enforced in others during the different phases and waves of the pandemic. Work culture has also changed, shifting from physical presence in the workplace towards a fully or partially virtual workplace. During the pandemic, this form of work prevailed even in companies or industries that had used teleworking or remote working only sparingly before the outbreak of the health crisis. Current discussions are concentrated on the future model of work and whether to introduce a hybrid model based on the experiences gleaned from the COVID-19 crisis. Virtual mobility is flourishing as a result of the digitalisation of work while remote working is being adopted to meet the needs of the 'new normal' caused by the coronavirus.

All of the above developments have practical implications for the pre-COVID-19 European social security coordination system. The effect of the pandemic in combination with the digitalisation of work is clearly visible and has become a topic of debate and research in national contexts.

4.1.2 Implications for the social security rights of frontier and cross-border workers

It is not unusual for individuals who reside in one EU country to take up work in another, particularly if they live within close proximity of the border. These workers commute daily to the neighbouring country to perform work and return home after work (or at least on a regular basis). Special provisions of Regulation 883/2004 apply to such migrant workers to facilitate their commute between countries and to protect their social security rights and those of their families.

The changes in remote working arrangements caused by the COVID-19 pandemic may have a major impact on these workers' social security coverage stipulated in the provisions of Regulation 883/2004. Article 13 paragraph 1 of Regulation 883/2004 applies to persons who pursue an activity as employed workers in two or more Member States. According to the Article, the worker is subject to the legislation of the Member State of residence if he/she performs a *substantial* part of his/her activity in *that* Member State. Alternatively, if he/she does not carry out a substantial part of his/her activity in the Member State of residence, the principle of *lex loci laboris* applies.[14] This reference to the law of the workplace points to the existence of an interface between social security coordination law and labour law.[15]

Given the new working arrangements, many frontier or cross-border workers are now performing work remotely and are thus carrying out the substantial part of their activities in their country of residence, which in turn may have implications for the applicable legislation *lex loci laboris*. If the work performed remotely exceeds 25 per cent of an employee's total working time, the applicable social security legislation changes, namely from the legislation applicable in the country of employment to that applicable in the country of residence.[16] The accumulation of insurance periods and entitlement to benefits may be affected as well. Moreover, employers may face additional administrative and financial burdens in terms of social security contributions if the contribution

---

[14] Article 13(1)(b) of Regulation (EC) No. 883/2004. The application of Article 13 must be read in conjunction with Articles 14, 16 and 19 of Regulation (EC) No. 987/2009 of the European Parliament and of the Council of 16 September 2009 laying down the procedure for implementing Regulation (EC) No. 883/2004 on the coordination of social security systems (Text with relevance for the EEA and for Switzerland), OJ L 284, 30.10.2009, pp. 1-42. For an analysis of the provisions of Article 13 of Regulation 883/2004 with practical examples and case law, see Stamatia Devetzi in: Hauck/Noftz, EU-Sozialrecht, Art. 13, Berlin, 2021.

[15] On the elements of co-existence of the fields of social security and labour law in the social security coordination framework, see Rob Cornelissen and Guido Van Limberghen, Social security for mobile workers and labour law, in Frans Pennings and Gijsbert Vonk (eds), Research Handbook on European social security law, Cheltenham/Northampton, 2015, pp. 344-384.

[16] Article 14(8) of Regulation (EC) No. 987/2009 of the European Parliament and of the Council of 16 September 2009 laying down the procedure for implementing Regulation (EC) No. 883/2004 on the coordination of social security systems (Text with relevance for the EEA and for Switzerland) OJ L 284, 30.10.2009, pp. 1-42.

rates in the employee's country of employment differ from those payable in his/her country of residence.

An additional challenge that has been identified in the context of measures to contain the coronavirus is entitlement to compensation as a result of loss of earnings due to a quarantine obligation imposed on the frontier worker. Interestingly, if the German *Land* imposes quarantine on a worker in Germany, he/she is entitled to compensation in line with Section 56(1) sentence 2 of the German Infection Protection Act.[17] If, however, quarantine is imposed on the worker by the authority of *another* Member State (where he/she resides or teleworks from) as a consequence of mobility restrictions, the frontier worker is *not* entitled to such compensation. This compensation is paid to the worker's employer in order to continue paying the worker's wages during the period of quarantine. This has implications for the continuation of payment of wages of frontier workers because entitlement to such compensation depends on which authority (in which Member State) ordered the quarantine.[18] It is difficult to include such compensation payments in the material scope of Regulation 883/2004 because they are not covered in Article 3 thereof.[19]

4.1.3 Solutions at EU level and in selected EU countries

Many employers ordered cross-border workers to work from home to contain the spread of the virus and to protect the health and safety of workers. This change in working conditions potentially had an impact on cross-border workers' social security obligations and their rights and entitlements, as the applicable social security legislation might have changed in accordance with the social security coordination rules.

---

[17] Infektionsschutzgesetz (IfSG).
[18] This case has been analysed in view of the compatibility of this regulation with EU law and the principle of equal treatment in Thomas Giegerich, Entschädigungsansprüche von Grenzgänger in Corona-Quarantäne - § 56 Infektionsschutzgesetz aus unionsrechtlicher Sicht, ZEuS 2/2021, pp. 237-275, https://doi.org/10.5771/1435-439X-2021-2-237. Giegerich characterises this situation as an unequal distribution of wage risk.
[19] Measures mitigating the consequences of the COVID-19 pandemic for workers have been adopted in several Member States. Some of these may have implications for the material scope of Regulation 883/2004, as benefits or other measures may not qualify as triggering the application of the Regulation's provisions.

The European Union has introduced certain initiatives in this regard. In March 2020, the European Commission issued a set of guidelines on the free movement of workers during the pandemic.[20] More specifically, according to Guideline Number 7, Member States shall allow frontier workers to continue crossing their borders to reach their workplace if the performance of work in the given industry is still possible or permissible in the host Member State. Moreover, Guideline Number 8 asserts "in situations that could lead to a change in the Member State of insurance of the worker in cases of pluriactivity in two Member States,[21] the Member States are encouraged to make use of the exception provided for in Article 16 of Regulation (EC) No 883/2004 with a view to maintaining the social security coverage unchanged for the worker concerned. To apply for such an exception, the employer must submit a request to the Member State whose legislation the worker requests to be subject to".

The individual experiences of certain countries are also worth mentioning. For example, many individuals who reside in Sweden but work in Denmark or Norway were ordered by their employers to work from home. The authorities of the countries involved collaborated to arrive at pragmatic solutions to the arising questions.[22] Frontier workers who performed more than 25 per cent of their total working hours from home in Sweden continued to be covered by the social security system of their actual country of employment (i.e. Denmark or Norway). No changes were introduced to the applicable legislation and the workers' social insurance was also not affected, even though they were performing

---

[20] Communication from the Commission, Guidelines concerning the exercise of the free movement of workers during COVID-19 outbreak (2020/C 102 I/03).

[21] More specifically, a frontier or cross-border worker in this case refers to individuals who work in both the Member State of employment and of residence and are insured in the country of employment because their activity in the Member State of residence is not substantial. If the working time in the country of residence exceeds the threshold of 25 per cent of total working time as a result of remote working due to confinement measures imposed by certain Member States, then there is a risk that the applicable legislation will change, i.e. that the legislation of the country of residence will apply.

[22] Thomas Erhag, Social security during the pandemic – the case of Sweden, in Stamatia Devetzi and Angelos Stergiou (eds.), Social security in times of corona, Thessaloniki, 2021, pp. 171-173.

a substantial part of their activity in their country of residence due to remote working arrangements.[23]

The Netherlands, Belgium and Germany also agreed that working from home during the lockdowns imposed to contain the coronavirus would not affect the originally applicable legislation. Article 14 of Regulation 987/2009 establishes a margin of appreciation for the competent authorities in defining the notion "substantial part of the activity" under the given circumstances.[24] The agreement between these countries' authorities interpreted the relevant Article by disregarding the working from home element.[25] However, the modified work patterns had to directly be connected to the measures introduced as a result of the coronavirus pandemic.[26]

Despite the extraordinary conditions created by the coronavirus, no substantial changes with regard to the applicable legislation were observed. The geographic location of certain countries allowed for a swift response to this unprecedented situation. Member States engaged in dialogue and agreed with neighbouring Member States to keep the initially applicable conditions – in particular for frontier workers – in place for the duration of the emergency. These initiatives sought to ensure the continuity of the applicable social security legislation. Many countries drew on Article 16 of Regulation 883/2004.[27] Furthermore, a temporary emergency measure in response to a pandemic was not deemed a

---

[23] A similar agreement was concluded between Italy and Switzerland regulating cross-border teleworking during the COVID-19 pandemic providing that "on an entirely exceptional and provisional basis" days of work performed by frontier workers at home on behalf of a Swiss company "as a result of the measures taken to combat the spread of COVID-19" shall be counted as working days performed in Switzerland.

[24] Article 14(8) of Regulation 987/2009.

[25] Frans Pennings, Social security in the Netherlands in times of corona, in Stamatia Devetzi and Angelos Stergiou, Social security in times of corona, Thessaloniki, 2021, pp. 103-106.

[26] In Belgium, employers must declare the introduction of teleworking as of 1 April 2021: https://www.socialsecurity.be/site_fr/employer/applics/coronavirus/index.htm (last accessed on 12.02.2022). This obligation does not only affect employers of frontier and cross-border workers, but all workers, including in the public sector.

[27] See the county fiches included in the European Labour Authority report, Impact of teleworking during the COVID-19 pandemic on the applicable social security, July 2021.

relevant change in circumstances justifying a modification of the applicable legislation or of insurance coverage.[28] The question that arises in this regard is how long such an extraordinary emergency justifies derogations from the Regulation's application. In addition, it will be interesting to observe whether the post-covid era will bring permanent changes in the work organisation of frontier or cross-border workers. The change of the circumstances in that case may then justify a modification of the applicable legislation or of insurance coverage. Thus, it is still to be seen how such changes will affect the applicable legislation and insurance coverage in the long term.

4.2 Cross-border platform work

Platform work[29] refers to working in the crowd (or crowdwork) and work on demand in digital labour platforms[30] within the context of the sharing or gig economy. Work on demand usually entails services provided within a given country, and the cross-border element may not always be present.[31] Platform work consists of work divided into smaller tasks or units and is performed or delivered remotely. These tasks may require low-/medium- or high skills. Depending on the number of tasks performed, platform work may vary from being a worker's primary economic activity or a secondary job to supplement his/her main activity. The nature of these assignments is, by and large, marginal as they are offered sporadically and are generally intended to supplement the con-

---

[28] For example, the case of the Czech Republic: https://www.cssz.cz/web/en/coronavirus-disease-covid-19-and-certificate-a1-cz (last accessed 12.02.2022).

[29] Digital platforms are intermediaries for freelance, delivery or home services. According to a study prepared for the European Commission, the number of digital labour platforms (DLPs) active in the EU-27 has increased by around 12 per cent over the past five years from about 463 in 2016 to 520 in 2020: Willem Pieter de Groen, Zachary Kilhoffer, Leonie Westhoff, Doina Postica and Farzaneh Shamsfakhr, Digital Labour Platforms in the EU: Mapping and Business Models, 2021, p. 26. Available online at: https://ec.europa.eu/social/main.jsp?catId=738&langId=en&pubId=8399&furtherPubs=yes (last accessed 12 February 2022).

[30] This terminology is adopted by the proposal for a Directive of the European Parliament and of the Council on improving working conditions in platform work from 9 December 2021 (COM(2021) 762 final), preamble 17-18 and Article 2 which contains a definition of digital labour platform.

[31] With one exception, namely when the intermediary platform is located in a country other than that where the work is performed or the services are provided.

tractor's main economic activity. If a platform worker who performs only marginal work is recognised as being an employee and he/she also carries out a primary economic activity as an employee, he/she is considered to have multiple employment relationships.

Platform work is perceived as an atypical form of work made possible through the use of digital technologies and innovations of the 4th Industrial Revolution.[32] The perception of platform work as atypical work is inferred from the discrepancy of this type of work from the standard 'typical' open ended, full-time employment relationship. Standard in the sense of 'regulated' atypical forms of work include part-time work, temporary agency work and fixed-term work.[33] Working arrangements have continued to evolve, however, and new non-standard types of atypical work, such as platform work, have emerged. Challenges in terms of regulating platform work arise at both the national as well as European level.[34] The EU's current initiatives in this regard aim to improve the working conditions of platform workers while at the same time supporting the sustainable growth of digital labour platforms in the EU.[35] The protection of social security in platform work is an issue that will most likely be intensively discussed in coming years once the legal landscape of labour protection becomes clearer.

---

[32] Ivana Vukopera, Cross-Border Platform Work: Riddles for Free Movement of Workers and Social Security Coordination, 70 ZBORNIK PFZ 481, 2020, pp. 481-512, DOI: 10.3935/zpfz.70.4.02.

[33] For possible applicability of the Fixed-Term Work Directive (1999/70/EC (FTWD)) to platform workers, see Annika Rosin, Platform work and fixed-term employment regulation, European Labour Law Journal, 2021, Vol. 12/2, pp. 156-176, DOI:10.1177%2F2031952520959335.

[34] For an international perspective on theoretical and practical regulatory problems of platform work, see Lourdes Mella Méndez & Alicia Villalba Sánchez (eds), Regulating the Platform Economy, International Perspectives on New Forms of Work, Oxon/New York, 2020.

[35] See the proposal for a Directive of the European Parliament and of the Council on improving working conditions in platform work from 9 December 2021 (COM(2021) 762 final). This initiative addresses the ongoing misclassification of employment status in platform work by establishing certain legal criteria under which a platform qualifies as an employer. On discussions regarding the introduction and impact of a rebuttable legal presumption for platform workers within the EU's legal framework, see Miriam Kullmann, 'Platformisation' of Work: An EU Perspective on Introducing a Legal Presumption, European Labour Law Journal, 2021, pp. 1-15, DOI:10.1177%2F20319525211063112.

The phenomenon of platform work has been the focus of labour law for quite some time.[36] As this form of work does not only have implications for labour law but for social security law as well, the social protection needs of such workers must be acknowledged.[37] Recent studies explore the relationship between platform work and social security law in general[38] or in more specific national contexts.[39] The triad of platform work, labour law and social security law has not yet been investigated in depth; labour law studies only explore certain elements of social security law and vice versa.

The type of platform work that could be of relevance for social security coordination is work that involves an invisible (virtual) relocation (of the work) to foreign countries.[40] This invisible (non-tangible) transnational element poses several challenges associated with cross-border labour flows. The typology of digital platforms is relevant in this regard. Some platforms operate online and are web-based while others are location-based.[41] Tasks that can be performed

---

[36] See, for example, Rogen Blanpain, Frank Hendrickx and Bernd Waas (eds), New Forms of Employment in Europe, Alphen aan den Rijn 2016; Jeremias Prassl, Humans as a Service, Oxford 2018; Bernd Waas, Wilma B. Liebmann, Andrew Lyubarsky, Katsutoshi Kezuka, Crowdwork – A Comparative Law Perspective, HSI-Schriftenreihe, Band 22, 2017.

[37] This need is acknowledged in the German context in Wiebke Brose, Von Bismarck zu Crowdwork: Über die Reichweite der Sozialversicherungspflicht in der digitalen Arbeitswelt, NZS 2017, pp. 7-14.

[38] See the literature review by Olga Chesalina, Platform Work: Critical Assessment of Empirical Findings and its Implications for Social Security, in Ulrich Becker and Olga Chesalina (eds), Social Law 4.0, New Approaches for Ensuring and Financing Social Security in the Digital Age, Baden Baden, 2021, pp. 39-72. For a comparative law overview, see Isabelle Daugareilh, Christophe Degryse and Philippe Pochet (eds), The platform economy and social law: Key issues in comparative perspective, ETUI Working Paper 2019.10, available online at: https://www.etui.org/publications/working-papers/the-platform-economy-and-social-law-key-issues-in-comparative-perspective (last accessed 12 February 2022), as well as the special issue Isabelle Daugareilh (guest editor), A European & Comparative Legal Approach on Digital Workers, Comparative Labour Law & Policy Journal, Vol. 41/2, 2020.

[39] Martin Gruber-Risak, Soziale Sicherung von Plattformarbeitenden, Expertise für den Dritten Gleichstellungsbericht der Bundesregierung, 2020, available at: https://www.dritter-gleichstellungsbericht.de/de/article/242.soziale-sicherung-von-plattformarbeitenden.html.

[40] See Olga Chesalina, Platform Work: Critical Assessment of Empirical Findings and its Implications for Social Security, in Ulrich Becker and Olga Chesalina (eds), Social Law 4.0, New Approaches for Ensuring and Financing Social Security in the Digital Age, Baden Baden, 2021, p. 53 et seq (including references to relevant literature).

[41] For different typologies of digital labour platforms (Eurofound, ILO and COLLEEM), see Willem Pieter de Groen, Zachary Kilhoffer, Leonie Westhoff, Doina Postica and Farzaneh

online via web-based platforms include online clerical and data entry tasks, online professional services, online creative and multimedia services, online sales and marketing support, online software development and technology, online writing and translation, online micro tasks or online interactive services. Typical location-based tasks include personal transportation services, delivery services or domestic work.

Social security coverage and entitlements depend on the type of contractual relationship. If a platform worker is classified as an employee, he/she will be entitled to benefits that differ from those of self-employed persons or freelancers.

The contractual relationship of platform work involves three parties: the online digital platform, the client and the worker. The nature of the contractual relationship between these three parties depends on the national legal framework within which the digital platform operates. It is therefore a question of national legislation and its interpretation by the national courts whether the relationship between the digital platform or between the client and the platform worker is one of employment.[42] There are extensive debates on how to extend platform workers' labour protection to include at least a set of rights, if not full labour law rights.[43]

Shamsfakhr, Digital Labour Platforms in the EU: Mapping and Business Models, 2021, p. 17 et seq. Available online at: https://ec.europa.eu/social/main.jsp?catId=738&langId=en&pubId=8399&furtherPubs=yes (last accessed 12 February 2022).

[42] There are numerous constellations of contractual relationships. Most digital platforms follow the business model of an IT company which operates as an intermediary relying on a crowd of independent, self-employed contractors to carry out services. These platforms position themselves as intermediaries between the client and the service provider-platform's worker and can thereby shift most of the costs, risks and liabilities to other parties. Only a minority of platforms actually employ their workers who usually perform location-based work. See Willem Pieter de Groen, Zachary Kilhoffer, Leonie Westhoff, Doina Postica and Farzaneh Shamsfakhr, Digital Labour Platforms in the EU: Mapping and Business Models, 2021, p. 64 et seq. Available online at: https://ec.europa.eu/social/main.jsp?catId=738&langId=en&pubId=8399&furtherPubs=yes (last accessed 12 February 2022).

[43] The experiences of countries such as the U.S., Germany and Japan, provide useful insights into the need for regulation in different national contexts facing the same challenges in terms of crowdwork in Bernd Waas, Wilma B. Liebman, Andrew Lyubarsky and Katsutoshi Kezuka, Crowdwork – A Comparative Law Perspective, HIS-Schriftenreihe, Band 22, Frankfurt am Main, 2017.

Whether platform workers are covered by Regulation 883/2004 depends on the qualification of their legal status under national law which may (or may not) grant them entitlement to social security benefits. In addition, it may be challenging to apply the principle of non-discrimination to platform workers because of the specificity of their contractual relationship and their entitlement to benefits across borders. Finally, determining which legislation applies to cross-border platform workers or to platform workers with multiple employment relationships is not always straightforward because platform work is usually performed marginally, i.e. it is a side activity or the income from such assignments is generally low.

4.2.1 The divide between the employee and self-employment status: relevance for social security coordination regulation

The personal scope of application of the coordination Regulation is quite broad. According to Article 2 of Regulation 883/2004, its scope covers all Member State citizens (including citizens in Norway, Iceland and Liechtenstein) as well as refugees and stateless persons who legally reside in a Member State and are subject or have been subject to the legislation of one or more Member States. Moreover, the Regulation applies to family members and descendants thereof, even when they are third-country nationals. Other third-country nationals were not initially covered, but with the adoption of Regulation (EU) No. 1231/2010,[44] the protection of Regulation 883/2004 was extended to third-country nationals.[45]

The scale of coordination varies for different categories of persons. What is of crucial importance is whether the individual is considered an insured worker (meaning most of the coordination rules would apply), or whether he/she is an

---

[44] Regulation (EU) No. 1231/2010 of the European Parliament and of the Council of 24 November 2010 extending Regulation (EC) No. 883/2004 and Regulation (EC) No. 987/2009 to third-country nationals who are not already covered by these Regulations solely on the ground of their nationality, OJ L 344, 29.12.2010, pp. 1-3.

[45] For the conditionality of such a coverage see Rob Cornelissen, 60 years of European social security coordination. Achievements, controversies and challenges, in Franz Marhold, Ulrich Becker, Eberhard Eichenhofer, Gerhard Igl, Giulio Prosperetti (eds), Arbeits- und Sozialrecht für Europa: Festschrift für Maximilian Fuchs, Baden Baden, 2020, p. 422 et seq, https://doi.org/10.5771/9783748909231-417.

economically inactive union citizen covered by limited social security coordination rules.[46]

Moreover, the legal status as an employee or self-employed person under a given national legislation may afford different levels of social protection. Since national social security systems in the EU are not harmonised but coordinated by the Regulation, differences in the level of protection may arise when an individual moves from one country to another – and thus from one national social security system to another. Apart from physical movement, virtual movement as a result of change in work organisation due to digitalisation may also entail a cross-border element, which would qualify as migratory movement and would depart from a clear national context.

One of the guiding principles of Regulation 883/2004 and an objective of the free movement of persons within the EU is to ensure that no individual who crosses internal EU borders remains without social protection. Article 11(3)(a) of the Regulation provides that "a person pursuing an activity as an employed or self-employed person in a Member State shall be subject to the legislation of that Member State". Article 1(a) of the Regulation 883/2004 defines the "activity as an employed person" as "any *activity* or *equivalent situation treated as such* for the purposes of the social security legislation of the Member State in which such activity or equivalent situation exists". The element of relevant activity for the national social security system is significant but may lead to a referral circle. The solution proposed is that the notion of activity must hypothetically be fulfilled so that the applicable legislation can be determined.[47]

4.2.2 Legal status and diversity of classification in national legal orders

The legal status of platform workers is, in principle, subject to national legislation. The qualification as an employee and his/her social protection coverage hinges on the national legal order. Traditional labour rules divide the labour

---

[46] Jaan Paju, The European Union and Social Security Law, 2017, Oxford/Portland, Oregon, p. 26.

[47] Ulrich Preis and Stephan Seiwerth, Der Beschäftigtenbegriff im Europäischen Sozialrecht, in Franz Marhold, Ulrich Becker, Eberhard Eichenhofer, Gerhard Igl, Giulio Prosperetti (eds), Arbeits- und Sozialrecht für Europa: Festschrift für Maximilian Fuchs, Baden Baden, 2020, p. 640 et seq, https://doi.org/10.5771/9783748909231-417.

market into a binary system with two distinct categories of economically active persons, namely employees and self-employed persons.[48] Although platform workers are often treated as self-employed or independent contractors, this construct could be challenged by the fact that their contractual relationship with the platform may exhibit characteristics of what is usually considered to be an employment relationship.[49] In case of bogus-self-employment,[50] certain subordination criteria may furthermore be met, such as economic dependence, control, surveillance and the assessment of work performance by the platform, resulting in a misclassification of the worker's legal status,[51] which would also imply inadequate access to social protection.[52]

Therefore, the notion of activity as defined in Article 1(a) of Regulation 883/2004 might be appropriate if a teleological interpretation is followed which takes the Regulation's objective into consideration. It may seem that an autonomous EU definition of 'activity as an employed person' is still out of reach, but an understanding of such an activity at the national level is not without limitations and needs to be in conformity with EU law.[53] The national definition of

---

[48] In some countries, there is an intermediary category between employees and self-employed persons, i.e. 'employee-like' persons. See Bernd Waas, Guus Heerma van Voss (eds) and Effrosyni Bakirtzi, Marta Otto (assistant eds), Restatement of Labour Law in Europe, Vol. I, The Concept of Employee, Oxford/Portland, Oregon, 2017, p. lxiii et seq.

[49] For two examples of labour law rulings that illustrate the complexities involved in the qualification of platform workers as employees and the associated access to social security, see Daniel Hlava, Social Security of Posted Workers and Platform Workers – Selected Challenges, in this book.

[50] Persons are hired as self-employed persons, but in practice are employees.

[51] See PPMI, Study to support the impact assessment of an EU initiative on improving working conditions in platform work, 2021, p. 50. Available at: https://ec.europa.eu/social/main.jsp?catId=738&langId=en&pubId=8428&furtherPubs=yes (last accessed at 12.02.2022).

[52] For a proposal to decouple social protection from employment as a means to address the challenges of digital platform work on social protections systems, see Christina Behrendt, Quynth Anh Nguyen and Uma Rani, Social protection systems and the future of work: ensuring social security for digital platform workers, International Social Security Review, Vol. 72/3, 2019, p. 27 et seq.

[53] Ulrich Preis and Stephan Seiwerth, Der Beschäftigtenbegriff im Europäischen Sozialrecht, in Franz Marhold, Ulrich Becker, Eberhard Eichenhofer, Gerhard Igl, Giulio Prosperetti (eds), Arbeits- und Sozialrecht für Europa: Festschrift für Maximilian Fuchs, Baden Baden, 2020, p. 643 et seq, https://doi.org/10.5771/9783748909231-417. Also Grega Strban, Social Law 4.0 and the Future of Social Security Coordination, in Ulrich Becker and Olga Chesalina, Social Law 4.0, New Approaches for Ensuring and Financing Social Security in the Digital Age, Baden Baden, 2021, p. 344 with the respective references to case law of the CJEU, https://doi.org/10.5771/9783748912002-335.

activity as an employed persons in light of the Regulation's wording could diverge from the national definition of employee.[54]

Moreover, distinct classifications of platform workers in different Member States might raise issues with regard to the coordination of social security systems. While they are excluded from social protection in some countries because of their marginal or merely ancillary activity, they will not be covered by the social security coordination system. If, however, they are covered because *all* residents of the given country are covered, then the social security coordination rules *will* apply to them.[55]

Platform workers' social protection can be covered by private or voluntary insurance schemes. For example, Uber has entered a partnership with AXA to strengthen the protection of independent workers in France. UberEats concluded a similar agreement to offer delivery riders an insurance package in Europe. This programme is funded by Uber at no cost to eligible partners and provides protection for accident, injury, illness as well as maternity and paternity benefits.[56] Furthermore, coverage has been extended across Europe through a new partnership with Allianz.[57] These cases cover location-based platform work, but could potentially be extended to online web-based digital labour platforms as well. Such schemes are not subject to the social security coordination regulation because they do not fall within the scope of Article 3 of Regulation 883/2004.

---

[54] It is suggested that the word "activity", which has not yet been defined by the CJEU, should not be attributed a limited understanding by Ulrich Preis and Stephan Seiwerth, Der Beschäftigtenbegriff im Europäischen Sozialrecht, in Franz Marhold, Ulrich Becker, Eberhard Eichenhofer, Gerhard Igl, Giulio Prosperetti (eds), Arbeits- und Sozialrecht für Europa: Festschrift für Maximilian Fuchs, Baden Baden, 2020, p. 644 et seq.

[55] Grega Strban, Social Law 4.0 and the Future of Social Security Coordination, in Ulrich Becker and Olga Chesalina, Social Law 4.0, New Approaches for Ensuring and Financing Social Security in the Digital Age, Baden Baden, 2021, p. 345, https://doi.org/10.5771/9783748912002-335.

[56] Terry Gangcuangco (2018), 'Uber and AXA tie-up to provide driver coverage across Europe', Insurance Business Magazine, 24 May, available at: https://www.eurofound.europa.eu/et/data/platform-economy/records/uber-and-axa-tie-up-to-provide-driver-coverage-across-europe (last accessed at 12.02.2022).

[57] https://www.allianz.com/en/press/news/business/insurance/211206_Allianz-Partners-and-Uber-are-partnering-to-provide-benefits-and-protection-insurance-for-independent-drivers-and-couriers-in-Europe.html (last accessed at 12.02.2022).

4.2.3 The potentially marginal nature of platform work and the impact on the applicable legislation

Platform workers usually engage in platform work as a secondary (side) activity, i.e. their temporal commitment to platform work or their dependence on the income from such activity is limited. What is of relevance with regard to coverage of the social security coordination system is whether their activity is considered marginal and as such is excluded from the material scope of Regulation 883/2004. Currently, the decision whether an activity is marginal or not is based on Article 14(8) of Regulation 987/2009, which sets certain indicative criteria to determine whether a substantial part of the employed or self-employed person's activity is performed in one Member State for the purpose of identifying the applicable legislation in case of activity in two or more Member States under Article 13(1) and (2) of Regulation 883/2004. The criteria to be considered are "in the case of an employed activity, the working time and/or the remuneration, and in the case of a self-employed activity, the turnover, working time, number of services rendered and/or income. In the framework of an overall assessment, a share of less than 25 % in respect of the criteria mentioned above shall be an indicator that a substantial part of the activities is not being pursued in the relevant Member State". The Administrative Commission for the Coordination of Social Security Systems proposes that activities accounting for less than 5 per cent of the worker's regular working time and/or less than 5 per cent of his/her overall remuneration should be considered marginal work.[58] In addition, Article 14(5)b provides that when a platform worker simultaneously works in different Member States, his/her marginal activities will be disregarded for the purpose of determining the applicable legislation.[59]

---

[58] Grega Strban, Social Law 4.0 and the Future of Social Security Coordination, in Ulrich Becker and Olga Chesalina, Social Law 4.0, New Approaches for Ensuring and Financing Social Security in the Digital Age, Baden Baden, 2021, p. 348, https://doi.org/10.5771/9783748912002-335.

[59] Ivana Vukopera, Cross-Border Platform Work: Riddles for Free Movement of Workers and Social Security Coordination, 70 ZBORNIK PFZ 481, 2020, pp. 500-1, DOI: 10.3935/zpfz.70.4.02.

5 Enforcement of EU rules on social security coordination: The role of the European Labour Authority

With regard to platform work, especially in cross-border situations, the enforcement of social rights is challenging because of the lack of traceability and transparency in the virtual world of work. National authorities lag behind in terms of access to data on digital platforms and their workers. When platforms operate across borders, traceability becomes even more problematic. This fact in combination with the phenomenon of undeclared platform work[60] complicates the enforcement by national authorities of different obligations even further, especially in terms of collecting social security contributions. This challenge is addressed in the proposal for a Directive of the European Parliament and of the Council on improving working conditions in platform work from 9 December 2021 (COM(2021) 762 final). The enhancement of transparency, traceability and awareness of developments in platform work and improving the enforcement of the applicable rules for all platform workers, including those operating across borders, is a stated objective of this proposal.[61] Chapter IV of the proposal for a Directive on transparency on platform work aims to achieve this.[62] Article 11 of the proposed Directive stipulates that "without prejudice to the Regulations (EC) 883/2004 and 987/2009 of the European Parliament and of the Council, Member States shall require digital platforms which are employers to declare work performed by platform workers to the competent labour and social protection authorities of the Member State in which the work is performed and to share relevant data with those authorities, in accordance with the rules and procedures laid down in the law of the Member States concerned". This provision focusses in particular on cross-border platform work because its

---

[60] EESC – European Economic and Social Committee, Impact of digitalization and the on-demand economy on labour markets and the consequences for employment and industrial relations, 2017, p. 54, available at: https://www.eesc.europa.eu/en/our-work/publications-other-work/publications/impact-digitalization-and-demand-economy-labour-markets-and-consequences-employment-and-industrial-relations#downloads (last accessed on 12.02.2022).

[61] See explanatory memorandum of the proposal for a Directive of the European Parliament and of the Council on improving working conditions in platform work from 9 December 2021 (COM(2021) 762 final), p. 3.

[62] See also the chapter of Daniel Hlava, Social Security of Posted Workers and Platform Workers – Selected Challenges, in this book.

practical implementation is quite problematic. The exchange of information between Member States on platform workers, their contractual status and the general terms and conditions applicable to their relationships would have to be coordinated or embedded within the existing structure of social security systems coordination. Therefore, an amendment of Regulation 883/2004 would be necessary in this respect to cover cross-border platform workers and to enforce their rights.

The newly established European Labour Authority (hereafter ELA) could ensure fairness in the internal market by monitoring and enforcing the EU rules on social security coordination.[63] The Authority is tasked "to assist the Member States and the European Commission in strengthening the access to information, support compliance and cooperation between the Member States in the consistent, efficient and effective application and enforcement of the Union law related to labour mobility across the Union, and the coordination of social security systems within the Union, and mediate and facilitate solutions in the case of disputes".[64] Moreover, the ELA shall assist in the coordination of social security systems without prejudice to the tasks and activities of the Administrative Commission for the Coordination of Social Security Systems.[65] More specifically, the ELA shall contribute to the improvement of the availability, quality and accessibility of information[66] and conduct risk assessments and analyses on labour mobility and social security coordination across the Union.[67] In addition, there is a clear distinction between the competencies of the ELA and the Administrative Commission on Social Security Coordination.

The monitoring and enforcement of social security rights would cover not only cross-border platform work, but remote cross-border working arrangements as

---

[63] Preamble 6 of Regulation (EU) No. 2019/1149 of the European Parliament and of the Council of 20 June 2019 establishing a European Labour Authority, amending Regulations (EC) No. 883/2004, (EU) No. 492/2011, and (EU) 2016/589 and repealing Decision (EU) 2016/344 (Text with relevance for the EEA and for Switzerland), OJ L 186, 11.7.2019, pp. 21-56. On the role of the European Labour Authority in general, see Jan Cremers, The European Labour Authority and rights-based labour mobility, ERA Forum, (2020) 21:21–34, https://doi.org/10.1007/s12027-020-00601-1.
[64] According to the Preamble 6 of Regulation (EU) 2019/1149.
[65] According to the Preamble 11 of Regulation (EU) 2019/1149.
[66] Article 5 of Regulation (EU) 2019/1149.
[67] Article 10 of Regulation (EU) 2019/1149.

well.[68] The purpose of the ELA's establishment is to ensure control of compliance of cross-border labour mobility due to the limited, fragmented and dispersed national competencies, shortage of specialised staff, lack of mandate in the host country and difficulty accessing the necessary information.[69] Several unresolved issues have been identified.[70] One of these is of relevance for digital cross-border work, namely concerted joint inspections as part of the ELA's mission to facilitate and enhance cooperation between Member States in the enforcement of relevant Union law across the EU.[71] This is not an EU-wide mandate that is comparable to the competence of joint activities of other EU authorities. It remains to be seen whether this EU authority will succeed in fighting regime-shopping and regulatory arbitrage used by legal entities operating in a cross-border context, such as digital labour platforms.

6 Concluding remarks

The phenomenon digitalisation of work creates new direct and indirect challenges for the coordination of social security systems, which could not have been anticipated at the time the Regulation was adopted. The continuously changing world of work and work organisation has an impact on transnational entitlements to benefits and the recognition of social security rights. Crossing national borders to pursue economic activities takes place both physically and virtually. Regulation 883/2004 was drafted and adopted at a time when physical

---

[68] The European Labour Authority issued a report on the impact of teleworking during the corona crisis on the applicable social security: European Labour Authority, Impact of teleworking during the COVID-19 pandemic on the applicable social security: Overview of measures and/or actions taken in EU Member States to facilitate a flexible approach to the applicable social security of teleworking cross-border workers, 2021, available at: https://www.ela.europa.eu/en/analyses-and-risk-assessment#ecl-inpage-290 (last accessed on 12.02.2022).

[69] See the findings of several projects which highlight that national competent enforcement and compliance authorities face difficulties in meeting their obligations in cases of cross-border labour mobility in Jan Cremers, The European Labour Authority and rights-based labour mobility, ERA Forum, 2020, p. 24 et seq, https://doi.org/10.1007/s12027-020-00601-1.

[70] Jan Cremers, The European Labour Authority and rights-based labour mobility, ERA Forum, 2020, p. 31 et seq, https://doi.org/10.1007/s12027-020-00601-1.

[71] Article 2(b) of the Regulation (EU) 2019/1149.

mobility prevailed. At the time of its adoption, the dimensions of virtual mobility were neither perceptible nor predictable.

Legislative initiatives and the adaptation of rules on the coordination of social security systems might be helpful, but since the commencement of the extended negotiation procedures in 2016 (which have not yet been concluded) to revise the Regulation, it has become abundantly clear that consensus on such initiatives cannot always be easily reached. In times of virtual mobility and transitions in working arrangements, the regulations on labour mobility and social security coordination must be aligned to close existing gaps in social protection and in the interpretation of entitlements to transnational social rights to dynamically adapt to the demands of the future of (digital) work. The application of different spheres of law and the participation of more than one jurisdiction cause legal complexities and uncertainties. Currently, as already mentioned above, the European Commission is seeking to improve the working conditions of platform workers in recognition of the emergence of this form of work and issues associated with their labour law protection. However, one should always keep in mind that the cross-border element of platform work may very often complicate the situation in terms of not only the labour protection of platform workers in general, but also their social protection, social security coverage and entitlements. This latter element is a matter that the coordination of social security systems in Europe will certainly need to focus on now and in the future.

References

Behrendt, Christina/Anh Nguyen, Quynth/Rani, Uma, Social protection systems and the future of work: ensuring social security for digital platform workers, International Social Security Review, Vol. 72, 3/2019, pp. 17-41.

Blanpain, Rogen/Hendrickx, Frank/Waas, Bernd (eds), New Forms of Employment in Europe, Alphen aan den Rijn, 2016.

Brose, Wiebke, Von Bismarck zu Crowdwork: Über die Reichweite der Sozialversicherungspflicht in der digitalen Arbeitswelt, NZS 2017, pp. 7-14.

Chesalina, Olga, Platform Work: Critical Assessment of Empirical Findings and its Implications for Social Security, in Becker, Ulrich/Chesalina, Olga (eds), Social Law

4.0, New Approaches for Ensuring and Financing Social Security in the Digital Age, Baden Baden, 2021, pp. 39-72.

COMMUNICATION FROM THE COMMISSION, Guidelines concerning the exercise of the free movement of workers during COVID-19 outbreak (2020/C 102 I/03).

Cornelissen, Rob, 60 years of European social security coordination. Achievements, controversies and challenges, in Marhold, Franz/Becker, Ulrich/Eichenhofer, Eberhard/Igl, Gerhard/Prosperetti, Giulio (eds), Arbeits- und Sozialrecht für Europa: Festschrift für Maximilian Fuchs, Baden Baden, 2020, pp. 417-434, https://doi.org/10.5771/ 9783748909231-417.

Cornelissen, Rob/Van Limberghen, Guido, Social security for mobile workers and labour law, in Pennings, Frans/Vonk, Gijsbert (eds), Research Handbook on European social security law, Cheltenham/Northampton, 2015, pp. 344-384.

Cremers, Jan, The European Labour Authority and rights-based labour mobility, ERA Forum, 2020, pp. 21-34 et seq, https://doi.org/10.1007/s12027-020-00601-1.

Devetzi, Stamatia in Hauck/Noftz, EU-Sozialrecht, Kommentar, Artikel 13, Berlin, 2021.

Daugareilh, Isabelle/Degryse, Christophe/Pochet, Philippe (eds), The platform economy and social law: Key issues in comparative perspective, ETUI Working Paper 2019.10, available online at: https://www.etui.org/publications/working-papers/the-platform-economy-and-social-law-key-issues-in-comparative-perspective (last accessed 12 February 2022).

Daugareilh, Isabelle (guest editor), Special Issue: A European & Comparative Legal Approach on Digital Workers, Comparative Labour Law & Policy Journal, Vol. 41/2, 2020.

Devetzi, Stamatia/Stergiou, Angelos (eds), Social security in times of corona, Thessaloniki, 2021,

EESC – European Economic and Social Committee, Impact of digitalization and the on-demand economy on labour markets and the consequences for employment and industrial relations, 2017, available at: https://www.eesc.europa.eu/en/our-work/publications-other-work/publications/impact-digitalization-and-demand-economy-labour-markets-and-consequences-employment-and-industrial-relations# downloads (last accessed on 12.02.2022).

Erhag, Thomas, Social security during the pandemic – the case of Sweden, in Devetzi, Stamatia/Stergiou, Angelos (eds), Social security in times of corona, Thessaloniki, 2021, pp. 155-175.

Eurofound, New forms of employment, Publications Office of the European Union, Luxembourg, 2015, p. 82 et seq.

European Economic and Social Committee, The definition of worker in the platform economy: Exploring workers' risks and regulatory solutions, 2021 (accessible at: https://www.eesc.europa.eu/sites/default/files/files/qe-05-21-286-en-n_0.pdf).

European Labour Authority, Impact of teleworking during the COVID-19 pandemic on the applicable social security: Overview of measures and/or actions taken in EU Member States to facilitate a flexible approach to the applicable social security of teleworking cross-border workers, 2021, available at: https://www.ela.europa.eu/en/analyses-and-risk-assessment#ecl-inpage-290 (last accessed on 12.02.2022).

European Parliament, Directorate General for Research, WORKING PAPER, Social Affairs Series – W 16A – Frontier Workers in the European Union, available at: https://www.europarl.europa.eu/workingpapers/soci/w16/summary_en.htm.

European Pillar of Social Rights Action Plan, Publications Office of the European Union, Luxembourg, 2021.

Gangcuangco, Terry (2018), 'Uber and AXA tie-up to provide driver coverage across Europe', Insurance Business Magazine, 24 May, available at: https://www.eurofound.europa.eu/et/data/platform-economy/records/uber-and-axa-tie-up-to-provide-driver-coverage-across-europe (last accessed at 12.02.2022).

Giegerich, Thomas, Entschädigungsansprüche von Grenzgänger in Corona-Quarantäne – § 56 Infektionsschutzgesetz aus unionsrechtlicher Sicht, ZEuS 2/2021, pp. 237-275, https://doi.org/10.5771/1435-439X-2021-2-237.

de Groen, Willem Pieter/Kilhoffer, Zachary/Westhoff, Leonie/Postica, Doina/Shamsfakhr, Farzaneh, Digital Labour Platforms in the EU: Mapping and Business Models, 2021, available online at: https://ec.europa.eu/social/main.jsp?catId=738&langId=en&pubId=8399&furtherPubs=yes (last accessed 12 February 2022).

Gruber-Risak, Martin, Soziale Sicherung von Plattformarbeitenden, Expertise für den Dritten Gleichstellungsbericht der Bundesregierung, 2020, available at: https://www.dritter-gleichstellungsbericht.de/de/article/242.soziale-sicherung-von-plattformarbeitenden.html.

Hlava, Daniel, Social Security of Posted Workers and Platform Workers – Selected Challenges, in this book.

Kullmann, Miriam, 'Platformisation' of Work: An EU Perspective on Introducing a Legal Presumption, European Labour Law Journal, 2021, pp. 1-15, DOI:10.1177%2F20319525211063112.

Mandl, Irene, Overview of New Forms of Employment, in Blanpain, Roger/Hendrickx, Frank/Waas, Bernd (eds), New Forms of Employment in Europe, Bulletin of Comparative Labour Relations, Alphen aan den Rijn, 2016, pp. 7-22.

Mella Méndez, Lourdes/Villalba Sánchez, Alicia (eds), Regulating the Platform Economy, International Perspectives on New Forms of Work, Oxon/New York, 2020.

Otting, Albrecht in: Hauck/Noftz, EU-Sozialrecht, Artikel 1 Definitionen, Berlin, 2021.

Paju, Jaan, The European Union and Social Security Law, Oxford/Portland, Oregon, 2017.

Pennings, Frans, Social security in the Netherlands in times of corona, in Devetzi, Stamatia/Stergiou, Angelos (eds), Social security in times of corona, Thessaloniki, 2021, pp. 91-107.

PPMI, Study to support the impact assessment of an EU initiative on improving working conditions in platform work, 2021, available at: https://ec.europa.eu/social/main.jsp?catId=738&langId=en&pubId=8428&furtherPubs=yes (last accessed at 12.02.2022).

Prassl, Jeremias, Humans as a Service, Oxford, 2018.

Preis, Urlich/Seiwerth, Stephan, Der Beschäftigtenbegriff im Europäischen Sozialrecht, in Marhold, Franz/Becker, Ulrich/Eichenhofer, Eberhard/Igl, Gerhard/Prosperetti, Giulio (eds), Arbeits- und Sozialrecht für Europa: Festschrift für Maximilian Fuchs, Baden Baden, 2020, pp. 639-650, https://doi.org/10.5771/9783748909231-417.

Risak, Martin/Dullinger, Thomas, The concept of "worker" in EU law: Status quo and potential for change, ETUI Report 140, 2018.

Rosin, Annika, Platform work and fixed-term employment regulation, European Labour Law Journal, 2021, Vol. 12/2, pp. 156-176, DOI:10.1177%2F2031952520959335.

Strban, Grega, Social Law 4.0 and the Future of Social Security Coordination, in Becker, Ulrich/Chesalina, Olga (eds), Social Law 4.0, New Approaches for Ensuring and Financing Social Security in the Digital Age, Baden Baden, 2021, pp. 335-362, https://doi.org/10.5771/9783748912002-335.

European Economic and Social Committee, The definition of worker in the platform economy: Exploring workers' risks and regulatory solutions, 2021 (accessible at: https://www.eesc.europa.eu/sites/default/files/files/qe-05-21-286-en-n_0.pdf).

Temming, Felipe, Systemverschiebungen durch den unionsrechtlichen Arbeitnehmerbegriff – Entwicklungen, Herausforderungen und Perspektiven, Soziales Recht, Ausgabe 4, 2016, pp. 158-168.

Terwey, Franz, Sozialversicherung als digitale Netzstruktur innerhalb der EU, Vom Online-Management zum plattformgestützten Universaldienst, ZESAR, Vol. 1, 2022, pp. 3-10, https://doi.org/10.37307/j.1868-7938.2022.01.04.

Vukopera, Ivana, Cross-Border Platform Work: Riddles for Free Movement of Workers and Social Security Coordination, 70 ZBORNIK PFZ 481, 2020, pp. 481-512, DOI: 10.3935/zpfz.70.4.02.

Waas, Bernd/Heerma van Voss, Guus (eds)/Bakirtzi, Effrosyni/Otto, Marta (assistant eds), Restatement of Labour Law in Europe, Vol. I, The Concept of Employee, Oxford/Portland, Oregon, 2017.

Waas, Bernd/Liebmann, Wilma B./Lyubarsky, Andrew/Kezuka, Katsutoshi, Crowdwork – A Comparative Law Perspective, HSI-Schriftenreihe, Band 22, Frankfurt am Main, 2017.

9 Recent Case Law on the Coordination of Social Security Systems under Regulation 883/2004

Anna Tsetoura

1 Introductory remarks

There are various issues arising from the implementation of the Regulation on Coordination of social security systems. Generally, many practical questions are answered through the case law of the Court of Justice of the European Union (CJEU). This is also true for the recent case law of the CJEU to be presented. The Court deals with preliminary rulings concerning different practical matters and quite often certain complications that emerge from the application of the Coordination Regulation in practice. Our search, which covered a 5-year period, identified 36 judgements of the CJEU. Some of the judgements have been excluded from our analysis, however, because Regulation 883/2004 is of only little relevance to them and they are of insignificant legal consequence. We present 30 selected judgements of the CJEU which address a wide range of issues from social security benefits (old-age, sickness, invalidity, family and unemployment benefits) to special non-contributory benefits, social security contributions and applicable legislation, including the posting and third-country nationals[1] under Regulation 883/2004. A comprehensive assessment of these

---

[1] Old-age benefits (4 cases), sickness benefits (4 cases), invalidity benefits (1 case), family benefits (6 cases), unemployment benefits (2 cases), special non-contributory benefits (1 case), social security contributions (3 cases), applicable legislation (including cases of posting and third-country nationals) (9 cases).

cases is provided based on comparisons with previous cases brought before the Court.[2]

2 Old-age benefits

2.1 Distinction between pre-retirement benefits and old-age benefits

In *Czerwiński*,[3] the Court reviewed the differences between pre-retirement benefits and old-age benefits, focussing on the characteristics of so-called 'bridging pensions' in Poland's social security system.

The applicant Czerwiński had completed contribution and non-contribution periods in Poland as well as in both Germany and Norway for periods of work as a second engineer and a chief engineer on a boat, respectively. The Polish authorities, referring to Article 9 of Regulation No. 883/2004, claimed that bridging pensions fall within the scope of pre-retirement benefits, whereas the referring court concluded that such pensions should be classified as old-age benefits.

The distinction between pre-retirement benefits and old-age benefits is crucial because the aggregation rule of Article 6 Regulation 883//2004 does not apply to pre-retirement benefits (Article 66 Regulation 883/2004). The Court seems to have adhered to the EU social security law perspective by closely scrutinising the characteristics of Poland's national social security benefits to determine whether the claimant's bridging pension ought to be classified as an old-age benefit or as a pre-retirement benefit. The description of the dispute mentions "contribution periods", which are compared with "insurance periods", which used to be the key determinant of a pension applicant's status. The concept of reciprocity applies in this regard between the type of pension the applicant is requesting and his or her contribution record (as opposed to his or her insurance record); it is not connected to the applicant's social security status or to

---

[2] There is no reference to the revision of the Regulation, as it is still ongoing. See European Parliament, Legislative Train 8.2021 – 7 Employment and Social Affairs – EMPL, Revision of Regulation on Social Security Coordination- Labour Mobility Package.2016-2.

[3] Judgement of the Court of 30 May 2018, Case C–517/16, Stefan *Czerwiński* v Zakład Ubezpieczeń Społecznych Oddział w Gdańsku, ECLI:EU:C:2018:350.

the criterion of residence or employment. The key question is whether the applicant has contributed to a social security system (even if that system also provides for non-contribution periods).

The Court first clarified that the declaration of Article 9(1) Regulation 883/2004 in view of Member State's assessment, which is bound by the principle of sincere cooperation, is not decisive for the classification of a benefit. The Court then reviewed whether the applicant's pension was to be classified as an old-age benefit within the meaning of Article 3(1)(d) of Regulation 883/2004 or as a 'pre-retirement benefit' within the meaning of Article 3(1)(i) of Regulation 883/2004.

More specifically, the Court referred to the principle of sincere cooperation, as stipulated in Article 4(3) TEU, according to which all Member States shall assist each other for the purposes of the declarations covered by Article 9(1) of Regulation 883/2004, while pointing out that the fact that a national law or rule is not explicitly mentioned in Article 9 of Regulation 883/2004 does not, in itself, prove that that law or rule does not fall within the scope of the Regulation[4] (para. 32). The Court therefore held that *the classification of a benefit under one of the branches of social security* listed in Article 3 of Regulation 883/2004 as established by the competent national authority in the declaration to be provided by the Member State in accordance with Article 9(1) of that Regulation *is not definitive*. The classification of a social security benefit can be determined by the respective national court, autonomously and on the basis of the elements that constitute that specific social security benefit, and by referring, if necessary, a question to the Court for a preliminary ruling (para. 40).

By comparing old-age benefits with pre-retirement benefits, the Court concluded that the essential characteristic of an old-age benefit lies in the fact that it is intended to safeguard the subsistence of persons who, when reaching a certain age, leave employment and are no longer required to be available for work at their employment office[5] (para. 45). By contrast, a *pre-retirement ben-*

---

[4] To that effect, see the judgements of 11 July 1996, *Otte*, C-25/95, EU:C:1996:295, para. 20 and the case law cited, and of 19 September 2013, *HliddalandBornand*, C-216/12 and C-217/12, EU:C:2013:568, para. 46.
[5] Judgement of 5 July 1983, *Valentini*, 171/82, EU:C:1983:189, para. 14.

efit (even if it bears certain similarities with an old-age benefit in terms of content and purpose, namely, amongst other things, to safeguard the subsistence of persons who have reached a certain age), differ notably from an old-age benefit insofar as it *pursues an objective that is connected with employment policy inasmuch as it helps to release posts held by workers who are close to retirement age for the benefit of younger unemployed persons, an objective that became quite apparent in the context of the economic crisis Europe was facing at the time*[6] (para. 46). It follows that pre-retirement benefits are more closely connected to financial crises in business, to restructuring, redundancies and rationalisation (para. 47).

The concept of 'pre-retirement benefit' is defined in Article 1(x) of the Regulation, and refers to all cash benefits other than unemployment benefits or early old-age benefits, which are provided to workers who have reached a certain age and who have reduced, ceased or suspended their remunerative activity until they qualify for an old-age pension or an early retirement pension, the receipt of which is not conditional upon the individual being available to the competent State's employment services (para. 48). Under this provision, 'pre-retirement benefits' differ from 'early old-age benefits' in that the latter is provided *before* the individual has reached the standard pension entitlement age and either continues to receive this benefit once he or she reaches that age or until that benefit is replaced with another old-age benefit (para. 49)[7]. Furthermore, to the extent that the national legislation at issue explicitly refers to the worker's age but makes no reference to the objective of releasing employment

---

[6] To that effect, see judgement of 5 July 1983, *Valentini*, 171/82, EU:C:1983:189, paras 16 and 17.

[7] As regards the subject matter and the purpose of the benefit, Article 3 of the Law on Bridging Pensions, in particular paras 1 and 3, states that bridging pensions apply to workers who performed work that involved risks and was carried out under particular conditions and could result in permanent damage to the worker's health or might – despite technological progress – require special mental or physical capacities which, as a result of the ageing process, are reduced or diminish before the worker reaches retirement age, making it difficult for him or her to continue performing his or her tasks; or they apply to workers who can no longer guarantee that they can perform work of a particular nature, such as tasks involving a certain level of responsibility or requiring certain capacities, and who, as a result of mental and physical decline due to the ageing process, can no longer carry out that work without placing their health or the lives of others at risk (para. 51).

positions for younger unemployed workers, *the benefit at issue in the main proceedings appears to be more similar to an old-age benefit* (para. 53).

Finally, the Court stated that Article 4 of the *law on bridging pensions outlines the general conditions relating to age, length of service and evidence of long contribution and non-contribution periods, which, as a rule, are requirements that are connected with entitlement to old-age benefits, unlike the conditions generally laid down for entitlement to pre-retirement benefits* (para. 55). Since the bridging pension continues to be provided once the standard age for old-age pension entitlement has been reached or is replaced by another old-age benefit (para. 56), the Court concluded that a benefit such as that at issue must be considered to be an 'old-age benefit' within the meaning of Article 3(1)(d) of Regulation 883/2004.

2.2 Early retirement benefits and equivalent benefits

In *Bocero Torrico*[8], while the question referred for a preliminary ruling related explicitly to Article 48 TFEU, the referring court also mentioned the provisions of Regulation No 883/2004.

Mr Bocero Torrico and Mr Bode applied to the INSS for an early retirement pension, having completed contribution periods in Spain and Germany. The pension applications were rejected on grounds that the amount payable was below the minimum monthly pension corresponding to the applicants' family situation on their 65th birthday. According to Spanish social security legislation, the amount of pension to be received must be higher than the minimum pension due to the respective person when he or she reaches the age of 65 and becomes eligible for an early retirement pension. The national courts reflected the intention of the Spanish legislation to avoid supplementing retirement pensions up to the statutory minimum of persons who have not yet reached the statutory retirement age, thus retaining them in the labour market.

---

[8] Judgement of the Court of 5 December 2019, Joined Cases C-398/18 and C-428/18, Antonio *Bocero Torrico* (C-398/18), Jörg Paul Konrad Fritz Bode (C-428/18) v Instituto Nacional de la Seguridad Social, Tesorería General de la Seguridad Social, ECLI:EU:C:2019:1050.

In this regard, the Court pointed out that no provision in Title I of Regulation 883/2004, which comprises the general provisions of that Regulation, or in Title III, Chapter 5 of that Regulation, which covers the applicable special provisions, inter alia, old-age pensions, precludes such a rule (para. 26). However, the applicants in the main proceedings disputed the interpretation of the competent institutions and the Spanish courts to determine eligibility for an early retirement pension, namely that the concept of the amount of 'pension to be received' only refers to the pension payable by the Kingdom of Spain, and does not include pensions from other Member States that might be due to the respective person (para. 28).

As the Advocate General stated in point 45 of his Opinion, Article 5 of Regulation 883/2004 must be considered as being applicable to situations such as those at issue in the main proceedings. The 'receipt of social security benefits', according to the provision, refers to the pension the applicants in the main proceedings are entitled to (para. 31). On the other hand, the factual situations addressed in the main proceedings do not fall within the scope of Article 6 of Regulation 883/2004. Instead, the issue was whether the amount of pension due to the applicants in another Member State should be taken into account for the purpose of determining eligibility for an early retirement pension (para. 32).

As regards old-age pensions, the Court had previously interpreted the concept of 'equivalent benefits' in Article 5(a) as referring to two types of old-age benefits that are comparable in terms of their objective and the legislation that established them[9] (para. 36). The refusal of one Member State's competent authorities to take the pension benefits to which a worker who has exercised his or her right to free movement is entitled in another Member State into account to determine eligibility for an early retirement pension, is likely to put that worker in a less favourable position than a worker who has spent his or her entire career in only one Member State (para. 42).

As the Advocate General noted in point 49 of his Opinion, even if such considerations were to represent general interest objectives within the meaning of the

---

[9] To that effect, see judgement of 21 January 2016, *Vorarlberger Gebietskrankenkasse and Knauer*, C-453/14, EU:C:2016:37, paras 33 and 34.

case law, the arguments put forward by the INSS and the Spanish government do not justify discriminatory application of such a requirement to the detriment of workers who have exercised their right to freedom of movement (para. 45).

Thus, the Court concluded that Article 5(a) of Regulation 883/2004 must be interpreted as precluding the legislation of a Member State which requires that – as a condition for a worker to be eligible for an early retirement pension – the amount of pension to be received must be higher than the minimum pension that would be due to that worker upon reaching statutory retirement age under the respective legislation, where the term 'pension to be received' is interpreted as referring only to the pension from that particular Member State, and does not include the pension that worker might receive through equivalent benefits payable by one or several other Member States.

2.3 Calculation of pension benefits and equal treatment – migrants are at a disadvantage

In *Crespo Rey*[10], the Court dealt with the calculation of a pension benefit according to the minimum contribution rate of the Spanish social security institution. Crespo Ray, a Spanish national, who, after paying social security contributions in Spain in an amount exceeding the minimum rate established by the Spanish social security scheme, moved to Switzerland and paid contributions to the Swiss social security system. He then returned to Spain and signed a special agreement with the Spanish social security institution ('special agreement of 1 December 2007') specifying that from that date onwards until 1 January 2014, he would pay contributions based *on the minimum contribution rate* established by the Spanish social security scheme.

As pointed out by the Court, by requiring migrant workers to conclude a special agreement to pay contributions that are based on the minimum contribution rate, the national legislation at issue in the main proceedings gives rise to a difference in treatment, which places migrant workers at a disadvantage com-

---

[10] Judgement of the Court of 28 June 2018, Case C-2/17, Instituto Nacional de la Seguridad Social (INSS) v Jesús *Crespo Rey*, third party Tesorería General de la Seguridad Social, ECLI:EU:C:2018:511.

pared to non-migrant workers who spent their entire working life in the respective Member State (para. 63). The Court stated that it is for the national court dealing with the dispute to identify the most appropriate means in national law for achieving equal treatment between migrant and non-migrant workers. The Court noted that this objective ought to, in principle, be achieved by granting migrant workers who conclude a special agreement the option to pay social security contributions retroactively based on contribution rates that exceed the minimum rate and to consequently be able to claim their right to a retirement pension based on those higher rates (para. 75).

Consequently, the Court concluded that the Agreement on the Free Movement of Persons must be interpreted as precluding the legislation of a Member State, such as the one at issue in the main proceedings, which requires a migrant worker, who concludes a special agreement with the social security institution of the respective Member State, to pay contributions based on the minimum contribution rate, with the result that the competent body of the respective Member State treats the period covered by that agreement in the calculation of the theoretical amount of the worker's retirement pension as a period that has been completed in that same Member State, and will only take the contributions paid under the special agreement into consideration, even though that worker had previously paid social security contributions in the respective Member State that exceeded the minimum before exercising his or her right to free movement, and a non-migrant worker, who did not exercise that right and who also concluded a special agreement, has the option of paying contributions that exceed the minimum contribution rate (para. 76).

2.4 Pension insurance periods and raising a disabled child

In *Caisse d'assurance retraite et de la santé au travail d'Alsace-Moselle*[11], the Court reviewed the period during which a mother raised her disabled child while receiving a carer's allowance for the purpose of calculating her retirement pension.

---

[11] Judgement of the Court of 12 March 2020, Case C-769/18, *Caisse d'assurance retraite et de la santé au travail d'Alsace-Moselle* v SJ, Ministre chargé de la Sécurité sociale, ECLI:EU:C:2020:203

SJ, a French national residing in Germany, and the mother of a disabled child, worked in France and Germany. From 10 November 1995 onwards, SJ received a carer's allowance for a child with a disability which assists families in the integration of mentally disabled children and youth (para.35a, Book VIII of the German Social Code) ('the German assistance'). On 7 July 2010, SJ became eligible for a French retirement pension. On 27 July 2011, she applied to the Deutsche Rentenversicherung Bund (German Pension Fund) for payment of her pension, which forwarded her request to Carsat. Carsat granted her a retirement pension without taking the circumstances into account that had given rise to her eligibility for 'the German assistance', namely without treating the period during which SJ received the carer's allowance for a child with a disability in Germany as an insurance period and thus without an 'increase in the pension rate' which is provided to parents who are raising a disabled child and who are entitled to relevant allowances in accordance with French legislation[12].

The Court examined whether 'the German assistance' constitutes a benefit within the meaning of Article 3 of Regulation 883/2004 and whether it falls within the material scope of that Regulation (para. 23). The Court concluded that 'the *German assistance*' is not subject to objective criteria such as, inter alia, a specific rate or level of incapacity or disability (para. 30). Therefore, the Court held that Article 3 of Regulation 883/2004 must be interpreted as meaning that 'the German assistance' does not constitute a benefit within the meaning of Article 3 and therefore, does not fall within the material scope of that Regulation (para. 36).

Nonetheless, *in view of the procedure laid down in Article 267 TFEU providing for cooperation between national courts and the Court of Justice*, the Court

---

[12] On 18 March 2012, SJ submitted a complaint to the commission de recours amiable de la Carsat (Carsat appeals board) concerning (i) the effective date of her pension, and (ii) the failure to take into account, for the purposes of determining the number of periods of contribution and periods treated as such for the calculation of the amount of that pension, of the increase in the insurance period by one quarter per 30-month period of child-rearing, up to a maximum of eight quarters, provided for in Article L. 351-4-1 of the French Social Security Code, for which socially insured persons qualify where they raise a child and are entitled to the child-rearing allowance for a disabled child and to any supplement thereto, pursuant to Article L.541-1 of that code ('increase in the pension rate').

reformulated the second question referred to it[13] (para. 39). The dispute in the main proceedings concerned the question whether – for the purpose of determining a person's entitlement to a higher pension rate as provided for in French legislation – the circumstances that gave rise to entitlement to 'the German assistance', namely assistance received by that person as a migrant worker in accordance with the legislation of the host Member State, must be taken into account (para. 41).

The Court, in line with its case law[14], held that such an increase in the pension rate can fall within the material scope of Regulation 883/2004 as an old-age benefit within the meaning of Article 3(1)(d) of that Regulation (para. 46). First, an increase in the pension rate is granted to beneficiaries without an individual and discretionary assessment of their personal needs on the basis of a legally defined situation, namely that they raised a child with a disability and were entitled to a carer's allowance for a child with a disability under French legislation (para. 47). Secondly, the benefit at issue intends to offset any disadvantages suffered by the beneficiary in terms of career advancement because he or she had to raise a disabled child, by granting an increase of his or her contribution periods which is proportionate to the period he or she spent raising the disabled child. This is then reflected in the amount of pension he or she receives. Accordingly, this benefit – in so far as it is intended to safeguard the subsistence of persons who, after reaching a certain age, leave their employment and are no longer required to be available for work – is linked to the risk covered by old-age benefits within the meaning of Article 3(1)(d) of Regulation 883/2004[15] (para. 48). Further, the Court noted that the increase in the pension rate is provided on the basis of the occurrence of a fact within the meaning of Article 5(b) of Regulation 883/2004, namely that the child's permanent incapacity must be at least equal to a certain level of disability (para. 50). It follows that the

---

[13] Judgement of 13 June 2019, *Moro*, C-646/17, EU:C:2019:489, para. 39 and the case law cited.
[14] Judgement of 14 March 2019, *Dreyer*, C-372/18, EU:C:2019:206, para. 32 and the case law cited, Judgement of 25 July 2018, *A (Assistance for a disabled person)*, C-679/16, EU:C:2018:601, para. 33 to be presented analytically below.
[15] To that effect, see judgement of 16 September 2015, *Commission v Slovakia*, C-361/13, EU:C:2015:601, para. 55 and the case law cited.

principle of the equal treatment of facts, enshrined in the aforementioned Article 5(b), applies in circumstances such as those at issue in the main proceedings (para. 51).

Accordingly, the competent French authorities must take similar facts that arose in Germany into account, and cannot limit their assessment of the permanent incapacity of the disabled child concerned solely to the criteria laid down to that end by the scale-guide applicable in France under Article R. 541-1 of the French Social Security Code (para. 53). Consequently, to determine whether the level of the child's permanent incapacity as specified in that Code justifies an increase in the parent's pension rate, the authorities cannot refuse to take similar facts that arose in Germany into account and which can be established by evidence, in particular by medical reports, certificates or prescriptions for treatment or medicines (para. 54). Finally, the Court added that in the context of such checks, the authorities must also observe the principle of proportionality by ensuring, inter alia, that the principle of equal treatment of facts does not give rise to objectively unjustified results in accordance with recital 12 of Regulation 883/2004 (para. 55).

3 Sickness benefits

3.1 Cross-border healthcare without prior authorisation and the superior criterion of medical assessment

3.1.1 Refusal of authorisation

In *Veselības ministrija*[16], the Court highlighted the medical justification as a superior criterion within the scope of assessment of the authorisation application for a scheduled healthcare service in a Member State of the European Union other than the State of affiliation. The applicant's son, a minor who was suffering from a congenital heart defect, needed open-heart surgery. The applicant, who was affiliated to the healthcare system in Latvia, refused to consent to a blood transfusion during his son's surgery on grounds that he was a Jehovah's Witness. As the surgery in question is not possible in Latvia without a blood

---

[16] Judgement of the Court of 29 October 2020, Case C-243/19, A v *Veselības ministrija*, ECLI:EU:C:2020:872.

transfusion, the applicant requested the Latvian National Health Service to issue an S2 form for his son so he could have the surgery in Poland. The National Health Service refused to issue such a form. In a decision of 15 July 2016, the Ministry of Health in Latvia upheld the National Health Service's decision on grounds that the surgery at issue could be performed in Latvia and that a person's medical condition and physical limitations alone must be taken into consideration for issuing such a form. The applicant's son had heart surgery in Poland on 22 April 2017.

In the present case, it was not denied that the treatment at issue in the main proceedings is provided for in Latvian law, and that the first condition of the second sentence of Article 20(2) of Regulation 883/2004 had been met (para. 26). The Court stated that the review of all circumstances of each specific case that must be considered in line with Article 20(2) of Regulation 883/2004 to determine whether the same or an equally effective treatment is available in the insured person's Member State of residence, constitutes an objective medical assessment. Accordingly, the prior authorisation system provided for in Article 20 of Regulation 883/2004 *exclusively considers the patient's medical condition*, not his or her personal preferences for medical care (para. 30).

The Court thus concluded that there was no medical justification for the applicant's son to seek treatment outside Latvia (para. 32). Consequently, to the extent that the second condition in the second sentence of Article 20(2) of Regulation 883/2004 exclusively entails a review of the patient's medical condition and history, the likely course of his or her illness, the degree of his or her pain and/or the nature of his or her disability, and does not, therefore, involve taking the patient's personal preference in terms of treatment into account, the decision of the Latvian authorities to refuse to issue an S2 form cannot be considered incompatible with that provision (para. 33).

Hence, when the insured person's Member State of residence refuses to grant the prior authorisation provided for in Article 20(1) of Regulation 883/2004, that Member State is implementing EU law within the meaning of Article 51(1) of the Charter, i.e. the fundamental rights guaranteed by the Charter must be respected, including in particular those enshrined in Article 21[17] (para. 34). Furthermore, the prohibition of all discrimination based on religion or belief is mandatory as a general principle of EU law. Such prohibition, laid down in Article 21(1) of the Charter, is in itself sufficient to confer on individuals a right they can resort to in disputes in a sphere covered by EU law[18] (para. 36).

The Court pointed out, however, that the number of hospitals, their geographical distribution, the mode of their organisation and the facilities they have and even the nature of the medical services they are able to offer, are all factors for which planning, generally designed to meet various needs, must be possible. Such wastage would be all the more damaging because it is generally recognised that the healthcare sector generates considerable costs and must meet increasing needs, while the financial resources which may be made available for healthcare are not unlimited, whatever the mode of funding applied[19] (para. 46). Consequently, it cannot be excluded that the possible risk of seriously undermining the financial balance of a social security system may constitute a legitimate objective that may justify a difference in treatment based on religion. The objective of maintaining a balanced medical and hospital service open to all may also fall within the derogations on grounds of public health in so far as it contributes to the attainment of a high level of health protection[20] (para. 47).

Such additional costs are difficult to foresee if – in order to avoid a difference in treatment based on religion – the competent institution is required to take account of the insured person's religious beliefs when implementing Article 20 of Regulation 883/2004, as such beliefs fall within that individual's 'forum internum' and are, by their very nature, subjective[21] (para. 50). If the competent

---

[17] Judgement of 11 June 2020, *Prokuratura Rejonowa w Słupsku*, C-634/18, EU:C:2020: 455, para. 42 and the case law cited.
[18] Judgements of 17 April 2018, *Egenberger*, C-414/16, EU:C:2018:257, para.76, and of 22 January 2019, *Cresco Investigation*, C-193/17, EU:C:2019:43, para. 76.
[19] Judgements of 12 July 2001, *Smits and Peerbooms*, C-157/99, EU:C:2001:404, paras 76 to 79; of 16 May 2006, *Watts*, C-372/04, EU:C:2006:325, paras 108 and 109; and of 5 October 2010, *Elchinov*, C-173/09, EU:C:2010:581, para. 43.
[20] See, by analogy, in the area of freedom to provide services, judgement of 5 October 2010, *Elchinov*, C-173/09, EU:C:2010:581, para. 42 and the case law cited.
[21] To that effect, see judgement of 22 January 2019, *Cresco Investigation*, C-193/17, EU:C: 2019:43, para. 58 and the case law cited.

institution were required to take account of the insured person's religious beliefs, such additional costs could, given their unpredictability and potential scale, be capable of entailing a risk in relation to the need to protect the health insurance system's financial stability, which is a legitimate objective recognised by EU law. Accordingly, a prior authorisation system which does not take account of the insured person's religious beliefs, but which is based exclusively on medical criteria, may reduce such a risk and therefore appears to be appropriate for the purpose of achieving that objective (para. 52). As regards the necessity for the legislation at issue in the main proceedings, it must be borne in mind that it is for the Member States to determine the level of protection it wishes to afford for public health and how that level is to be achieved. Since that level may vary from one Member State to another, Member States should be allowed a measure of discretion[22] (para. 53).

The Court concluded that Article 20(2) of Regulation 883/2004, read in the light of Article 21(1) of the Charter, must be interpreted as not precluding the insured person's Member State of residence from refusing to grant that person the authorisation provided for in Article 20(1) of that Regulation, where hospital care, the medical effectiveness of which is not contested, is available in that Member State, although the method of treatment is contrary to that person's religious beliefs (para. 56). Further, the Court held that Article 8(5) and (6)(d) of Directive 2011/24, read in the light of Article 21(1) of the Charter, must be interpreted as precluding a patient's Member State of affiliation from refusing to grant that patient the authorisation provided for in Article 8(1) of that Directive, where hospital care, the medical effectiveness of which is not contested, is available in that Member State, although the method of treatment is contrary to that patient's religious beliefs, unless that refusal is objectively justified by a legitimate aim relating to maintaining treatment capacity or medical competence, and is an appropriate and necessary means of achieving that aim, which it is for the referring court to determine (para. 85).

---

[22] Judgement of 12 November 2015, *Visnapuu*, C-198/14, EU:C:2015:751, para. 118 and the case law cited.

3.1.2 Absence of an application for authorisation: Regulation 883/2004 and Directive 2011/24

In *Vas Megyei Kormányhivatal*[23], the Court examined a claim for reimbursement for cross-border healthcare services for an (urgent) treatment without prior authorisation. In 1987, WO, a Hungarian national, suffered a retinal detachment in his left eye and lost his vision in that eye. In 2015, WO was diagnosed with glaucoma in his right eye. The treatment he received in several medical establishments in Hungary were not effective, and his visual field continued to decrease and his eye pressure remained high. On 29 September 2016, WO contacted a doctor in Germany and set up an appointment with that doctor for a medical examination on 17 October 2016. The doctor recommended that WO extend his stay, in case eye surgery would have to be performed. In the meantime, WO's intra-ocular pressure was assessed in a medical examination in Hungary and was considerably above 21mmHG, the level at which intra-ocular pressure is considered to be abnormal. On 17 October 2016, the German doctor determined that eye surgery had to be urgently performed to save WO's eyesight. WO's surgery on 18 October 2016 was successful. The application WO submitted for reimbursement of cross-border healthcare services was rejected because eye surgery is considered to be a scheduled treatment for which WO had not obtained prior authorisation on the basis of which he could be reimbursed.

The referring court sought guidance on the interpretation of Article 56 TFEU, establishing the freedom to provide services, and of various provisions of secondary EU legislation, namely Article 20 of Regulation 883/2004, Article 26 of Regulation 987/2009 and Articles 8(1) and 9(3) of Directive 2011/24 (para. 32).

Initially, the Court noted that 'scheduled treatment' for the purposes of those provisions is distinct from the treatment referred to in Article 19 of Regulation 883/2004 and Article 25 of Regulation 987/2009, namely unexpected treatment received by the insured person in the Member State to which he or she travelled for reasons relating to tourism or education, for example, and which becomes necessary on medical grounds with a view to preventing that person

---

[23] Judgement of the Court of 23 September 2020, Case C-777/18, WO v *Vas Megyei Kormányhivatal* ECLI:EU:C:2020:745.

from being forced to return – before the end of the planned duration of his or her stay – to the competent Member State to undergo the necessary treatment[24] (para. 39). Any healthcare services received on his or her own initiative in a Member State other than the State in which the insured person resides on grounds that according to him or her, that particular treatment or treatment with the same outcome was unavailable in his or her Member State of residence within a time frame that is medically justifiable, falls within the definition of 'scheduled treatment' within the meaning of Article 20 of Regulation 883/2004, read in conjunction with Article 26 of Regulation 987/2009. Under those circumstances, such treatment is subject to prior authorisation by the Member State of residence in accordance with Article 20(1) of the first Regulation (para. 44).

Consequently, the Court held that the combined provisions of Article 20 of Regulation 883/2004 and Article 26 of Regulation 987/2009, read in the light of Article 56 TFEU, must be interpreted as meaning that (para. 55):

- healthcare services received on a person's own initiative in a Member State other than that in which the insured person resides on the ground that according to him or her, that particular treatment or treatment with the same outcome was unavailable in his or her Member State of residence within a time frame that is medically justifiable, falls within the definition of 'scheduled treatment' within the meaning of those provisions. Receipt of such treatment, in accordance with the conditions laid down in Regulation 883/2004, is in principle subject to prior authorisation by the competent institution of the Member State of residence;
- an insured person who has received scheduled treatment in a Member State other than his or her Member State of residence, without having applied for prior authorisation from the competent institution pursuant to Article 20(1) of that Regulation, is entitled to reimbursement of the cost of that treatment under the conditions laid down in that Regulation, if:
- first, between the date on which the appointment for a medical examination and possible treatment in another Member State was made, and the date

---

[24] See, by analogy, judgement of 15 June 2010, *Commission v Spain*, C-211/08, EU:C: 2010:340, paras 59 to 61.

on which that treatment was provided to the insured person in the Member State he or she travelled to, that person, *for reasons relating to his or her state of health or the need to receive urgent treatment in that Member State, finds him- or herself in a situation that prevented him or her from applying for prior authorisation* from the competent institution in the Member State of residence or was not able to wait for the institution's decision regarding his or her application, and

– second, that any additional conditions for the assumption of the costs of the benefits in kind, pursuant to the second sentence of Article 20(2) of that Regulation are also met.

It is for the referring court to carry out the necessary verifications in that respect.

Subsequently, the Court examined whether Article 56 TFEU and Article 8(1) of Directive 2011/24 must be interpreted as precluding national legislation that makes the reimbursement of costs of healthcare services received by an insured person in another Member State subject, in all cases, to prior authorisation, even when there is, while waiting for such authorisation to be granted, a genuine risk that that person's state of health will irreversibly deteriorate (para. 56).

The Court acknowledged that the objectives that may justify such a restriction to the freedom to provide services include the prevention of the possible risk of seriously undermining the financial balance of a Member State's social security system, the maintenance of balanced medical and hospital services that are open to all, the maintenance of treatment capacity or medical competence on national territory, and making it possible to create a plan seeking, first, to ensure that there is sufficient and permanent access to a balanced range of high-quality hospital treatment in the Member State concerned and, second, to ensure cost control and to prevent, as far as possible, any wastage of financial, technical and human resources[25] (para. 59).

In this context, the Court has established a distinction between medical services provided by practitioners in their offices or at the patient's home and hospital care or healthcare services that entail the use of highly specialised and

---

[25] See, by analogy, *Elchinov*, paras 42 and 43 and the case law cited.

cost-intensive medical equipment ('major non-hospital care')[26] (para. 60). Consequently, the Court concluded that (para. 86):

- Article 56 TFEU and point (a) of the first subpara. of Article 8(2) of Directive 2011/24 must be interpreted as precluding national legislation which, in the absence of prior authorisation, excludes reimbursement, within the limits of the coverage provided by the health insurance scheme in the Member State of affiliation, of the costs of a medical consultation incurred in another Member State.
- Article 56 TFEU and Article 8(1) of Directive 2011/24 must be interpreted as precluding national legislation in a case in which the insured person was prevented from applying for such prior authorisation or was not able to wait for the competent institution's decision regarding his or her application for prior authorisation for reasons relating to his or her state of health or to the need to receive urgent hospital or major non-hospital care, even though all other conditions for such costs are presume to have been met, which, in the absence of prior authorisation, excludes reimbursement, within the limits of the coverage provided by the health insurance scheme in the Member State of affiliation, of the costs of that care provided to that person in another Member State.

Finally, the Court noted that Article 9(3) of Directive 2011/24 requires Member States to set reasonable periods of time within which requests for cross-border healthcare must be dealt with and when considering such requests, must in accordance with subparagraphs (a) and (b) of that provision, that into account 'the specific medical condition' of the applicant and 'the urgency and individual circumstances', respectively (para. 88). Therefore, the Court concluded that Article 9(3) of Directive 2011/24 must be interpreted as not precluding national legislation which provides for a time limit of 31 days to grant prior authorisation for the assumption of costs of cross-border healthcare services and 23 days to reject such authorisation, while allowing the competent institution to take the

---

[26] To that effect, see judgments of 28 April 1998, *Decker*, C-120/95, EU:C:1998:167, paras 39 to 45; of 28 April 1998, *Kohll*, C-158/96, EU:C:1998:171, paras 41 to 52; of 12 July 2001, *Smits and Peerbooms*, C-157/99, EU:C:2001:404, para. 76; and of 5 October 2010, *Commission* v *France*, C-512/08, EU:C:2010:579, paras 33 to 36.

individual circumstances and the urgency of the case in question into account (para. 91).

Even though the Court held that it is for the national court to decide whether the criteria of Regulation 883/2004 on prior authorisation were met, it stated that an additional criterion that ought to be taken into consideration was, if by reasons relating to the applicant's state of health or the need to receive urgent treatment in another Member State, the person concerned was in a situation that prevented him or her from applying for such prior authorisation. This approach is reasonable and offers some guidance for national judges and can be validated based on the interpretation of Directive 2011/24. Thus, according to the Court, Directive 2011/24 precludes such a legislation that does not take the abovementioned additional criterion into account. The Court highlighted the substantive criterion of the medical state of the person concerned (the right to health or, in other words, the right to remain healthy), at the same time balancing the national social security systems' financing requirements. The Court referred to the reasonable periods of time within which requests for cross-border healthcare must be dealt with in the context of Directive 2011/24. Indeed, the Court provided some specific guidelines, stating that a time limit of 31 days for granting prior authorisation for the assumption of costs of cross-border healthcare, and 23 days to reject such an application is compatible with the purposes of Article 9(3) of Directive 2011/24.

3.2 Rehabilitation allowance as a sickness benefit

In *Pensionsversicherungsanstalt*[27], the Court was asked to determine whether a rehabilitation allowance was to be considered a sickness benefit or an invalidity benefit (or an unemployment benefit). An Austrian national, after residing and working in Austria, moved her place of residence to Germany, where she had been living since then and where she worked until 2013. She completed periods of insurance in both Austria and in Germany. On 18 June 2015, while she was still residing in Germany, she applied to the Austrian Pension Insur-

---

[27] Judgement of the Court of 5 March 2020, Case C-135/19, *Pensionsversicherungsanstalt v CW*, ECLI:EU:C:2020:177.

ance Institution for an invalidity pension or, as an alternative, a medical rehabilitation measure and a rehabilitation allowance or, as another alternative, an occupational rehabilitation measure. The Austrian institution rejected the application on grounds that the respondent did not suffer from an invalidity and that, in any event, she was not covered by the Austrian statutory social security scheme and had not sufficiently demonstrated close ties with that scheme. The national court of Austria acknowledged that the respondent had suffered temporary invalidity that was expected to last for at least six months and held that she had a right to receive a medical rehabilitation measure and a rehabilitation allowance from the Austrian social security system for the duration of her temporary invalidity. On the other hand, that same court dismissed her application for an invalidity pension and for occupational rehabilitation measures.

The Court was essentially asked to answer whether a benefit such as the rehabilitation allowance at issue in the main proceedings is a sickness benefit, an invalidity benefit or an unemployment benefit within the meaning of Article 3(1)(a), (c) and (h) of Regulation 883/2004 (para. 29).

The Court pointed out that a sickness benefit within the meaning of Article 3(1)(a) of Regulation 883/2004 covers the risk connected to a state of ill health which entails the temporary suspension of the individual's gainful activity[28] (para. 32). By contrast, an invalidity benefit within the meaning of Article 3(1)(c) of that Regulation intends, as a general rule, to cover risks associated with a disability of a predefined degree, which is likely to be permanent or long term[29] (para. 33). An unemployment benefit covers the risk associated with the loss of income suffered by a worker following the loss of employment, even though he or she is still capable of working. A benefit granted if that risk, namely loss of employment, materialises and which is no longer payable once the beneficiary finds paid employment, must be regarded as constituting an unemployment benefit[30] (para. 34).

---

[28] See, by analogy, judgement of 21 July 2011, *Stewart*, C-503/09, EU:C:2011:500, para. 37.
[29] See, by analogy, judgement of 21 July 2011, *Stewart*, C-503/09, EU:C:2011:500, para. 38 and the case law cited.
[30] Judgement of 19 September 2013, *Hliddal and Bornand*, C-216/12 and C-217/12, EU:C: 2013:568, para. 52 and the case law cited.

As regards classification of a rehabilitation allowance as an invalidity or sickness benefit, it follows that a benefit such as the rehabilitation allowance at issue in the main proceedings is intended to cover the risk of temporary disability and must therefore be considered a sickness benefit within the meaning of Article 3(1)(a) of that Regulation (para. 39). This conclusion is supported by the fact that according to para. 143a(1) and (2) and para. 143b of the ASVG, the rehabilitation allowance is paid by the sickness insurance institution and that the amount of that allowance is based on the amount of the sickness allowance (para. 40). Consequently, the Court concluded that a benefit such as the rehabilitation allowance at issue in the main proceedings is a sickness benefit within the meaning of Article 3(1)(a) of Regulation 883/2004 (para. 41).

Subsequently, the Court noted that the respondent in the main proceedings falls within the scope of Article 11(3)(e) of Regulation 883/2004, which applies to all persons other than those covered by Article 11(3)(a) to (d) of that Regulation, including, inter alia, persons who are not economically active[31] (para. 50). Under Article 11(3)(e) of Regulation 883/2004, the national legislation applicable to a situation such as that at issue in the main proceedings is that of the Member State of residence of the person concerned, namely in the present case, *German legislation* (para. 51). A person who is in a situation in which – as in the case in the main proceedings – he or she has ceased to be insured under the social security system of his or her Member State of origin after terminating his or her employment and moving his or her place of residence to another Member State, is no longer covered by the social security system of his or her State of origin (para. 52).

Thus, in the present case, in accordance with the Court's case law, the competent institution of the Member State of origin, namely the Republic of Austria, cannot be criticised for refusing to grant the claimant the rehabilitation allowance. This refusal did not have the effect of excluding a person to whom that legislation applies pursuant to Regulation 883/2004 from the scope of the legislation at issue and, therefore, of leaving him or her without social security coverage because no legislation is applicable to him or her (para. 53).

---

[31] To this effect, see judgement of 8 May 2019, *Inspecteur van de Belastingdienst*, C-631/17, EU:C:2019:381, paras 35 and 40.

According to the Court, Regulation 883/2004 must be interpreted as not precluding a situation in which a person who is no longer insured under the social security system of his or her Member State of origin after terminating his or her employment and moving his or her place of residence to another Member State, where he or she continued working and completed the majority of his or her insurance periods, is refused a benefit such as the rehabilitation allowance at issue in the main proceedings by the competent institution of his or her Member State of origin, since that person is no longer subject to the legislation of the State of origin but to that of the Member State of his or her place of residence (para. 54).

3.3 Services provided to people with disabilities being outside the scope of Regulation 883/2004

In A (Assistance for a disabled person)[32], the Court examined whether a benefit such as personal assistance falls within the concept of a sickness benefit within the meaning of Regulation 883/2004.

The claimant in the main proceedings resides in Finland and requires a substantial amount of help, including in his everyday activities. The Finnish municipality provided him with a personal carer to allow him to conclude his secondary school studies in Finland. In August 2013, A applied to the Finnish municipality of Espoo to receive personal assistance in the form of coverage for the costs of household chores. At the time of his application, A was in the process of moving to Estonia to attend a three-year, full-time law course: hence, he would be spending three or four days a week in Tallinn (Estonia) and return to Espoo (Finland) at weekends. The services he applied for would therefore have to be provided outside Finland. The municipality of Espoo asserted that it was under no obligation to provide such services and support outside of Finland, since the claimant's stay in Estonia corresponded to the concept of 'habitual residence'.

---

[32] Judgement of the Court of 25 July 2018, Case C-679/16, A (Assistance for a disabled person) Intervener: Espoon kaupungin sosiaali- ja terveyslautakunnan yksilöasioiden jaosto, ECLI:EU:C:2018:601.

As regards care insurance more specifically, the Court, in essence, held that whilst benefits relating to risk of reliance on care have features that are peculiar to them, they must be treated as sickness benefits within the meaning of Article 3(1) of Regulation 883/2004[33] (para. 42). However, treating the risk of reliance on care in the same way as the risk of sickness assumes that the purpose of benefits designed to provide coverage against the risk of reliance on care is to improve the state of health and the quality of life of persons who are reliant on care[34] (para. 43).

This is the case, in particular, when, irrespective of the method of the financing of such schemes, the expenses incurred by the insured person's reliance on care which arise, at the very least concurrently, from the care provided to that person and to the improvement of that person's everyday life, for example, through the provision of equipment and assistance by third parties[35] (para. 44). It has also been held that benefits relating to the risk of reliance on care are at most supplementary to the 'classic' sickness benefits that fall within Article 3(1)(a) of Regulation 883/2004 *stricto sensu* and are not necessarily an integral part of them[36] (para. 45). Consequently, the Court held that Article 3(1)(a) of Regulation 883/2004 must be interpreted as meaning that a benefit such as the personal assistance at issue in the main proceedings, which entails, inter alia, coverage of the costs of assistance provided to a severely disabled person for their everyday activities, with the aim of enabling that person, who is not economically active, to complete higher education, does not fall within the concept of 'sickness benefit' within the meaning of that provision, and is therefore outside the scope of Regulation 883/2004 (para. 52).

---

[33] To that effect, see, inter alia, judgements of 5 March 1998, *Molenaar*, C-160/96, EU:C:1998:84, paras 23 to 25; of 30 June 2011, *da Silva Martins*, C-388/09, EU:C:2011:439, paras 40 to 45; and of 1 February 2017, *Tolley*, C-430/15, EU:C:2017:74, para. 46.

[34] To that effect, see judgements of 8 March 2001, *Jauch*, C-215/99, EU:C:2001:139, para. 28; of 21 February 2006, *Hosse*, C-286/03, EU:C:2006:125, paras 38 to 44; and of 30 June 2011, *da Silva Martins*, C-388/09, EU:C:2011:439, para. 45.

[35] See, inter alia, judgements of 5 March 1998, *Molenaar*, C-160/96, EU:C:1998:84, para. 23; of 8 July 2004, *Gaumain-Cerri and Barth*, C-502/01 and C-31/02, EU:C:2004:413, paras 3, 21 and 26; and of 12 July 2012, *Commission v Germany*, C-562/10, EU:C:2012:442, para. 46.

[36] See, inter alia, judgements of 30 June 2011, *da Silva Martins*, C-388/09, EU:C:2011:439, para. 47; and of 1 February 2017, *Tolley*, C-430/15, EU:C:2017:74, para. 46 and the case law cited.

The Court therefore held that, although the person claiming that benefit lived in a Member State other than the Member State concerned, the fact that there was a genuine and sufficient connection with the latter Member State could be established on the basis of factors other than the claimant's residence in that Member State prior to her claim, such as the relationship between the claimant and the social security system of that Member State as well as the claimant's family circumstances[37] (para. 70).

In that context, the Court, echoing the question raised by the Advocate General in his Opinion, draws attention to the fact that the personal assistance at issue in the main proceedings can continue to be awarded when the person concerned attends a higher education institution in a Finnish municipality that may be a long way from his or her home municipality. The home municipality's ability to monitor the use of the personal assistance granted in that situation is not much more limited than it is in a situation such as that at issue in the main proceedings, in which A pursues his studies outside Finland in a neighbouring region, returning to his Finnish home municipality every weekend (para. 75).

Consequently, the Court concluded that Articles 20 and 21 TFEU preclude the home municipality of a resident of a Member State, who is severely disabled, from refusing to grant that person a benefit, such as the personal assistance at issue in the main proceedings, on grounds that he spends more time in another Member State where he is pursuing a higher education (para. 79).

4 Invalidity status and entitlement to invalidity benefits

In *Vester*[38], the Court, interpreting Articles 45 and 48 TFEU, dealt with the right of a migrant to invalidity benefits that were consecutively regulated by different legislations precluding entitlement of the person concerned to invalidity benefits, despite the fact that this invalidity status has been confirmed. Ms Vester, a Dutch national, worked in the Netherlands from 10 November 1997 until 31

---

[37] Judgement of 21 July 2011, *Stewart*, C-503/09, EU:C:2011:500, paras 97 to 102, 104 and 109.
[38] Judgement of the Court of 14 March 2019, Case C-134/18, Maria *Vester* v Rijksinstituut voor ziekte- en invaliditeitsverzekering, ECLI:EU:C:2019:212.

March 2015 and then moved to Belgium. Although she did not satisfy the conditions laid down by Belgian law, the competent Belgian institution granted her incapacity benefits until 6 April 2016 based on the principle of the aggregation of insurance periods laid down in Article 6 of Regulation 883/2004. Ms Vester's invalidity status was established in Belgium on 7 April 2016. By letter of 17 May 2016, Ms Vester applied to the Employees Insurance Institute, Netherlands ('the UWV') for payment of invalidity benefits in the Netherlands, which rejected her application. It informed Ms Vester that according to Netherlands law, the recognition of invalidity status and the payment of the related benefits was only possible following completion of a 'primary period of incapacity for work' of 104 weeks and that since she had only completed 52 weeks of this primary period in Belgium, it could not pay her invalidity benefits, as she was only eligible for such benefits from 4 April 2017. By decision of 18 August 2016, the INAMI informed Ms Vester that since she had only completed a 4-day insurance period in Belgium by the date of her declaration of incapacity for work, which was followed by recognition of her invalidity status, she failed to meet the conditions for entitlement to invalidity benefits in Belgium and the INAMI therefore refused to grant her those benefits on the basis of Article 57 of Regulation 883/2004. From 4 April 2017, the date on which Ms Vester completed her 104-week 'primary period of incapacity for work' required by Netherlands law, during which she had not received any invalidity benefits which, in principle, are only granted to workers who complete this period, her invalidity status was recognised in the Netherlands and invalidity benefits were paid by the competent Netherlands institution.

The invalidity insurance schemes in Belgium and the Netherlands make recognition of a person's invalidity status subject to the completion of a 'primary period of incapacity for work' during which he or she receives benefits for incapacity for work. It is only upon the expiry of that period that the invalidity status of that worker is recognised and invalidity benefits are paid. However, the legislation of Belgium and the Netherlands differ as regards the duration of that period, establishing that that period shall last for one and two years, respectively (para. 34).

According to the Court, although the Netherlands legislation at issue in the main proceedings does not, a priori, make a distinction between migrant and sedentary workers, as it generally provides for the transfer of an invalidity status at the end of a two-year period of incapacity for work, in practice, it places migrant workers who are in a situation similar to Ms Vester's at a disadvantage during their second year of incapacity for work relative to non-migrant workers, and results in the former losing a social security advantage which that legislation is actually supposed to provide for (para. 41). Under those circumstances, it must be held that the application of the Netherlands applicable regulations at issue in the main proceedings to a migrant worker in a situation such as Ms Vester's produces effects that are incompatible with the objective of Article 45 TFEU due to the fact that Ms Vester's right to invalidity benefits was consecutively regulated by different legislations (para. 44).

The Court has already held that where such a difference in legislation exists, the principle of cooperation in good faith laid down in Article 4(3) TFEU requires the competent authorities in the Member State to use all means at their disposal to achieve the aim of Article 45 TFEU[39] (para. 45). The arrangements applicable to members of the group placed at an advantage remain, for want of correct application of EU law, the only valid point of reference[40] (para. 46).

Consequently, the Court concluded that the answer to the questions referred to it is that Articles 45 and 48 TFEU must be interpreted as precluding a situation, such as that at issue in the main proceedings, in which a worker who is incapacitated for work for one year and whose invalidity status has been recognised by the competent institution of the Member State of his or her residence, without him or her being entitled to receive invalidity benefits on the basis of that Member State's legislation, is required by the Member State's competent institution in which he or she completed all of his or her insurance periods to complete an additional one-year period of incapacity for work in order to be granted invalidity status and receive pro-rata invalidity benefits, without receiving any benefits for incapacity for work during that period (para. 49).

---

[39] To that effect, see judgement of 1 October 2009, *Leyman* C-3/08, EU:C:2009:595, para. 49 and the case law cited.

[40] Judgements of 13 July 2016, *Pöpperl*, C-187/15, EU:C:2016:550, para. 46 and the case law cited, and of 28 June 2018, *Crespo Rey*, C-2/17, EU:C:2018:511, para. 73.

5 Family benefits

5.1 Family allowances for EU nationals

5.1.1 Lawful residence as a requirement for family benefit entitlement does not amount to discrimination prohibited under Article 4 of Regulation 883/2004

In the case *European Commission v United Kingdom of Great Britain and Northern Ireland*[41], the Court referred to the British child benefit and child tax credit, two cash benefits with the objective of helping cover family expenses and are funded not from recipients' contributions but from compulsory taxation.

After receiving numerous complaints from nationals of other Member State residents in the United Kingdom that the competent United Kingdom authorities had refused to grant them certain social benefits on grounds that they did not have a right to reside in that Member State, the Commission sent a request for clarification to the United Kingdom in 2008. The United Kingdom confirmed, by two letters dated 1 October 2008 and 20 January 2009, that, under national legislation, whilst the right to reside in the United Kingdom is conferred on all United Kingdom nationals, under certain circumstances, nationals of other Member States are not considered to have a right to reside. According to the United Kingdom, that restriction is based on the concept of 'right of residence' within the meaning of Directive 2004/38 and on the limitations upon that right which were established by the Directive, in particular the requirement that an economically inactive person must have sufficient financial resources to prevent becoming an unreasonable burden on the Member State's social assistance system.

In the light of the judgement of 19 September 2013 in *Brey* (C-140/12, EU:C: 2013:565), the Commission decided to limit its review to child benefits and child tax credit ('the social benefits at issue'), to the exclusion of the 'special non-

---

[41] Judgement of the Court of 14 June 2016, Case C-308/14, ACTION under Article 258 TFEU for failure to fulfil obligations, brought on 27 June 2014, *European Commission*, represented by D. Martin and M. Wilderspin, acting as agents, applicant, v *United Kingdom of Great Britain and Northern Ireland*, represented by M. Holt and J. Beeko, acting as agents, and J. Coppel QC, ECLI:EU:C:2016:436.

contributory cash benefits' that were also subject of the reasoned opinion and which, in accordance with that judgement of the Court, can be classified as 'social assistance' within the meaning of Article 7(1)(b) of Directive 2004/38 (para. 27).

As the Court pointed out, despite its name, child tax credit is periodically paid to recipients by the competent authority and seems to be associated with their status as taxpayers. This benefit replaced a range of additional payments that were made to persons claiming various income-linked maintenance allowances in respect of children for whom they were responsible, and the overall aim of which was to fight child poverty (para. 59).

According to the Court's case law, benefits that are automatically granted to families that meet certain objective criteria relating in particular to their size, income and capital resources, without any individual and discretionary assessment of their personal needs, and which are intended to meet family expenses, must be considered social security benefits[42] (para. 60). The result of applying the criteria referred to in the previous paragraph of the present judgement to the social benefits at issue is that the latter must be classified as 'social security benefits', as referred to in Article 3(1)(j) of Regulation 883/2004, read in conjunction with Article 1(z) thereof (para. 61).

It is clear from the Court's case law that nothing, in principle, prevents the granting of social benefits to Union citizens, who are not economically active, being made subject to the requirement that those citizens meet the conditions to lawfully reside in the host Member State[43] (para. 68). The conflict rule laid down in Article 11(3)(e) of Regulation 883/2004 is thus not distorted by the right to reside test, as that test forms an integral part of the conditions for the granting of the social benefits at issue (para. 69). Consequently, the main complaint put forward by the Commission was dismissed (para. 73).

---

[42] To this effect, see in particular, judgements of 16 July 1992 in *Hughes*, C-78/91, EU:C:1992:331, para. 22, and of 10 October 1996 in *Hoever and Zachow*, C-245/94 and C-312/94, EU:C:1996:379, para. 27.

[43] To this effect, see in particular judgements of 19 September 2013 in *Brey*, C-140/12, EU:C:2013:565, para. 44, and of 11 November 2014 in *Dano*, C-333/13, EU:C:2014: 2358, para. 83.

As regards the proportionality of the right to reside test, as observed by the Advocate General in point 92 of his Opinion, verification by the national authorities in connection with the granting of the social benefits at issue that the claimant does not unlawfully reside in their territory must be regarded as a situation which involves checks on the lawfulness of the residence of Union citizens in accordance with the second subpara. of Article 14(2) of Directive 2004/38, and must therefore comply with the requirements set out in the Directive (para. 81). Moreover, the fact that under the national legislation at issue in the present case, for the purpose of granting the social benefits at issue, the competent United Kingdom authorities shall require the residence of nationals of other Member States in their territory, who claim such benefits, must be lawful, does not amount to discrimination prohibited under Article 4 of Regulation 883/2004 (para. 86). Consequently, the Court concluded that the claim must be dismissed in its entirety.

5.1.2 Eligibility for family benefits regardless of activity

In *Bogatu*[44], the Court dealt with the eligibility requirements for family benefits. Mr Bogatu, a Romanian national and father of two children who lives in Romania, was employed in Ireland between 26 May 2003 and 13 February 2009, the date on which he lost his job. He received a contributory unemployment benefit (from 20 February 2009 to 24 March 2010), followed by a non-contributory unemployment benefit (from 25 March 2010 to 4 January 2013) and ultimately, a sickness benefit (from 15 January 2013 to 30 January 2015). He submitted a claim for family benefits on 27 January 2009. By letters dated 12 January 2011 and 16 January 2015, the Minister notified Mr Bogatu of his decision to approve that claim, with the exception for the period from 1 April 2010 to 31 January 2013.

The Court held that as is apparent from the wording of Article 67 Regulation 883/2004, although it refers to a 'person' who is entitled to family benefits, the Article does not state that such a person must have a specific status and, therefore, it does not explicitly require that the person be an 'employed person'. That

---

[44] Judgement of the Court of 7 February 2019, Case C-322/17, Eugen *Bogatu* v Minister for Social Protection, ECLI:EU:C:2019:102.

being said, the Article does not set out conditions to which that person's eligibility for family benefits are subject, but refers, in that regard, to the relevant Member State's legislation (para. 22). As that provision refers to a number of conditions that give rise to entitlement to family benefits, including activity as an employed person, Article 67 of Regulation 883/2004 cannot be considered to exclusively apply to entitlement on the basis of such activity (para. 25). Second, with regard to the objective pursued by Article 67 of Regulation 883/2004, it should be noted that the objective of the EU legislature in adopting that regulation was, inter alia, to extend the scope of that Regulation to categories of person other than employed persons falling under Regulation 1408/71 and, in particular, to economically inactive persons who were not covered by the latter (para. 26).

According to the Court, as regards family benefits in particular, that objective is reflected in Article 67 of Regulation 883/2004 of the word 'person', where Article 73 of Regulation 1408/71, which was succeeded by the former provision, refers to an 'employed person'. In this respect, Article 67 of Regulation 883/2004 reflects the intention of the EU legislature to no longer restrict entitlement to family benefits exclusively to employed persons, but to extend it to other categories of persons (para. 28).

In the light of these findings, the Court concluded that Regulation 883/2004 and, in particular, Article 67, read in conjunction with Article 11(2) thereof, must be interpreted as meaning that in a situation such as that in the main proceedings, to be eligible for family benefits in the competent Member State, it is not necessary for a person to either be employed in that Member State or to be in receipt of cash benefits from that Member State because or as a consequence of such employment activity (para. 33).

5.1.3 Payment of the difference between parental allowance paid in the Member State with primary competence and childcare allowance provided by the Member State with secondary competence

In *Moser*[45], the Court proceeded with an interpretation of Articles 67-68 of Regulation 883/2004 and of Article 60 of Regulation 987/2009. Mr and Mrs Moser lived in Germany with their two daughters. Mr Moser was employed in Germany while Mrs Moser was employed in Austria. Following the birth of her first daughter on 14 June 2011, she took parental leave until 31 January 2013. Following the birth of her second daughter on 29 August 2013, she arranged with her Austrian employer to take a further period of parental leave until 28 May 2015. From the end of her maternity protection period, she received the German parental allowance, together with the German allowance for parents whose children do not visit a childcare facility. In addition, the Austrian Health Insurance Fund paid Mrs Moser an allowance supplementing the Austrian income-dependent childcare allowance for the period from 25 October 2013 to 31 May 2014. Following an application brought by Mrs Moser before the Austrian Regional Court requesting receipt of an additional supplementary allowance covering a period extending beyond that for which the first supplementary allowance was granted to her, namely for the periods from 25 October 2013 to 28 June 2014 and from 29 August to 28 October 2014, which the Court granted. The Austrian Health Insurance Fund paid the allowance she had applied for.

Mr Moser took parental leave between 29 June and 28 August 2014, during which he received the German parental allowance. He also brought an application before the Austrian Regional Court seeking payment of the additional supplementary allowance consisting of the difference between the amount of the German parental allowance received and that of the Austrian income-dependent childcare allowance. By judgment of 10 November 2015, that Court dismissed his application. On appeal, by decision of 27 April 2017, the Oberlandesgericht Innsbruck (Higher Regional Court, Innsbruck) granted Mr Moser's application in part and ordered the Austrian Health Insurance Fund to pay a daily supplementary allowance of EUR 29.86, amounting to a total of

---

[45] Judgement of the Court of 18 September 2019, Case C-32/18, Tiroler Gebietskrankenkasse v Michael *Moser*, ECLI:EU:C:2019:752.

EUR 1,821.46. The Austrian Health Insurance Fund brought an appeal on a point of law (*revision*) against that decision before the Oberster Gerichtshof (Supreme Court, Austria).

According to the Court, Article 67 of Regulation 883/2004 establishes the principle that a person may claim family benefits for family members who reside in a Member State other than the Member State competent for paying those benefits as though they were residing in the latter Member State[46] (para. 35). In that case, the spouse of the worker is also entitled to rely on that Article[47] in accordance with the respective provision included in Article 67 of Regulation 883/2004, which stipulates that the entire family shall be taken into account as if all persons involved were subject to the legislation of the Member State concerned and residing there (para. 38). In the event that the granting of a family benefit is made subject to the condition that the person concerned has worked in the national territory of the competent Member State, as was the case in the main proceedings, which makes entitlement to the allowance conditional upon the completion of insurance periods in the Austrian territory, that condition must be considered to have been fulfilled where the person concerned has worked in the territory of another Member State (para. 39). However, the principle of equal treatment established in Article 67 of Regulation 883/2004 is not absolute, in the sense that where several entitlements are payable under different laws, the rules against overlapping benefits laid down in Article 68 of Regulation 883/2004 apply[48] (para. 40).

In accordance with Article 68(1)(b) of Regulation 883/2004, where, during the same period and for the same family members, benefits are provided for under the legislation of more than one Member State on the same basis, the priority of rights available on the basis of an activity as an employed or self-employed person is given to the legislation of the children's Member State of residence. Para. 2 of that Article provides that in the case of overlapping entitlements, family benefits are provided in accordance with the legislation designated as

---

[46] Judgement of 22 October 2015, *Trapkowski*, C-378/14, EU:C:2015:720, para. 35.
[47] Judgement of 7 November 2002, *Maaheimo*, C-333/00, EU:C:2002:641, para. 33.
[48] See, as regards Article 73 of Regulation 1408/71, judgement of 14 October 2010, *Schwemmer*, C-16/09, EU:C:2010:605, paras 42 and 43 and the case law cited.

having priority, entitlements to family benefits under other legislation being suspended up to the amount provided for in the first legislation and a differential supplement being provided, if necessary, for the sum exceeding that amount (para. 41).

The Court held that such a rule against overlapping entitlements seeks to ensure that the person entitled to benefits paid by several Member States receives a total amount of benefits which is equal to the amount of the most favourable benefit to which he or she is entitled under the legislation of a single Member State[49] (para. 42). It should be added that the application of Article 60 of Regulation 987/2009, like the payment of the differential supplement resulting therefrom, does not require a cross-border element with regard to the entitled person in question (para. 47).

As the Court noted, since the wording 'legislation of the Member State concerned' in Article 60 of Regulation 987/2009 is not subject to any limitation, the second sentence of Article 60(1) of Regulation 987/2009 must be interpreted as meaning that the obligation laid down in that provision to take into account, for the purpose of determining the scope of a person's entitlement to family benefits, 'the entire family... as if all the persons involved were subject to the legislation of the Member State concerned' applies both in the case where benefits are provided in accordance with the legislation designated as having priority under Article 68(1)(b)(i) of Regulation 883/2004, and in the case where benefits are payable in accordance with one or several other laws (para. 48).

Subsequently, the Court clarified that the present case differed from the case that gave rise to the judgement of 15 December 2011, *Bergström* (C-257/10, EU:C:2011:839), in that the interpretation accepted in that judgement, consisting of calculating the amount of a parental allowance by reference to notional income unrelated to the income actually earned, cannot be transposed to the situation at issue in the main proceedings, in which Mr Moser was entitled to a family benefit under Articles 67 and 68 of Regulation 883/2004 (para. 51). The Austrian childcare allowance, in its income-dependent variant, constitutes a benefit in replacement of income, thus enabling the worker to receive a benefit

---

[49] Judgement of 30 April 2014, *Wagener*, C-250/13, EU:C:2014:278, para. 46 and the case law cited.

in an amount proportionate to the amount of remuneration he or she was receiving at the time the allowance was granted. Consequently, to achieve that objective, the amount of remuneration must be assessed in the Member State of employment, particularly when in border situations, earnings are generally higher in the worker's Member State of employment (para. 54). The Court concluded that Article 68 of Regulation 883/2004 must be interpreted as meaning that the amount of the differential supplement to be granted to a worker under the legislation of a Member State with secondary competence in accordance with that Article must be calculated taking reference to the income actually earned by that worker in his or her Member State of employment (para. 55).

5.2 The right to family benefits of third-country nationals

In *Martinez Silva*[50], the Court considered a specific family benefit provided by the Italian social security system as a social security benefit within the meaning of Regulation 883/2004.

Mrs Martinez Silva, a third-country national, resided in Italy and was the holder of a single work permit valid for more than six months. Since she was the mother of three children under the age of 18 years and her income was below the limit laid down by Law No. 448/1998, she applied for ANF in 2014, which was rejected on grounds that she was not in possession of a long-term EC residence permit. She brought a civil action before the District Court, Genoa, Italy, against the Municipality of Genoa and the INPS for payment of EUR 1,833.26 for 2014 and recognition of her right to ANF for the following years, arguing that the refusal was contrary to Article 12 of Directive 2011/98.

Since Article 12(1)(e) of Directive 2011/98 provides that third-country workers as referred to in Article 3(1)(b) and (c) of the Directive are to enjoy equal treatment with nationals of the Member State where they reside with regard to the branches of social security as defined in Regulation 883/2004, the Court first examined whether a benefit such as ANF is a social security benefit which is

---

[50] Judgement of the Court of 21 June 2017, Case C-449/16, Kerly Del Rosario *Martinez Silva* v Istituto nazionale della previdenza sociale (INPS), Comune di Genova, ECLI:EU: C:2017:485.

included among the family benefits referred to in Article 3(1)(j) of that Regulation, or whether it is a social assistance benefit which is excluded from the scope of that Regulation under Article 3(5)(a) of the Regulation, as asserted by the Italian government (para. 19).

Whether a particular benefit can be classified as a family benefit referred to in Article 3(1)(j) of Regulation 883/2004, the Court noted that in accordance with Article 1(z) of that Regulation, the term 'family benefit' means all benefits in kind or in cash intended to meet family expenses, excluding advances of maintenance payments and special childbirth and adoption allowances mentioned in Annex I to the Regulation. The Court held that the phrase 'to meet family expenses' is to be interpreted as referring, in particular, to a public contribution to a family's budget to alleviate the financial burdens involved in the maintenance of children[51] (para. 23).

As regards the benefit at issue in the main proceedings, it appears from the documents before the Court, first, that ANF is paid to recipients who apply for it, where the conditions relating to the number of minors and to income laid down in Article 65 of Law No. 448/1998 are met. The benefit is consequently granted without any individual and discretionary assessment of the claimant's personal needs on the basis of a legally defined situation. Secondly, ANF consists of subsidy paid to recipients every year to meet family expenses. It is therefore a cash benefit intended, by means of a public contribution to a family's budget, to alleviate the financial burdens involved in the maintenance of children (para. 24).

Thus, a benefit such as ANF is a social security benefit that is included among the family benefits referred to in Article 3(1)(j) of Regulation 883/2004 (para. 25). Therefore, the Court concluded that Article 12 of Directive 2011/98 must be interpreted as precluding national legislation, such as that at issue in the main proceedings, under which a third-country national holding a single permit within the meaning of Article 2(c) of that Directive cannot receive a benefit such as ANF established by Law No. 448/1998 (para. 32).

---

[51] To that effect, see judgement of 19 September 2013, *Hliddal and Bornand*, C-216/12 and C-217/12, EU:C:2013:568, para. 55 and the case law cited.

Further, in the case *Istituto nazionale della previdenza sociale (INPS)*[52], the Court reclaimed the foregoing judgement to answer the question referred to it that Article 12(1)(e) of Directive 2011/98 must be interpreted as precluding the legislation of a Member State under which, for the purpose of determining entitlement to a social security benefit, family members of the holders of a single permit, within the meaning of Article 2(c) thereof, who do not reside in the territory of that Member State but in a third country, are not to be taken into account, whereas family members of nationals of that Member State residing in a third country are taken into account (para. 47).

5.3 Interpretation of Decision H3 – Currency conversion of child allowance

In *Bundesagentur für Arbeit – Familienkasse Baden-Württemberg West*[53], the Court referred to Decision H3 of the Administrative Commission for the purposes of currency conversion of child allowance.

The applicant in the main proceedings, GP, and her husband reside in Germany and performed paid employment in Switzerland. They had two children.

---

[52] Judgement of the Court of 25 November 2020, Case C-302/19, *Istituto nazionale della previdenza sociale (INPS)* v WS ECLI:EU:C:2020:957. According to the order for reference, WS was a third-country national who had held a work permit for Italy since 9 December 2011, and a single work permit since 28 December 2015, pursuant to Legislative Decree No. 40/2014. During the periods from January to June 2014 and July 2014 to June 2016, his wife and two children resided in Sri Lanka, their country of origin. The INPS, having refused to pay him the family unit allowance during those periods on the basis of Article 2(6-bis) of Law No. 153/1988, WS brought an action before the Tribunale del lavoro di Alessandria (Labour Court, Alessandria, Italy), claiming infringement of Article 12 of Directive 2011/98 and the discriminatory nature of the refusal to pay him the family unit allowance. The Court dismissed his action. The referring Court stated in that regard that the family unit referred to in Article 2 of Law No. 153/1988 not only serves as the basis for calculating the family unit allowance, but is also the beneficiary of that allowance through the intermediary of the person receiving the remuneration or pension to which the allowance is tied. That allowance is a financial supplement to which all employees who work on Italian territory are eligible, provided they are members of a family unit whose annual income does not exceed a certain threshold. For the period from 1 July 2018 to 30 June 2019, this amount, at the full rate, was EUR 137.50 per month for annual incomes not exceeding EUR 14,541.59. It is paid by the employer together with the worker's salary.

[53] Judgement of the Court of 4 September 2019, Case C-473/18, GP v *Bundesagentur für Arbeit – Familienkasse Baden-Württemberg West*, ECLI:EU:C:2019:662.

From February 2012 onwards, the husband received two monthly child allowance payments in Switzerland. On 19 August 2015, GP applied to the Family Allowances Office (FAO) for the payment of a differential supplement to child allowance. The FAO rejected GP's application for the period from April 2012 to December 2014. The FAO referred to Article 90 of Regulation 987/2009 and to Decision H3 in finding that, in order to determine whether there was an entitlement to a differential supplement and, if so, the amount thereof, the exchange rate to be used was that published on the first day of the month preceding the month during which the calculation was made. Since that calculation had been made on the day when the decision of 8 September 2015 was adopted, the relevant exchange rate was that published on 1 August 2015. On the basis of that rate, the amount of CHF 200 equated to EUR 188.71, i.e., an amount greater than the amount of child allowance granted for the years 2012 to 2014 by the Federal Republic of Germany, namely EUR 184 per month for the first two children. Accordingly, the FAO asserted that no differential supplement to child allowance was payable for the period in question.

The Court examined whether – as regards the currency conversion of child allowance to determine the amount of any differential supplement under Article 68(2) of Regulation 883/2004 – the application and interpretation of Article 90 of Regulation 987/2009 and of Decision H3 were affected by the fact that that allowance was paid in Swiss francs by a Swiss institution (para. 23). The circumstances of GP, who resided in Germany and worked in Switzerland, as did her husband who received a family allowance granted by a Swiss institution, fell within the scope of Regulations 883/2004 and 987/2009 and of Decision H3[54] (para. 25).

It follows that under those EU acts, the aforementioned allowances and the currency conversion of the amount concerned must be treated the same way as allowances received in an EU Member State. In particular, with regard to Question 3(a) of the referring Court relating to the significance of the exclusion under point 2 of the first sentence of para. 65(1) of the EStG of the child allowance in Germany, when a comparable benefit is granted abroad – in the case

---

[54] See, by analogy, judgement of 14 March 2019, *Dreyer*, C-372/18, EU:C:2019:206, para. 30.

in point, in Switzerland – a rule against overlapping entitlements laid down by a Member State's national law cannot be applied if the application thereof is found to be contrary to EU law[55] (para. 26).

Accordingly, the Court held that as regards the currency conversion of child allowance to determine the amount of any differential supplement under Article 68(2) of Regulation 883/2004, the application and interpretation of Article 90 of Regulation 987/2009 and of Decision H3 are not affected by the fact that that allowance is paid in Swiss francs by a Swiss institution (para. 28).

According to the Court, the benefit at issue in the main proceedings, which is a differential supplement potentially payable in respect of monthly family allowances, has its basis in Article 68 of Regulation 883/2004 (para. 33). To ensure that the total amount paid is equal to the amount of the most favourable benefit in a case where the sums to be compared are in different currencies, it is necessary to use the reference exchange rate published by the European Central Bank on a date as close as possible to that of the payment of the benefits. In a situation where benefits are paid at regular intervals – in the case in point, monthly – over a long period of time, this entails the use of a different exchange rate for each payment (para. 35). To apply a single rate of conversion for such a period, even though rates are liable to be subject to significant fluctuations over the course of that period, could either deprive the recipient of the benefits of part of the amount of the most favourable benefit or result in him or her being awarded an amount in excess of that benefit (para. 36).

As regards the provisions of Decision H3, which may be applicable to the dispute in the main proceedings, para. 2 of that decision provides that unless otherwise stated in the decision, the rate of conversion to be used is the rate published on the day when the transaction is performed by the institution (para. 38). However, the Court pointed out that the wording of para. 2 of Decision H3 makes the residual nature of that paragraph clear in that it is to be applied to determine the rate of conversion to be used in accordance with the provisions of Regulations 883/2004 and 987/2009 that are covered by Decision H3, unless that Decision provides otherwise. Consequently, the Court examined

---

[55] To that effect, see judgement of 12 June 2012, *Hudzinski and Wawrzyniak*, C-611/10 and C-612/10, EU:C:2012:339, para. 71.

whether paras 3 to 5 of Decision H3 apply to a situation such as that at issue in the main proceedings (para. 40). The Court stated that since paras 3 to 5 of Decision H3 do not apply in a situation such as that at issue in the main proceedings, para. 2 must be applied as is apparent from para. 40 of the present judgement (para. 47).

Accordingly, the Court concluded that Decision H3 must be interpreted as meaning that para. 2 thereof is applicable when the currency in which the child allowance is paid is converted to determine the amount of any differential supplement under Article 68(2) of Regulation 883/2004 (para. 48). As regards Question 2(a), referred to the Court in the event that para. 2 of Decision H3 is held to be applicable to a situation such as that at issue in the main proceedings, the referring Court in essence asked what the scope of the concept of 'the day when the transaction is performed by the institution' is within the meaning of that provision (para. 49).

It is not until the benefit has been paid by the State of employment and the amount has been converted into the currency of the State of residence that the person concerned may be entitled to that supplement in the latter State, if the amount converted is lower than the amount due by way of the same benefit under the legislation of the State of residence[56] (para. 50). That interpretation is consistent with the purpose of the rule against overlapping entitlements in Article 68(2) of Regulation 883/2004, as set out in para. 34 of the present judgement (para. 51). Accordingly, the Court concluded that para. 2 of Decision H3 must be interpreted as meaning that in a situation such as that at issue in the main proceedings, the concept of 'the day when the transaction is performed by the institution', within the meaning of that provision, refers to the day on which the competent institution of the State of employment transfers the payment of the family benefit in question (para. 52).

---

[56] See, by analogy, judgement of 30 April 2014, *Wagener*, C-250/13, EU:C:2014:278, paras 45 and 47.

6 Unemployment benefits

In *Klein Schiphorst*[57], the Court interpreted Article 64(1)(c) Regulation 883/2004.

Mr Klein Schiphorst, a Dutch national, was living in the Netherlands and was receiving unemployment benefits since 2 May 2011 under the WW. He informed the Management Board of the Employee Insurance Agency in the Netherlands ('the Uwv') on 19 July 2012 that he intended to move to Switzerland to look for work and requested retention of his entitlement to unemployment benefits and asked the Uwv, pursuant to Regulation 883/2004, for the period of export of his unemployment benefits to be extended beyond three months. The Uwv rejected both his request and the appeal against that refusal.

As the Advocate General noted in point 78 of his Opinion, a Member State remains within the limits permitted by EU law in adopting measures under which an extension of the unemployment benefit export period up to a maximum of six months may be granted only when certain conditions are met (para. 53). Thus, the Court held that Article 64(1)(c) of Regulation 883/2004 must be interpreted as not precluding a national measure such as that at issue in the main proceedings, which requires the competent institution to reject, as a matter of principle, any request to extend the unemployment benefit export period beyond three months, provided the institution deems that rejection of such a request will not lead to an unreasonable result (para. 54).

Further, in *Bundesagentur für Arbeit*[58], the Court, reclaiming amongst others the foregoing judgement, proceeded with the interpretation of Article 62 (1) and (2) Regulation 883/2004.

The applicant in the main proceedings was a German national residing in Germany. Between 1 July 1990 and 31 October 2014, he worked as a frontier worker for a company located in Switzerland. From 1 November 2014, he was employed in Germany. That activity was terminated by his employer and the

---

[57] Judgement of the Court of 21 March 2018, Case C-551/16, J. *Klein Schiphorst* v Raad van bestuur van het Uitvoeringsinstituut werknemersverzekeringen ECLI:EU:C:2018:200.

[58] Judgement of the Court of 23 January 2020, Case C-29/19, ZP v *Bundesagentur für Arbeit* ECLI:EU:C:2020:36.

Agency granted the applicant unemployment benefits for a period of 2 years calculated on the basis of a notional reference pay of EUR 73.73 per day. Since the remuneration received by the applicant for his former activity as an employed person in Switzerland was not used as the basis for calculating his unemployment benefits, the applicant lodged a complaint with the Agency, which was rejected.

The Court stated that, as follows from Article 62(1) and (2) of Regulation 883/2004, first, where the legislation of a Member State provides that the calculation of benefits is based on the amount of the person's previous salary, account must exclusively be taken of the salary earned by the person concerned for his or her last employment activity under that legislation and, second, if that legislation provides for and specifies a reference period for the purpose of determining the salary to be used as the basis for calculating unemployment benefits, that reference period must include periods of employment completed both under that legislation and under the legislation of other Member States (para. 32).

That interpretation is also consistent with the objectives of Regulation 883/2004, the purpose of which as follows from recitals 4 and 45 is to coordinate Member States' social security systems to guarantee that the right to free movement of persons can be exercised effectively[59]. Accordingly, that regulation seeks to prevent the situation in which a worker who, having exercised his or her right of free movement, has worked in more than one Member State is treated, without objective justification, less favourably than a worker who has completed his or her entire career in only one Member State[60] (para. 33).

As regards in particular the calculation of unemployment benefits provided for in Article 62(1) of Regulation 883/2004, it is apparent from the Court's case law that the corresponding provision of Regulation 1408/71 was intended to facilitate the mobility of workers by ensuring that the persons concerned received benefits that took into account, as far as possible, the conditions of employment

---

[59] Judgment of 21 March 2018, *Klein Schiphorst*, C-551/16, EU:C:2018:200, para. 31.
[60] To that effect, see judgement of 19 September 2019, *van den Berg and Others*, C-95/18 and C-96/18, EU:C:2019:767, para. 75 and the case law cited.

and, in particular, of the remuneration they earned under the legislation of the Member State in which they were last employed[61] (para. 35).

The Court concluded that Article 62(1) and (2) of Regulation 883/2004 must be interpreted as precluding the legislation of a Member State which, while providing that the calculation of unemployment benefits is to be based on the amount of the beneficiary's previous salary, does not allow – where the period during which the person concerned was in receipt of a salary in respect of his or her last employed activity pursued under that legislation is shorter than the reference period laid down by that legislation for determining the salary to be used as the basis for calculating unemployment benefits – for account to be taken of the salary earned by the person concerned in respect of that activity (para. 43).

Further, according to the Court, the date on which the salary is paid to the person concerned has no bearing on the pursuit of the objective of ensuring that that person receives benefits that take account, in so far as possible, of the conditions of employment, in particular remuneration he or she earned under the legislation of the Member State where he or she was employed. On the other hand, making the right guaranteed in Article 62(1) of Regulation 883/2004 dependent on the date on which the salary is calculated and paid may hamper the free movement of workers within the European Union (para. 50).

Consequently, the Court concluded that Article 62(1) and (2) of Regulation 883/2004 must be interpreted as precluding legislation of a Member State which, while providing that the calculation of unemployment benefits shall be based on the amount of the beneficiary's previous salary, does not allow – where the salary received by the respective person for the last activity he or she pursued as an employed person under that legislation was not calculated or paid until after his or her employment relationship came to an end – for account to be taken of the salary earned by the person concerned for that activity (para. 51).

---

[61] To that effect, see judgement of 28 February 1980, *Fellinger*, 67/79, EU:C:1980:59, para. 7.

7 Special non-contributory benefits

In *Jobcenter Krefeld*[62], the Court interpreted Articles 3 and 4 Regulation 883/2004 on special non-contributory benefits under Article 70 Regulation 883/2004 in conjunction with Regulation 492/11 and Directive 2004/38.

JD, a Polish national, was married and had two daughters. JD separated from his wife between 2012 or 2013. In late 2012 and early 2013, all members of the family settled in Germany. The two daughters essentially moved in with their father in 2015. JD's wife moved to Poland in 2016. The daughters attended school in Germany. From March 2015 onwards, JD was in paid employment in Germany. From 4 October to 7 December 2016, JD was incapacitated for work and for that reason continued to receive payment of his wages from his employer until 31 October 2016, when the employment relationship ended. He received sickness benefits until 7 December 2016 and subsequently received unemployment benefits from 23 February to 13 April 2017 and from 12 June to 23 October 2017. JD began working again full time on 2 January 2018. JD and his two daughters received basic social protection benefits from 1 September 2016 until 7 June 2017 under SGB II, namely 'subsidiary unemployment benefits' (*Arbeitslosengeld II*) for JD and 'social allowances' (*Sozialgeld*) for his two daughters (together 'the subsistence benefits at issue in the main proceedings'). In June 2017, JD, on behalf of himself and his daughters, applied for continued payment of the subsistence benefits at issue in the main proceedings. Jobcenter Krefeld rejected his application on grounds that JD had not retained the status of worker and that he was residing in Germany solely to seek employment.

The Court stated that Article 7(2) and Article 10 of Regulation 492/2011 must be interpreted as precluding legislation of a Member State which provides that a national of another Member State and his or her minor children, all of whom have a right of residence in the former Member State based on Article 10 of that Regulation, by virtue of those children attending school in that State, are automatically and under all circumstances excluded from entitlement to bene-

---

[62] Judgement of the Court of 6 October 2020, Case C-181/19, *Jobcenter Krefeld – Widerspruchsstelle v JD*, ECLI:EU:C:2020:794.

fits to cover their subsistence costs. That interpretation is not called into question by Article 24(2) of Directive 2004/38 (para. 79). Further, according to the Court, the fact that under a provision of national law such as point 2(c) of the second sentence of para. 7(1) of SGB II, persons who, like JD and his daughters, are nationals of another Member State and derive their right of residence from Article 10 of Regulation 492/2011 are excluded from any entitlement to subsistence benefits, constitutes a difference in treatment in relation to social security benefits compared to national citizens (para. 86).

Moreover, the Court stated that derogation from the principle of equal treatment in relation to social assistance provided for in Article 24(2) of Directive 2004/38 is not applicable to a situation such as that at issue in the main proceedings, where nationals of other Member States have a right of residence under Article 10 of Regulation 492/2011.

In that regard, the situation that arises in the present case must be distinguished from those at issue in the cases that gave rise to the judgements of 15 September 2015, *Alimanovic* (C-67/14, EU:C:2015:597) and of 25 February 2016, *García-Nieto and Others* (C-299/14, EU:C:2016:114), where the applicability of that derogation led the Court to recognise a corresponding derogation from the principle of equal treatment laid down in Article 4 of Regulation 883/2004 (para. 87).

Thus, the Court held that the exclusion laid down in point 2(c) of the second sentence of para. 7(1) of SGB II, which states that nationals of other Member States who have a right of residence based on Article 10 of Regulation 492/2011 are categorically and automatically refused any entitlement to the subsistence benefits at issue in the main proceedings, is contrary to Article 4 of Regulation 883/2004 (para. 88).

8 Applicable legislation

8.1 Worker pursuing an activity as an employed person and an activity as a self-employed person in different Member States – Dual affiliation

In V^{63}, the Court in essence dealt with the transition from Regulation 1408/71 to Regulation 883/2004 and the question whether the person concerned in the context of this transition had to make a request for the purpose of determining the applicable legislation.

Mr V worked as a lawyer registered with the Brussels Bar (Belgium) from September 1980 to 30 September 2007. During that period, he was registered with Inasti and affiliated with the Belgian social insurance fund Securex. On 30 September 2007, Mr V requested his name to be removed from the Bar Council Register and, as a result, his affiliation to Securex was terminated. On the same day, the law firm for which he was working went into liquidation and Mr V was appointed liquidator. As of 1 October 2007, Mr V worked as legal director of a company established in Luxembourg and, as an employed person, was subject to the Luxembourg social security scheme. Inasti asked Mr V for detailed information concerning his duties as liquidator and he replied that the emoluments he received as liquidator from the law firm in liquidation did not mean that he should be treated as a self-employed person or should be subject to the social security scheme for self-employed persons. On 23 December 2013, Securex informed Mr V that in the light of information provided by Inasti, he was to be considered subject to the Belgian social security scheme as a self-employed worker on a supplementary basis from 1 October 2007 onwards and that he had to therefore pay Securex a balance of EUR 35,198.42 in respect of contributions and increases payable for the period from 2007 to 2013. Mr V brought an action before the Belgian Labour Court, challenging his supplementary liability to the Belgian social security scheme as a self-employed person and the request for payment of social security contributions made by Securex.

---

[63] Judgement of the Court of 6 June 2019, Case C-33/18, *V* Institut national d'assurances sociales pour travailleurs indépendants (Inasti), Securex Integrity ASBL, ECLI:EU:C: 2019:470.

It is apparent from the order for reference that Mr V was no longer subject to the Belgian social security scheme as of 30 September 2007, the date on which he ceased to work as a lawyer. The referring court therefore raised the question whether Mr V, who on the date of application of Regulation 883/2004, was only subject to the Luxembourg social security system, was nevertheless required to submit an express request within 3 months in accordance with Article 87(8) of Regulation 883/2004 to be able to benefit from the application of that Regulation (para. 20).

According to the Court, Article 87(8) of Regulation 883/2004, which is a transitional provision, covers persons who, as a result of Regulation 883/2004, are 'subject to the legislation of a Member State other than that determined in accordance with Title II of [Regulation 1408/71]' (para. 36). Moreover, as the Advocate General pointed out in point 35 of his Opinion, Regulation 883/2004 abolished all exceptions to the principle that the legislation of only one Member State shall apply, which was the case under Regulation 1408/71 (para. 44). Under those circumstances, an interpretation of Article 87(8) of Regulation 883/2004, which takes account of the context of that provision, cannot promote the continuation of derogating rules providing for dual affiliation, which is inconsistent with the system established by that Regulation based on the principle that the legislation of only one Member State is to apply (para. 45).

With regard to the purpose of Article 87(8) of Regulation 883/2004, as the Advocate General stated in point 36 of his Opinion, it is apparent from the Practical Guide for determining the legislation applicable to workers in the European Union, the European Economic Area and in Switzerland, that it intends to prevent a high number of changes in the applicable legislation during the changeover to Regulation 883/2004, and to ensure that the persons concerned have a 'smooth transition' with regard to the applicable legislation if there is a discrepancy between the legislation applicable under Regulation 1408/71 and that applicable under the provisions of Regulation 883/2004 (para. 46).

Therefore, Article 87(8) of Regulation 883/2004 is to be interpreted as meaning that a person who, on the date of application of Regulation 883/2004, was engaged in paid employment in one Member State and self-employed in another and therefore subject at the same time to the social security legislation applicable in those two Member States, was not required to submit an express request to that effect (para. 51) to be subject to the legislation applicable under Regulation 883/2004.

8.2 Employer established in a Member State other than the worker's State of residence

In *Inspecteur van de Belastingdienst*[64], the Court interpreted Article 11 Regulation 883/2004 on the maintenance of residence in the Member State of origin and the applicable legislation of the State of residence. The person concerned (SF), a Latvian national residing in Latvia, was working as a seaman for an employer established in another Member State (the Netherlands) on board a vessel flying the flag of a third State (Bahamas) and travelling outside the territory of the European Union (sailing over the German part of the continental shelf of the North Sea). The dispute arose because the Netherlands' tax authorities issued SF with a notice of assessment in respect of income tax and social insurance contributions.

In that regard, the Court had already held that the mere fact that a worker carries on his or her activities outside the territory of the European Union is not sufficient to exclude the application of EU rules on free movement of workers, in particular Regulation 883/2004, as long as the employment relationship retains a sufficiently close connection with that territory[65] (para. 22). A sufficiently close connection between the employment relationship in question and the territory of the European Union derives, inter alia, from the fact that an EU citizen, who is a resident of a Member State, has been engaged by an undertaking established in another Member State on whose behalf he or she carries out activities[66] (para. 23). In addition, since SF worked as a seaman on board a vessel flying the flag of a third State, he also fell outside the general rule in

---

[64] Judgement of the Court of 8 May 2019, Case C-631/17, SF v *Inspecteur van de Belastingdienst*, ECLI:EU:C:2019:381.
[65] Judgement of 19 March 2015, *Kik*, C-266/13, EU:C:2015:188, para. 42 and the case law cited.
[66] Judgement of 19 March 2015, *Kik*, C-266/13, EU:C:2015:188, para. 43 and the case law cited.

Article 11(4) of Regulation 883/2004 designating the legislation of the flag Member State with regard to seafarers[67] (para. 28).

Considering not only the wording of the relevant provision but also its context and the objectives of the legislation of which it forms part[68] as well as its origins[69] (para. 29), the Court pointed out that, as is apparent from the wording of Article 11(3)(e) of Regulation 883/2004 that 'any other person to whom subparagraphs (a) to (d) do not apply shall be subject to the legislation of the Member State of residence, without prejudice to other provisions of this Regulation guaranteeing him/her benefits under the legislation of one or more other Member States' (para. 30). As the Advocate General stated in points 34 and 35 of his Opinion, it follows from a literal analysis of that provision that the EU legislature used general terms, in particular the words 'any other person' and 'without prejudice to other provisions of this Regulation', to make Article 11(3)(e) a residual rule which is intended to apply to all persons who find themselves in a situation that is not specifically regulated by other provisions of that Regulation and to introduce a complete system for determining the applicable legislation (para. 31).

Repeating its ruling in Walltopia and Commission v United Kingdom, the Court reaffirmed that Article 11(3) of Regulation 883/2004 applies, inter alia, to economically non-active persons[70] (para. 35). However, as the Advocate General stated in points 44 and 45 of his Opinion, a restrictive interpretation of Article 11(3)(e) of Regulation 883/2004 limiting its scope solely to economically non-active persons may deprive persons who do not fall under the situations referred to in subparas (a) to (d) of Article 11(3) or other provisions of Regulation 883/2004 of social security coverage because there is no legislation that is applicable to them (para. 36). As the Advocate General also stated in point 50 of

---

[67] To that effect, see judgement of 19 March 2015, *Kik*, C-266/13, EU:C:2015:188, para. 56.
[68] Judgements of 15 October 2014, *Hoštická and Others*, C-561/13, EU:C:2014:2287, para. 29 and the case law cited, and of 19 September 2018, *González Castro*, C-41/17, EU:C:2018:736, para. 39 and the case law cited.
[69] Judgement of 3 October 2013, *Inuit Tapiriit Kanatami and Others v Parliament and Council*, C-583/11 P, EU:C:2013:625, para. 50 and the case law cited.
[70] Judgement of 25 October 2018, *Walltopia*, C-451/17, EU:C:2018:861, para. 43 and the case law cited, judgements of 14 June 2016, *Commission v United Kingdom*, C-308/14, EU:C:2016:436, para. 63.

his Opinion, that interpretation cannot be called into question by the Commission's Explanatory Notes referred to in paragraph 14 above, or in the Practical Guide – the applicable legislation in the EU, EEA and in Switzerland, drawn up and approved by the Administrative Commission for the Coordination of Social Security Systems and published in December 2013. Even though those documents are useful tools for interpreting Regulation 883/2004, they are not legally enforceable and cannot, therefore, bind the Court in the interpretation of that Regulation (para. 41).

The Court concluded that the answer to the question referred to it is that Article 11(3)(e) of Regulation 883/2004 must be interpreted to the effect that a situation such as the one at issue in the main proceedings in which a person, whilst working as a seaman for an employer established in a Member State on board a vessel flying the flag of a third State and travelling outside the territory of the European Union, maintained his residence in his Member State of origin, falls within the scope of that provision, such that the applicable national legislation is that of that person's Member State of residence (para. 47).

8.3 Posting of workers

8.3.1 Failure of a Member State to fulfil the obligations under Article 11(1), Article 12(1) and Article 76(6) of Regulation 883/2004 and under Article 5 of Regulation 987/2009

In *European Commission v. Kingdom of Belgium*[71], the Court, in essence, examined the compliance of national legislation with the principle enshrined in Article 11 Regulation 883/2004.

On 21 November 2013, the Commission sent the Kingdom of Belgium a letter of formal notice relating to the incompatibility of Articles 23 and 24 of the Programme Law with Articles 11 and 12 and Article 76(6) of Regulation 883/2004,

---

[71] Judgement of the Court of 11 July 2018, Case C-356/15, ACTION under Article 258 TFEU for failure to fulfil obligations brought on 13 July 2015, *European Commission*, represented by D. Martin, acting as agent, with an address for service in Luxembourg, applicant, supported by: Ireland, represented by E. Creedon, M. Browne, G. Hodge and A. Joyce, acting as agents, and by C. Toland, Barrister-at-Law, intervener, v *Kingdom of Belgium*, represented by L. Van den Broeck and M. Jacobs, acting as agents, and by P. Paepe, Avocat, ECLI:EU:C:2018:555.

Article 5 of Regulation 987/2009 and Decision A1. The Belgian law entitled the competent national authorities to unilaterally require and without following the dialogue and conciliation procedure set out in the Regulations in question, that the national legislation on social security matters is to apply to posted workers who are already subject to a social security scheme in the Member State in which their employer normally carries out its activities, on grounds that the issuing of a document by the social security body of that Member State indicating that such workers are subject to the social security scheme of that Member State ('A1 certificate') is an abuse of rights pursuant to Regulations 883/2004 and 987/2009.

The Court reiterated that with regard to the complaints alleging a breach of Articles 11 and 12 and of Article 76(6) of Regulation 883/2004 and Article 5 of Regulation 987/2009, Article 5(1) of Regulation 987/2009 states, with regard to the legal value of documents issued by the institution of a Member State indicating the position of a person for the purpose of application of Regulations 883/2004 and 987/2009, and of the supporting evidence on the basis of which those documents were issued, that such documents are to be accepted by the institutions of the other Member States for as long as they have not been withdrawn or declared to be invalid by the Member State in which they were issued (para. 82). According to the Court, under Article 76(6) of Regulation 883/2004, in the event of difficulties in the interpretation or application of the Regulation, which could jeopardise the rights of the persons covered by it, the institution of the competent Member State or of the Member State of residence of the person concerned is to contact the institution of the Member State concerned. If no solution can be found within a reasonable period, the authorities concerned may call on the Administrative Commission to intervene (para. 83).

The Court, in line with previous case law[72], referred to the principle of sincere cooperation laid down in Article 4(3) TFEU and, largely following the same reasoning as in the case *Altun and Others*[73], the Court repeated its rulings. It pointed out the necessity to reconsider the grounds for issuing the certificate

---

[72] Judgements of 27 April 2017, *A-Rosa Flussschiff*, C-620/15, EU:C:2017:309, para. 39, and of 6 February 2018, *Altun and Others*, C-359/16, EU:C:2018:63, para. 37.

[73] To that effect, see judgement of 6 February 2018, *Altun and Others*, C-359/16, EU:C: 2018:63, para. 43 and the case law cited.

and, if appropriate, to withdraw the A1 certificate (para. 90). *Should the institutions concerned not reach an agreement,* in particular on how the specific facts of a given case are to be assessed, it is open to them to refer the matter to the Administrative Commission[74] (para. 91). *If the Administrative Commission does not succeed in reconciling* the points of view of the competent institutions, it is at least open to the Member State in which the workers concerned are posted to *bring infringement proceedings under Article 259 TFEU to enable the Court to examine* the question which legislation applies to those workers and, consequently, whether the particulars contained in the A1 certificate are accurate[75] (para. 92), even in case of a manifest error of assessment of the conditions regulating the application of Regulation 883/2004[76] (para. 93).

Accordingly, legislation such as Articles 23 and 24 of the Belgian Programme Law is contrary to the principle laid down in Article 11(1) of Regulation 883/2004, namely that workers are to be covered by only one social security scheme and to the principle of legal certainty which requires, inter alia, that the rules of law must be clear, precise and predictable as regards their effects, in particular if they could have negative consequences for individuals and undertakings[77] (para. 95).

In that context, the Court held that when in the dialogue provided for in Article 76(6) of Regulation 883/2004, the institution of the Member State to which the workers have been posted puts before the institution that issued the A1 certificates concrete evidence suggesting that those certificates were fraudulently obtained, it is the duty of the latter institution, by virtue of the principle of sincere cooperation, to review in the light of that evidence the grounds for issuance of those certificates and, where appropriate, to withdraw them[78] (para. 100). If the latter institution fails to carry out such a review within a reasonable period of

---

[74] To that effect, see judgement of 6 February 2018, *Altun and Others*, C-359/16, EU:C:2018:63, para. 44 and the case law cited.
[75] To that effect, see judgement of 6 February 2018, *Altun and Others*, C-359/16, EU:C:2018:63, para. 45.
[76] Judgement of 6 February 2018, *Altun and Others*, C-359/16, EU:C:2018:63, para. 46 and the case law cited.
[77] To that effect, see, inter alia, judgement of 12 December 2013, *Test Claimants in the Franked Investment Income Group Litigation*, C-362/12, EU:C:2013:834, para. 44 and the case law cited.
[78] Judgement of 6 February 2018, *Altun and Others*, C-359/16, EU:C:2018:63, para. 54.

time, it must be possible for that evidence to be relied on in judicial proceedings to satisfy the court of the Member State to which the workers have been posted that the certificates should be disregarded[79] (para. 101) However, the persons who are alleged in such proceedings to have used posted workers ostensibly covered by fraudulently obtained certificates must be given the opportunity to rebut the evidence on which those proceedings are based, with due regard to the safeguards associated with the right to a fair trial, before the national court decides, if appropriate, that the certificates should be disregarded and issues a ruling on the liability of those persons under the applicable national law[80] (para. 103).

The Court concluded that in the present case, the national legislation at issue did not satisfy the conditions set out in paragraphs 100 and 101 of this judgement (para. 104). Under those circumstances, the Commission's complaints that the Kingdom of Belgium failed to fulfil its obligations under Article 11(1), Article 12(1) and Article 76(6) of Regulation 883/2004 and Article 5 of Regulation 987/2009 must be upheld (para. 109).

With regard to the complaint alleging a breach of Decision A1, it is clear from settled case law that such a decision, although capable of providing assistance to social security institutions responsible for applying EU law in that sphere, cannot require those institutions to follow certain methods or to adopt certain interpretations when applying EU law[81] (para. 110). Accordingly, since Decision A1 is not a legislative act, there is no ground for claiming that the Kingdom of Belgium, by adopting Articles 23 and 24 of the Programme Law, infringed that decision (para. 111). Hence, the Court found that by adopting Articles 23 and 24 of the Programme Law, the Kingdom of Belgium failed to fulfil its obligations under Article 11(1), Article 12(1) and Article 76(6) of Regulation 883/2004 and under Article 5 of Regulation 987/2009 (para. 113).

---

[79] Judgement of 6 February 2018, *Altun and Others*, C-359/16, EU:C:2018:63, para. 55.
[80] Judgement of 6 February 2018, *Altun and Others*, C-359/16, EU:C:2018:63, para. 56.
[81] Judgements of 8 July 1992, *Knoch*, C-102/91, EU:C:1992:303, para. 52, and of 1 October 1992, *Grisvard and Kreitz*, C-201/91, EU:C:1992:368, para. 25.

8.3.2 Interpretation of Article 14(1) of Regulation 987/2009, read together with Article 12(1) of Regulation 883/2004

In *Walltopia*[82] the Court interpreted Article 14(1) of Regulation 987/2009, read together with Article 12(1) of Regulation 883/2004. Mr Punchev, a Bulgarian national, was hired by Walltopia (established in Bulgaria) with the purpose of being posted to the United Kingdom. Subsequently, the national authority concerned refused to issue Walltopia an A1 certificate attesting that Bulgarian legislation was applicable to Mr Punchev, on grounds that the latter had not been subject to that legislation for at least one month before his posting.

In respect of the four questions of the referring court, the Court examined whether a person recruited for the purpose of being posted to another Member State and who is in a situation such as that of Mr Punchev must be regarded as having been 'immediately before the start of his employment ... already subject to the legislation of the Member State in which his employer is established' within the meaning of Article 14(1) of Regulation 987/2009 (para. 40). It is clear from the file before the Court that Mr Punchev's residence, within the meaning of Article 1(j) of Regulation 883/2004, was in Bulgaria immediately before the commencement of his employment (para. 45). In the present case, it did not appear from the file before the Court that the legislation of a Member State other than the Republic of Bulgaria was applicable to Mr Punchev immediately before the commencement of his employment with Walltopia, which, however, is for the referring court to ascertain (para. 50).

According to the Court, Article 14(1) of Regulation 987/2009, read together with Article 12(1) of Regulation 883/2004, must be interpreted as meaning that an employee recruited for the purpose of being posted to another Member State must be regarded as having been 'just before the start of his employment ... already subject to the legislation of the Member State in which his employer is established', within the meaning of Article 14(1) of Regulation 987/2009, even if that employee was not an insured person under the legislation of that Member State immediately before the commencement of his or her employment, if, at

---

[82] Judgement of the Court of 25 October 2018, Case C-451/17, '*Walltopia*' AD v Direktor na Teritorialna direktsia na Natsionalnata agentsia za prihodite – Veliko Tarnovo, ECLI: EU:C:2018:861.

that time, that employee's residence was in that Member State, which is for the referring court to ascertain (para. 51).

8.3.3 The binding effect of the A1 certificate

In *Alpenrind*[83], the Court examined the binding effect of the A1 certificate. The case concerned the posting of employees of a Hungarian company to work for an Austrian company (Alpenrind). Employees of Martimpex, a company based in Hungary (country of origin), were regularly posted to Alpenrind, a company based in Austria (host country). If the conditions for posting are met, Hungary should have issued A1 certificates. A1 certificates would ensure the continued inclusion of posted workers in the Hungarian social insurance system (country of origin). Hungary issued A1 certificates retroactively after Austria (host country) recognised the inclusion of the posted workers from Hungary in the Austrian social security system. It is, of course, also possible to issue A1 certificates retroactively. However, the certificates were issued by Hungary while the conditions for posting were not met. Specifically, the condition of non-replacement was not met at the time.

The Court generally reaffirmed its previous judgements concerning postings and the validity of E101 certificates (now A1). Furthermore, as the Advocate General pointed out in point 35 of his Opinion, the assessments on which the case law of the Court of Justice on the binding validity of E 101 certificates is based also apply in Regulations 883/2004 and 987/2009 (para. 45).

Although the condition of non-substitution was not met, the Court acknowledged the binding nature and retroactive effect of A1 certificates for which there was no reason to issue them. It was based on the fundamental principle of sincere cooperation between Member States, which is enshrined in Article 4 (3) TFEU, but also follows from the provisions of Regulation 883/04. The importance of the principle of sincere cooperation derives from both Article 76 of Regulation 883/2004 and recital 2 as well as Article 20 of Regulation 987/2009

---

[83] Judgement of the Court of 6 September 2018, Case C-527/16, Salzburger Gebietskrankenkasse, Bundesminister für Arbeit, Soziales und Konsumentenschutz, Interested parties: Alpenrind GmbH, Martin-Meat Szolgáltató és Kereskedelmi Kft, Martimpex-Meat Kft, Pensionsversicherungsanstalt, Allgemeine Unfallversicherungsanstalt, (*Alpenrind and others*) ECLI:EU:C:2018:669.

(para. 45). At the same time, the Court established that the jurisdiction of the Member State of origin of the employees / issuance of certificates is decisive, asserting that the provision of Article 5 (1) of Regulation 987/2009 tends to indicate that only the authorities and courts of the issuer Member State may, in principle, on a case-by-case basis, revoke or declare an A1 certificate as being invalid (para. 39). The same had previously been accepted by the Court on the use of E101 certificates. An E101 certificate issued in accordance with Article 11a of Regulation 574/72, unless revoked or declared invalid, shall be binding on the competent institution of the Member State to which the worker is posted to perform work[84].

The Court held that Article 5(1) of Regulation 987/2009, read together with Article 19(2) thereof, must be interpreted as meaning that an A1 certificate, issued by the competent institution of a Member State under Article 12(1) of Regulation 883/2004, binds not only the institutions of the Member State in which the activity is being carried out, but also the courts of that Member State (para. 47).

The Court seems to be moving towards respecting the rules of the Coordination Rules, even in the event of their incorrect application (Hungary was proven to not be the competent Member State)[85]. This is justified by the need to preserve the functionality of a coordination mechanism that aims to combine the technical characteristics of different social security systems based on the sincere cooperation of the Member States[86]. If it were accepted that except in cases of fraud or abuse of rights, the competent national body could, by appealing to a court in that worker's host Member State, obtain a declaration of invalidity of the E101 certificate, cooperation between the competent bodies of the Member States would arise (para. 46). This would further hamper the free movement of persons. However, the Court has repeatedly emphasised that the coordination of social security legislation is a prerequisite for the realisation of the freedom of movement or otherwise of movement, established in Articles 45-48 TFEU[87].

---

[84] Judgement of the Court of 30.03.2000, Case C-178/97, Barry Banks and others, 2000 I-02005, para. 46.
[85] A. Tsetoura, Posting in social security: Posting of workers and the binding effect of A1 certificate, Social Security Law (Greek Review) 1/2019, p. 103 sub.
[86] Ibid.
[87] Judgement of 19.03.1964, Case 75/63, Unger, ECR 1964, p. 177, para. 1, judgement of 13.07.1966, Case 4/66, J. E. Labots (Nee Hagenbeek), widow of W. Labots, ECR 1966,

In the same vein, the Court in the *Banks* case accepted that the E 101 certificate may, on a case-by-case basis, have retroactive effect. The Court based its judgement on the possibility provided for in Article 17 of Regulation 1408/71 according to which Member States can agree on the application of legislation other than Articles 13-16 in the interest of the employee (also valid for different periods[88]). Referring to its judgement in the *Banks* case, the Court stated that under Regulation 883/04, the issuance of an A1 certificate during or even after the end of the relevant period of employment is possible (para. 72). Of course, it cannot be overlooked that acceptance of a retrospectively issued E 101 certificate calls into question the effectiveness of the checks carried out by the social security institutions with regard to posted workers[89]. However, the effectiveness of coordination is highlighted by the Court.

It is also crucial to underscore the illustrative role of the Administrative Committee. The Court held that A1 certificates are binding on both the social security institutions of the Member State in which it operates and the courts of that Member State, even if the Administrative Commission has concluded that the certificate had been wrongly issued and should be revoked (para. 64). As regards the condition of non-substitution, the Court gave a literal interpretation of Article 12(1) of Regulation 883/2004 (para.91).

The Court seems to be falling into an interpretive "trap", which it has also fallen into in the past[90] in its attempt to safeguard the interests of employees. Having extended its interpretation in relation to the binding effect of certificates recognising their retroactive effect in previous judgements, it is in a position to extend this binding effect even further. It could be said that this is an extension of the binding nature of retrospectively issued certificates, even in the case of (illegal) issuance despite the letter of the Regulation. It places the burden on the State

---

p. 425, b, judgement of 14.12.1989, Case C-168/88, Theo Dammer, ECR 1989, p. 4553, para. 21, of 06.12.1973, Case 140/73, Mancuso, ECR 1973 p. 01449, para. 6, of 25.11.1975, Case 50/75, Massonet, ECR 1975 01473, para. 10.

[88] Judgements of 17.05.1984, Case 101/83, Brusse, 1984, p. 2223, paras 20-21 and of 29.06.1995, Case C-454/93, Van Gestel, 1995, p. I-1707, para. 29.

[89] P. Schouckens and D. Pieters, "The rules within Regulation 883/2004 for determining the applicable legislation", *European Journal of Social Security*, 2009 (1-2), p. 86.

[90] A. Tsetoura, *The European Pensioner*, Sakkoulas publications, Athens - Thessaloniki, 2017, p. 432 sub.

concerned to initiate infringement proceedings under Article 259 TFEU to enable the Court to consider the question of the legislation to be applied to the worker and, consequently, the accuracy of the information included in the E 101[91] certificate (para. 61). This case law can be justified by the need to preserve the effectiveness and continuity of coordination, which is inextricably linked to the principle of free movement. Certificates may be declared invalid in accordance with the Court only in the event of fraud or abuse of power. As can be deduced from this judgement, fraud or abuse of power can be established through the procedure laid down in Article 259 TFEU.

Finally, the Court held that the recurrent use of posted workers to fill the same post, even though the employers responsible for posting workers are different, does not comply with the wording or the objectives of Article 12(1) of Regulation 883/2004 and is not consistent with the context of which that provision is part, so that a person posted cannot benefit from the special rule laid down in that provision if he or she replaces another worker (para. 99). Having regard to all of the foregoing considerations, the Court concluded that Article 12(1) of Regulation 883/2004 must be interpreted as meaning that if a worker who is posted by his or her employer to carry out work in another Member State is replaced by another worker posted by another employer, the latter employee must be considered to have been 'sent to replace another person' within the meaning of that provision, so that he or she cannot benefit from the special rules laid down in that provision to remain subject to the legislation of the Member State in which his or her employer normally carries out its activities. The fact that the employers of the two workers concerned have their registered offices in the same Member State or that they may have personal or organisational links is irrelevant in that respect (para. 100).

In the more recent case *Bouygues travaux publics*[92], the Court interpreted both Regulation 1408/71 and Regulation 883/2004 and their implementing Regulations 574/72 and 987/2009, respectively, with regard to the binding effect of

---

[91] See judgement of 27 April 2017, A-Rosa Flussschiff, C-620/15, EU:C:2017:309, para. 46 and case law cited.
[92] Judgement of the Court of 14 May 2020, Case C-17/19, *Bouygues travaux publics*, Elco construct Bucarest, Welbond armatures ECLI:EU:C:2020:379.

posting certificates in the context of a complicated case including various Member States.

After being awarded contracts for the construction of a new generation nuclear reactor, a pressurised water reactor known as 'EPR', in Flamanville (France), Bouygues, a company in France established a limited partnership with two other undertakings to realise those contracts. The contracts were subcontracted to an economic interest grouping that included, among others, Welbond, a company also established in France. The grouping also used subcontractors, including Elco, a company established in Romania, and Atlanco Ltd, a temporary employment company established in Ireland with a subsidiary in Cyprus and an office in Poland. Following a complaint about the accommodation provided for foreign workers, strike actions by temporary Polish employees against the lack and inadequacy of social security coverage for accidents. There were over 100 unreported workplace accidents, and an investigation initially by the Nuclear Safety Authority and then by the police resulted in convictions of Bouygues, Welbond and Elco for offences committed between June 2008 and October 2012, with charges of concealed employment and the unlawful provision of workers against Bouygues and Welbond, and a charge of concealed employment against Elco. Bouygues, Elco and Welbond brought an appeal before the Cour de cassation (Court of Cassation, France) against the judgement of the cour d'appel de Caen (Court of Appeal, Caen) of 20 March 2017, claiming, inter alia, that that Court had disregarded the effects attached to the E 101 and A 1 certificates issued to the workers concerned.

As regards the nature and effect of the declaration prior to the engagement of employees provided for by the *code du travail*, the requirement of which was at the heart of the dispute in the main proceedings, the Court noted that, according to the applicants in the main proceedings, the purpose of that declaration, although it is formally provided for by that code, is to verify whether a worker is affiliated to one or other branches of the social security scheme and, consequently, to ensure payment of social security contributions in France. That declaration shall be made by employers to the social security bodies and is thus the means whereby the latter can verify compliance with national social security rules to fight clandestine work (para. 49).

The present dispute did not concern the payment of social security contributions in that Member State, but the compliance of the applicants in the main proceedings with all the French rules of labour law (para. 50).

As noted by the Court, it is for the referring court to determine whether the sole purpose of the obligation to make a declaration prior to engaging employees as laid down in the *code du travail* is to ensure that the workers concerned are affiliated to one or other branches of the social security scheme and, therefore, to ensure compliance with the legislation in that area only, in which case the E 101 and A 1 certificates, provided by the issuing institution, would, in principle, preclude such an obligation, or alternatively, whether the purpose of that obligation is also, even in part, to protect the effectiveness of checks made by the competent national authorities to ensure compliance with conditions of employment and working conditions imposed by labour law, in which case those certificates would have no effect on that obligation, given that that obligation cannot, in any event, entail that the workers concerned are affiliated to one or other branches of the social security system (para. 53). Thus, the Court concluded that Article 11(1)(a), Article 12a(2)(a) and (4)(a) of Regulation 574/72 and Article 19(2) of Regulation 987/2009 must be interpreted as meaning that an E 101 certificate, issued by the competent institution of a Member State under Article 14(1)(a) or Article 14(2)(b) of Regulation 1408/71 to workers who are employed in the territory of another Member State, and an A 1 certificate, issued by that institution under Article 12(1) or Article 13(1) of Regulation 883/2004 to such workers are binding on the courts or tribunals of the latter Member State solely in the area of social security (para. 54).

8.3.4 Applicable legislation to posted third-country nationals who are temporarily residing and working in different Member States in the service of an employer established in a Member State

In *Balandin and others*[93], the Court interpreted Regulations 1231/2010, 987/2009 and 883/2004 as applicable legislation to third-country nationals. Mr Balandin and Mr Lukachenko were third-country nationals employed by HOI, a

---

[93] Judgement of the Court of 24 January 2019, Case C-477/17, Raad van bestuur van de Sociale Verzekeringsbank v D. Balandin, I. Lukachenko, Holiday on Ice Services BV *(Balandin and others)*, ECLI:EU:C:2019:60.

company legally established in the Netherlands which organises, ice-skating shows in different countries, including some Member States. All workers employed by HOI meet in the Netherlands for several weeks to prepare for the shows. Some of the skaters perform in a number of shows in the Netherlands, while the rest perform in shows in various other Member States, in particular in France and Germany. During the period of training and, where applicable, during the performance period, all third-country nationals legally reside in the Netherlands, with work permits being issued where necessary. They also legally reside in the other Member States where shows take place, often on the basis of a visa known as a 'Schengen visa'. For many years, the Svb issued A1 certificates to third-country nationals employed by HOI, establishing that they were covered by the social security legislation of the Netherlands and that compulsory contributions were also paid in the Netherlands. However, from the 2015/2016 season onwards, the Svb refused to issue such certificates, arguing that they had been incorrectly issued in previous years. It thus rejected HOI's applications for an A1 certificate. After consultations in particular as part of the interim relief granted by the court following hearings on interim applications in Amsterdam, the Netherlands, the Svb finally issued A1 certificates valid until 1 May 2016. However, the 2015/2016 season ended on 22 May 2016, so that the dispute continued for those final weeks in May 2016. In a judgement of 28 April 2016, the District Court, Amsterdam, the Netherlands, held, particularly on the basis of the principle of legitimate expectations, that the Svb should have issued A1 certificates covering the last weeks of that season as well. Svb appealed against this judgement to the referring court.

According to the Court, as reflected in Article 12(1)(e) and (2)(b) of Directive 2011/98, read in conjunction with Article 2(b) and Article 3(1)(b) and (c), (2)(i) and (3) of that Directive, third-country nationals admitted for work in a Member State, even temporarily, in principle, benefit from equal treatment with respect to branches of social security within the meaning of Regulation 883/2004 (para. 42). In the present case, it was apparent from the order for reference that the persons concerned in the main proceedings, who were employed by an undertaking established in the Netherlands, legally resided and worked in the territory of the Member States in which they had shows (para. 44). It follows that third-country nationals who are in the situation such as that at issue in the main proceedings are entitled to the application of the coordination rules laid down by Regulations 883/2004 and 987/2009 for the purpose of the determination of the applicable social security legislation (para. 45).

In that regard, it must be recalled in view of the factual findings made in para. 44 of the present judgement, that Article 13 of Regulation 883/2004 provides, inter alia, connecting factors that are applicable to persons pursuing activities as employed persons in two or more Member States. It is for the referring court to ascertain whether one of those connecting factors is applicable to the persons concerned in the main proceedings to determine whether they are subject to the Netherlands' social security legislation. If that is the case, the competent institution of the Member State whose legislation becomes applicable shall certify, by issuing an A1 certificate, that the legislation is indeed applicable and shall indicate, where applicable, until when and under what conditions the legislation applies pursuant to Article 19(2) of Regulation 987/2009 (para. 46). Therefore, the Court concluded that Article 1 of Regulation 1231/2010 must be interpreted as meaning that third-country nationals, such as those at issue in the main proceedings who temporarily reside and work in different Member States in the service of an employer established in a Member State, may rely on the coordination rules laid down by Regulations 883/2004 and 987/2009 to determine the social security legislation to which they are subject, provided that they are legally residing and working in the territory of those Member States (para. 47).

9 The 'race to the bottom' effect on labour and social security protection through the cases before the Court

9.1 Autonomous interpretation of the concept of "an undertaking" – the criterion of the actual performance of the hierarchical relationship between "employer" and "employee" in practice

In *AFMB Ltd and Others*[94], the Court reviewed the autonomous interpretation of the concept of 'an undertaking', while in parallel, it interpreted the concept of 'employer' and 'employee', as well as the hierarchical relationship between the

---

[94] Judgement of the Court of 16 July 2020, Case C-610/18, *AFMB Ltd and Others* v Raad van bestuur van de Sociale verzekeringsbank, ECLI:EU:C:2020:565.

employer and employees. The request was made in proceedings between AFMB Ltd, a company established in Cyprus, and international long-distance lorry drivers (residing in the Netherlands), on the one hand, and the Board of Management of the Social Insurance Bank, the Netherlands; 'the Svb', concerning decisions whereby the Svb declared that the social security legislation of the Netherlands was applicable to those long-distance lorry drivers. According to the terms of their contracts, AFMB was named as the employer of those workers and Cypriot employment law was declared to be applicable. AFMB made an application under Article 16 of Regulation 987/2009 to the Svb for confirmation that during the above period, the international long-distance lorry drivers with whom it had concluded those employment contracts were not subject under Article 13 of Regulation 883/2004 to the social security legislation of the Netherlands. The Svb declared that the Netherlands' social security legislation was applicable to the long-distance lorry drivers and issued A 1 certificates to that effect. AFMB and a number of the long-distance lorry drivers with whom it had concluded employment contracts brought an action before the District Court, Amsterdam, the Netherlands, challenging the latter decisions of the Svb.

According to the findings of the referring court, before the conclusion of those employment contracts, the international long-distance lorry drivers concerned had never lived nor worked in Cyprus. When those contracts were being carried out, they continued to live in the Netherlands and worked on behalf of those transport undertakings in two or more Member States, and also, in the case of some of those long-distance lorry drivers, in one or more European Free Trade Association (EFTA) States. It was also stated in the order for reference that during the abovementioned period, those long-distance lorry drivers did not carry out a substantial part of their activities in the Netherlands. Furthermore, some of those drivers had previously been employees of those undertakings.

The Court stated that that hierarchical relationship resulted from, inter alia, the fact that the undertaking in question paid the workers' wages and could dismiss them on the ground of faults he or she might have committed in the performance of the work at the premises of the entity making use of the work[95] (para. 56). Specifically, the Court stated that the institution concerned may, where appropriate, take account not only of the wording of contractual documents, but also of factors such as the way in which employment contracts between the employer and the worker concerned had previously been performed in practice, the circumstances surrounding the conclusion of those contracts and, more generally, the characteristics and conditions of the work performed by the undertaking concerned, in so far as those factors may throw light on the actual nature of the work in question[96] (para. 58).

The Court added that, if it is apparent from the relevant factors other than the contractual documents that an employed person's situation in fact differs from that described in those documents, the obligation to correctly apply Regulation 1408/71 means that it is incumbent on the institution concerned, whatever the wording of those contractual documents, to base its findings on the employed person's actual situation[97] (para. 59). To arrive at such a conclusion, regard must not only be given to the information formally contained in the employment contract but also to how the obligations under the contract incumbent on both the worker and the undertaking in question are performed in practice. Accordingly, whatever the wording of the contractual documents, it is necessary to identify the entity that actually exercises authority over the worker, which, in reality, bears the relevant wage costs and which has the actual power to dismiss that worker (para. 61).

However, the objective of those regulations, as stipulated in para. 63 of the present judgement, might be undermined if the interpretation adopted of the concepts mentioned in para. 48 of this judgement were to make it easier for employers to be able to resort to purely *artificial arrangements to exploit EU legislation* with the sole aim of obtaining an advantage from the differences that exist between the national rules. Such exploitation of that legislation would

---

[95] To that effect, see judgement of 17 December 1970, *Manpower*, 35/70, EU:C:1970:120, paras 17, 18 and 20.
[96] Judgement of 4 October 2012, *Format Urządzenia i Montaże Przemysłowe*, C-115/11, EU:C:2012:606, para. 45.
[97] To that effect, see judgement of 4 October 2012, *Format Urządzenia i Montaże Przemysłowe*, C-115/11, EU:C:2012:606, para. 46.

likely *have a 'race to the bottom' effect on the social security systems of the Member States and, ultimately, possibly reduce the level of protection offered by those systems* (para. 69).

Thus, regardless which EU legislation was applicable to the long-distance lorry drivers in the main proceedings, whether Regulation 1408/71 or Regulation 883/2004, the applicable social security legislation seems to be the legislation of the Netherlands, which, however, it is for the referring court to determine (para. 79). Thus, the Court concluded that the answer to the first question was that Article 14(2)(a) of Regulation 1408/71 and Article 13(1)(b)(i) of Regulation 883/2004 must be interpreted as meaning that the employer of an international long-distance lorry driver, for the purposes of those provisions, is the undertaking which has actual authority over that long-distance lorry driver, which, in reality, bears the costs of paying his or her wages, and which has the actual power to dismiss him or her, and not the undertaking with which that long-distance lorry driver has concluded an employment contract and which is formally named in that contract as being the employer of that driver.

The abovementioned ruling has been considered positive in as much as the Court tends to prevent circumvention of legislation through a teleological interpretation of the provisions of Coordination Regulation[98]. Besides, the interpenetration of labour and social security laws aiming at the enforcement of the framework of social protection of workers is promoted through common terms[99]. In other words, the Court approached this case from the perspective of "prolepsis" with regard to the 'race to the bottom' effect in the field of social security protection through artificial employment arrangements which potentially undermine the working person's rights. Below in the more recent case of Team Power Europe, the Court reaffirms its approach.

---

[98] Th. Bourlos, The concept of "employer" in the European social security law in the light of the case law of the Court of Justice of the European Union, *Social Security Law* (Greek Review) 4/2020, p. 725.

[99] B. Kouziorti and Ang. Stergiou, The wage in social security, *Labour Law Review* (Greek Review), 2014, p. 66.

9.2 The concept of a substantial part of activities as a balancing indicator between fair competition and social security coordination

In *TEAM POWER EUROPE*[100], the Court interpreted Article 12(1) of Regulation 883/2004, the scope of which is defined in Article 14(2) of Regulation 987/2009, highlighting the practical importance of the substantial part of the activity criterion.

The request was made in proceedings between 'TEAM POWER EUROPE' EOOD, a company (temporary work agency) incorporated under Bulgarian law and established in Varna (Bulgaria), and the Director of the Territorial Directorate of the National Public Revenue Agency for the City of Varna, Bulgaria ('the Director') concerning the latter's refusal to issue a certificate attesting that Bulgarian social security legislation was applicable to a temporary agency worker employed by that agency for the period during which that worker was assigned to a user undertaking established in Germany. The application was rejected on grounds that the situation at issue in the main proceedings did not fall within the scope of Article 12(1) of Regulation 883/2004. It took the view, first, that the direct relationship between Team Power Europe and the worker in question had not been maintained and, second, that that undertaking did not carry on any substantial activity in Bulgaria.

The Court repeated its rulings in case Walltopia with regard to the objectives of Article 12(1) of Regulation 883/2004, the scope of which is defined in Article 14(2) of Regulation 987/2009. Specifically, to prevent an undertaking established in a Member State from being required to register its workers, who are usually subject to the social security legislation of that State, with the social security system of another Member State to which they are posted to perform work of a short duration, Article 12(1) of Regulation 883/2004 allows the undertaking to keep its workers registered under the social security system of the first Member State[101] (para. 60).

---

[100] Judgement of the Court of 3 June 2021, Case C-784/19, *'TEAM POWER EUROPE'* EOOD V Direktor na Teritorialna direktsia na Natsionalna agentsia za prihodite – Varna ECLI:EU:C:2021:427.
[101] See judgement of 25 October 2018, *Walltopia*, C-451/17, EU:C:2018:861, para. 39 and the case law cited.

To allow temporary work agencies to exercise the freedom to provide services to benefit from that advantage when they orientate their activities of supplying temporary agency workers exclusively or primarily to one or more Member States other than that in which they are established, would be likely to encourage those undertakings to choose the Member State in which they wish establish themselves on the basis of the latter's social security legislation with the sole aim of benefiting from the legislation that is most favourable to them in that field, and thus to allow for *'forum shopping'* (para. 60).

However, the objective of those regulations – which is to promote the freedom of movement of workers, and in the case of the posting of workers, the freedom to provide services by offering an advantage in terms of social security for undertakings exercising those freedoms – might be undermined if the interpretation of Article 14(2) of Regulation 987/2009 were to make it easier for those undertakings to use EU legislation with the sole aim of exploiting the differences between the national social security systems. Such exploitation of that legislation would be likely to have a *'race to the bottom' effect* on the social security systems of Member States or might even lead to a reduction in the level of protection they offer (para. 64).

Furthermore, by allowing temporary work agencies to take advantage of the differences between Member States' social security systems, an interpretation of Article 12(1) of Regulation 883/2004 and Article 14(2) of Regulation 987/2009 according to which temporary agency workers recruited by those undertakings remain affiliated to the social security system of the Member State in which those undertakings are established, even though they do not carry out any significant activity assigning those workers to user undertakings that are also established there, would have the effect of creating a *distortion of competition* between the various possible modes of employment in favour of recourse to temporary agency work as opposed to undertakings directly recruiting workers, who would be affiliated to the social security system of the Member State in which they work (para. 65).

It follows that although a temporary work agency, which carries out its activities of assigning temporary agency workers exclusively or primarily to user undertakings established in a Member State other than that in which it is established, is entitled to rely on the freedom to provide services guaranteed by the Treaty on the Functioning of the European Union, such an undertaking cannot, by contrast, benefit from the advantage in terms of social security offered by Article 12(1) of Regulation 883/2004, which consists of keeping those workers affiliated to the legislation of the Member State in which the temporary work agency is established, since that advantage is subject to the exercise by that undertaking of a significant part of its activities of assigning workers for the benefit of user undertakings established and carrying out its activities in the territory of the Member State in which it is itself established (para. 66).

The Court concluded that the answer to the question referred to it is that Article 14(2) of Regulation 987/2009 must be interpreted as meaning that a temporary work agency established in a Member State must, in order for it to be considered as 'normally carrying out its activities' within the meaning of Article 12(1) of Regulation 883/2004 in that Member State, perform a significant part of its activities of assigning temporary agency workers for the benefit of user undertakings that are established and carry out their activities in the territory of that Member State (para. 68).

10 Social security contributions

10.1 Exemption of EU officials from social security contributions to their Member State of residence – their financial obligations with reference to social security are exclusively regulated by the EU Protocol and Staff Regulations

In *de Lobkowicz*[102], the Court referred to the obligations of EU officials to pay social security contributions in their Member State of residence.

Mr de Lobkowicz, a French national, was a Commission official from 1979 until his retirement on 1 January 2016. As such, he was subject to the joint social security scheme of the EU institutions. Pursuant to Article 13 of the Protocol, Mr de Lobkowicz's domicile for tax purposes was France. He earned an income from real estate in that Member State. For the years 2008 to 2011, that income was subject to CSG, the *contribution pour le remboursement de la dette sociale*

---

[102] Judgement of the Court of 10 May 2017, Case C-690/15, Wenceslas *de Lobkowicz* v Ministère des Finances et des Comptes publics, ECLI:EU:C:2017:355.

(social debt repayment contribution) ('CRDS'), the social levy of 2 per cent and the contributions additional to that levy at the rates of 0.3 per cent and 1.1 per cent, respectively. Following the tax authorities' refusal to grant his application for exemption from the abovementioned contributions and levies, Mr de Lobkowicz brought an action before the French Administrative Court, seeking exemption from those payments.

The Court noted that EU officials are subject to the joint social security scheme of the EU institutions, which, pursuant to Article 14 of the Protocol, is laid down by the European Parliament and the Council acting by means of regulations adopted under the ordinary legislative procedure and after consultation of the other institutions (para. 36). Therefore, the legal position of EU officials with regard to social security obligations comes within the scope of EU law by reason of their employment by the European Union[103] (para. 38). As the Court pointed out, the European Union alone, and not the Member States, has competence to establish the rules applicable to EU officials in respect of their social security obligations (para. 44).

National legislation, such as that at issue in the main proceedings, which subjects the income of an EU official to contributions and social levies specifically allocated for the funding of the social security schemes of the Member State concerned, therefore infringes the exclusive competence of the European Union under Article 14 of the Protocol and the relevant provisions of the Staff Regulations, in particular those that prescribe mandatory contributions to the funding of a social security scheme by EU officials (para. 46). In addition, such legislation might interfere with the equal treatment of EU officials and, therefore, discourage employment within an EU institution, since some officials would be required to contribute to a national social security scheme in addition to the joint social security scheme of the EU institutions (para. 47). An EU official such as Mr de Lobkowicz cannot, accordingly, be subject to those levies and contributions since his financial obligations relating to social security are

---

[103] To that effect, see judgement of 13 July 1983, *Forcheri*, 152/82, EU:C:1983:205, para. 9.

exclusively regulated by the Protocol and the Staff Regulations and, as such, fall outside the jurisdiction of the Member State[104] (para. 48).

The Court concluded that Article 14 of the Protocol and the provisions of the Staff Regulation on the joint social security scheme of the EU institutions must be interpreted as precluding national legislation which provides that income from real estate received in a Member State by an official of the European Union, whose domicile for tax purposes in that Member State is subject to contributions and social levies that are allocated for the funding of the social security scheme of that same Member State (para. 49).

10.2 Obligations for social security contributions of a Member State national while residing in a third country other than an EEA Member State or the Swiss Confederation

In *Jahin*[105], the Court interpreted Article 11 of Regulation 883/2004, taking into account the movement of capital from or to third countries with regard to obligations for social security contributions of a Member State national while residing in a third country other than an EEA Member State or the Swiss Confederation.

Mr Jahin, a French national, had lived in China since 2003. He pursued a professional activity in China and was affiliated with a private social security scheme there. Between 2012 and 2014, he was subject to various levies on income in France from real estate and capital gain realised on the transfer of immovable property[106].

---

[104] See, by analogy, with regard to Regulation 1408/71, judgement of 26 February 2015, *de Ruyter*, C-623/13, EU:C:2015:123, paras 23, 26, 28 and 29.
[105] Judgement of the Court of 18 January 2018, Case C-45/17, Frédéric *Jahin* v Ministre de l'Économie et des Finances, Ministre des Affaires sociales et de la Santé, ECLI:EU:C:2018:18.
[106] Having already been requested to deliver a preliminary ruling by the referring court, the Conseil d'État (Council of State, France), in another case relating to identical levies, which gave rise to the judgement of 26 February 2015, *de Ruyter* (C-623/13, EU:C:2015:123), the Court in essence held that such levies, in so far as they have a direct and relevant link with some of the branches of social security listed in Article 4 of Regulation 1408/71, fall within the scope of that Regulation and are subject to the principle that the legislation of a single Member State shall apply only, as laid down in Article 13(1) of that Regulation, even though they are imposed on the income from assets of taxable persons, irrespective of the pursuit of any professional activity. Following that

According to the Court, levies such as those described under the national legislation at issue in the main proceedings, in so far as they relate to income from real estate and to capital gains realised following the transfer of immovable property received in a Member State by a natural person who holds the nationality of that State but resides in a third country other than an EEA Member State or the Swiss Confederation, fall within the scope of 'movement of capital' within the meaning of Article 63 TFEU (para. 23). In the present case, it was acknowledged that the French legislation treats its nationals who reside in a third country other than an EEA Member State or the Swiss Confederation and are affiliated with a social security scheme in that third country in the same way as French nationals who reside in France and are affiliated with a social security scheme there, since in both cases they are equally subject to the levies on capital income provided for by that national legislation (para. 26). By contrast, more favourable tax treatment is reserved for EU nationals affiliated with a social security scheme in another Member State, an EEA Member State or the Swiss Confederation, given that they are exempt from those levies (para. 27). Such a difference in treatment is liable to dissuade natural persons affiliated with a social security scheme of a third country other than the EEA Member States or the Swiss Confederation from making investments in immovable property in the Member State whose nationality they hold and is therefore liable to hamper the movement of capital from such third countries to that Member State (para. 28).

According to the Court, there is an objective difference between, on the one hand, of the situation of a national of the Member State concerned, who resides in a third country other than an EEA Member State or the Swiss Confederation and is affiliated with a social security scheme in that third country and, on the other hand, the situation of an EU national affiliated with a social security scheme of another Member State, in so far as that latter national alone is liable to benefit from the principle that only the legislation of a single Member State shall apply to matters of social security, as laid down in Article 11 of Regulation

---

judgement, the referring court in a ruling of 27 July 2015 held that any natural person affiliated with a social security scheme in another Member State is entitled to seek the discharge of the contributions which were imposed in France on the income received from those assets.

883/2004, by reason of that person's movement within the European Union (para. 42).

The Court stated that since the TFEU does not contain any provision extending the free movement of workers to persons who migrate to a third country, it is important to ensure that the interpretation of Article 63(1) TFEU as regards relations with third countries, other than the EEA Member States or the Swiss Confederation, does not enable persons, who do not come within the territorial scope of the free movement of workers to profit from that freedom[107] (para. 46).

Thus, the Court concluded that Articles 63 and 65 TFEU must be interpreted as not precluding legislation of a Member State, such as that at issue in the main proceedings, under which a national of that Member State who resides in a third country other than an EEA Member State or the Swiss Confederation and is affiliated with a social security scheme in that third country is subject in that Member State to levies on income from assets for the purpose of contributing to the social security scheme established by that Member State, whereas an EU national covered by a social security scheme of another Member State is exempt therefrom by reason of the principle that the legislation of a single Member State only is to apply to matters of social security pursuant to Article 11 of Regulation 883/2004 (para. 47).

10.3 Proportionate calculation of the tax credit's social security component for the purpose of establishing the social security contributions payable by a worker

In *Zyla*[108], the Court reviewed whether the proportionate calculation of the tax credit's social security component for the purpose of establishing the social security contributions payable by a worker who falls under Regulation 883/2004 is compatible with Article 45 TFEU. The request was made in the context of a dispute between Ms K.M. Zyla and the Secretary of State for Finance, the Netherlands concerning the pro rata calculation of the tax credit's social security component to which she was entitled. Ms Zyla, a Polish national,

---

[107] To that effect, see judgement of 13 November 2012, *Test Claimants in the FII Group Litigation*, C-35/11, EU:C:2012:707, para. 100.
[108] Judgement of the Court 23 January 2019, Case C-272/17, K.M. *Zyla* v Staatssecretaris van Financiën, ECLI:EU:C:2019:49.

worked in the Netherlands from 1 January 2013 to 21 June 2013. During that time, she was insured under the Netherlands' general social security system and was liable to pay the corresponding social security contributions. Ms Zyla then returned to Poland, where she took up residence but did not perform any paid work in 2013. Ms Zyla received an income of EUR 9,401 for the work she performed in the Netherlands in 2013. A wage levy of EUR 1,399 was withheld at source from the wage amount. Ms Zyla was also liable in the amount of EUR 2,928 in respect of social security contributions. When her tax assessment was carried out for that year, as a resident in the Netherlands, she benefited under national law from a general tax credit on both income tax and social security contributions.

The legislation at issue in the main proceedings concerned levies allocated specifically and directly to the funding of social security. That legislation, therefore, has a direct and sufficiently relevant link to the laws that govern the branches of social security listed in Article 3 of Regulation 883/2004 and thus falls within the scope of that Regulation[109]. The dispute in the main proceedings thus concerned a possible restriction to the freedom of movement for workers as a result of a social security measure that forms an integral part of the national social security system (para. 30). The Court concluded that the answer to the question referred to it is that Article 45 TFEU must be interpreted as not precluding legislation of a Member State which, with a view to establishing the amount of social security contributions payable by a worker, provides that the social security component of the tax credit to which a worker is entitled for a calendar year is to be proportionate to the period during which that worker was insured under the social security system of that Member State, thus excluding from that annual credit a fraction proportionate to the period during which that worker was not insured under that system and lived in another Member State where he or she did not engage in a professional activity (para. 50).

---

[109] Judgement of 26 February 2015, *de Ruyter*, C-623/13, EU:C:2015:123, para. 7 and the case law cited.

10.4 Social security contributions and benefits under Article 3 of Regulation 883/2004

In *Dreyer*[110], the Court dealt with a special issue of matching the benefits under certain social security schemes to social security contributions in the context of interpretation of Article 3 Regulation 883/04.

Mr and Mrs Dreyer were French nationals who lived in France and were tax residents of that Member State. Mr Dreyer, who is now retired, spent his entire career working in Switzerland. He and his wife are insured under the Swiss social security scheme. By a tax adjustment notice of 31 October 2016, confirmed by a decision of 6 December 2016, the French tax authorities declared Mr and Mrs Dreyer subject to the general welfare contribution, the social debt repayment contribution, the social levy and additional contributions and the solidarity levy (together 'the contributions and levies at issue') for their income from assets received in France in 2015 in the form of income from choses in action[111]. On the basis that the allowances funded by the contributions and levies at issue administered by the FSV, the CADES and the CNSA were social security contributions, Mr and Mrs Dreyer disputed their liability to those contributions and levies before the French Administrative Court on grounds that they were already insured under the Swiss social security scheme and could not be required to contribute to the funding of the French social security scheme on account of the principle of a single applicable social legislation resulting from Regulation 883/2004.

According to the Court, it is clear from the provisions of the Social Assistance Code that a recipient's resources are not taken into account in conferring entitlement to the APA and PCH, but for the method of calculating those benefits, since the benefits must be granted if the applicant meets the conditions for eligibility, irrespective of his or her resources (para. 37). Taking into account a recipient's resources for the sole purpose of calculating the actual amount of

---

[110] Judgement of the Court of 14 March 2019, Case C-372/18, Ministre de l'Action et des Comptes publics v Mr and Mrs Raymond Dreyer, ECLI:EU:C:2019:206.
[111] The contributions and levies at issue fund three French bodies, namely the Fonds de solidarité vieillesse (Old-Age Solidarity Fund, 'the FSV'), the Caisse d'amortissement de la dette sociale (Social Security Debt Redemption Fund, 'the CADES') and the Caisse nationale de solidarité pour l'autonomie (National Solidarity Fund for Independent Living, 'the CNSA').

APA or PCH on the basis of legally defined objective criteria does not entail an individual assessment by the competent authority of the recipient's personal needs (para. 38). The need to assess, for the purposes of the APA and the PCH, the degree of the applicant's loss of independence or disability also does not entail an individual assessment of that applicant's personal needs. As is clear from the case file submitted to the Court, it cannot be maintained that the granting of the APA and the PCH depends on an individual assessment of the applicant's personal needs within the meaning of the case law cited in paragraph 32 above (para. 39). Furthermore, the APA and PCH cannot be considered 'special non-contributory cash benefits' within the meaning of Article 3(3) of Regulation 883/2004. As both cumulative conditions referred to in para. 32 of that judgement were met and the APA and PCH had to therefore be considered 'social security contributions', there is no need to ascertain whether each of the benefits can also be considered 'special non-contributory cash benefits', as the Court had previously held that both classifications are mutually exclusive[112] (para. 40). Hence, the Court concluded that Article 3 of Regulation 883/2004 must be interpreted as meaning that benefits such as the APA and PCH, must, for the purposes of their classification as 'social security contributions' within the meaning of that provision, be regarded as being granted without any individual assessment of a recipient's personal needs, since the recipient's resources are taken into account for the sole purpose of calculating the actual amount of those benefits on the basis of legally defined objective criteria (para. 41).

11 Conclusion

A review of Court's recent case law reveals that the Court follows a reasonable line of thinking. Generally, the Court's rulings can be considered sufficiently justified, and most importantly, offer efficient protection of social security rights that apply objective criteria which neither undermine the functionality of the coordination mechanism nor the financial balance of social security systems. However, the "problematic" situations that arise with regard to the posting of

---

[112] To that effect, see judgements of 21 February 2006, *Hosse*, C-286/03, EU:C:2006:125, para. 36, and of 16 September 2015, *Commission* v *Slovakia*, C-433/13, EU:C:2015:602, para. 45.

workers, as well as to certain phenomena of artificial arrangements are reflected in the respective judgements, which complicate the application of EU labour and social security laws. The Court seems to approach such cases from the perspective of "prolepsis" with regard to the 'race to the bottom' effect in the field of social security protection and working persons' rights. Ultimately, the Court appears to balance between the requirements of States' planning as far as their social security systems are concerned and the social security protection provided to persons who make use of the freedom of movement, extending the protection provided where possible and well-founded. In other words, the Court opts for the solution in favour of the persons concerned, taking into account the factual circumstances and the margin of Coordination Regulation to enhance social protection in practice.

References

Bourlos, Thanos, The concept of "employer" in the European social security law in the light of the case law of the Court of Justice of the European Union, Social Security Law (Greek Review) 4/2020, pp. 720-727.

Kouziorti, Vasiliki/Stergiou, Angelos, The wage in social security, Labour Law Review (Greek Review), 2014, pp. 65-76.

Schouckens Paul/Pieters, Danny, The rules within Regulation 883/2004 for determining the applicable legislation, European Journal of Social Security, 2009 (1-2), pp. 81-117.

Tsetoura, Anna, Posting in social security: Posting of workers and the binding effect of A1 certificate, Social Security Law (Greek Review) 1/2019, pp. 128-132.

Tsetoura, Anna, The European Pensioner, Athens/Thessaloniki, 2017.

10 Coordination as a Common Language for Social Security and as a Basis for European Solidarity

Angelos Stergiou

As long as no common concept of social security exists in the context of the European Union (EU), "communication" between the Member States on this concept hinges on the configuration of a "common language". It seems that the coordination of social security systems represents an arena within which this common language (lingua franca) between Member States has been evolving. The Coordination Regulation is not a mere extension of the "know-how" of the Bilateral Social Security Conventions. Replacing the latter, the Regulation attempts to unite the different notions and prevailing worldviews of social security in Europe, aiming to resolve (osmosis) the basic dilemma between Bismarck and Beveridge. Behind the declared respect for national approaches, coordination is emerging as a "topos" for the exchange of good practices and the elaboration of common concepts. The application of the Regulation has an impact on all national systems. In other words, the EU influences the reform of national systems subcutaneously both through coordination as well as 'soft law' (open method of coordination). The coordination of national systems ultimately results from the interaction between the coordination mechanism and the national approaches. It would be an exaggeration – albeit not entirely unfounded – to claim that coordination entails elements of harmonisation.[1]

---

[1] On the distinction between coordination and harmonisation, see Frans Pennings, European Social Security Law, 6th ed., 2015, p. 6-7.

Coordination is the interface where European systems meet and where many difference are reconciled; it can therefore also be considered a test of diversity. It may not seem like an overly ambitious goal at first glance, but coordination is more than simply a validation of Member States' systems. Coordination is neither a procedure only, nor is it entirely neutral. Coordination exercises indirectly influence national law through typological generalisations and common definitions, which are deemed necessary for its effective application. For example, the Court of Justice of the European Union (CJEU), through its case law, has provided certain legal definitions of terms such as insurance institution, insured person, contribution, benefit, social assistance, etc. Obviously, these definitions are not *ex ante data* and since they represent a precondition for the application of coordination regulations, *how* their content is formulated is crucial.

This, after all, is the reason why a discussion on Community concepts that do not fall within the competence of national legislators is even taking place. The need to find a common denominator arose because these concepts (signifier and signified) vary across national laws. The concepts at issue were formally formulated by the CJEU or diligently interpreted by the rules themselves. In fact, the Community judicature is not bound by statements made by Member States.[2] Were it not for the common definitions, the application of the Regulation could have easily been bypassed by national legislators. It is crucial for the legal concepts on which the coordination mechanism is based to be uniformly interpreted and applied across the Union. The terms, i.e. the substance of the rules, are (teleologically) defined in accordance with the objectives of coordination, which are no longer limited to facilitating the free movement of workers only.[3]

---

[2] A parallel system of coordination exists for special non-contributory benefits listed in Annex X. The basic characteristic of these hybrid benefits, which fall within the material scope of Regulation 883/2004 (Article 3, para. 3), is that they are either directly or indirectly financed from public means targeted at a social need. It is noteworthy that the CJEU considers the benefits included in Annex X of the Coordination Regulation to be non-decisive. In case CJEU, 8.3.2001, Jauch, C-215/99, the Court concluded that the benefit at issue should not have been included in Annex X.

[3] See Angelos Stergiou, The community judge and the coordination of social security systems, Sakkoulas publications, Athens-Thessaloniki, 1997, p. 44.

According to the CJEU, "contribution" refers to any amount intended for financing social security.[4] This is a very broad understanding of the term 'social security contribution'. Similarly, the Greek Supreme Court sought to broadly define the meaning of insurance contribution within the internal legal order.[5] Another example is the Watts judgment[6]: the CJEU did not reject the National Health Systems' (NHS) waiting lists. However, as EU law requires adequate care to be provided in a timely manner, the NHS was put under pressure to adapt its approach in line with the Court's case law. Generalising these two examples of coordination, we can conclude that the underlying purpose of coordination is the establishment of a system of protection at a high level based on a broad range of financing mechanisms.

Coordination has its own administrative framework. The Administrative Commission of the Coordination of Social Security Systems (Article 72) aims to promote cooperation and dialogue between Member States. The duty of mutual information and cooperation (Article 76 of Regulation 883/2004) facilitates the establishment of common perceptions of social security.

When concepts are not developed under the *ratio* of the Coordination Regulation but within the framework of other legal instruments, such as the Residence Directive, they become narrower and ethnocentric. For example, the concept "social assistance" has recently been treated differently in the context of the free movement of persons and Directive 2004/38/EC. It has been interpreted as "covering all assistance introduced by the public authorities, whether at national, regional or local level, that can be claimed by an individual who does not have resources sufficient to meet his own basic needs".[7] That is, the CJEU, abandoning Regulation 883/2004, has embraced a restrictive concept of European solidarity.[8] Ultimately, what the Dano case law clearly demon-

---

[4] CJEU,15.2.2000, Commission européenne c/ France, C-34/98.
[5] Greek Council of the State 89/2011.
[6] CJEU, 16.5.2006, Watts, C-372/04.
[7] CJEU, 19.9.2013, Brey, C-140/12, thought 61.
[8] The Court has consistently stated that a given benefit can be considered a social security benefit insofar as it is granted to recipients without any individual and discretionary assessment of his/her personal needs on the basis of a legally defined position (une position légalement définie). See CJEU, 15.3.1998, Molenaar C-160/96; CJEU, 27.3.1985, Hoeckx, 249/83; CJEU, 9.10.1974, Biason, 24/74.

strates is that solidarity is linked to the nation state and not to Europe.[9] But is this what we actually want? Does this really contribute to European integration?

Coordination as a common basis for European solidarity

In light of the absence of harmonisation of national laws, the EU took action early on to build bridges between social security systems, so that workers (initially) and individuals (later) could more freely move within the EU's borders without losing their acquired social security rights. The diversity of social security systems results in gaps and overlaps. Proper coordination, namely ensuring that the structure of the different systems converges, prevents negative conflicts, i.e. the possibility that an individual who makes use of his or her right to move freely is not covered by any social security legislation, as well as positive conflicts, i.e. the possibility of being subject to several national legislations, resulting in additional burdens.

In other words, the primary law of the EU does not guarantee that the social security rights of a worker who moves to another Member State other than his/her own will not be affected. Movement between Member States may thus be more or less advantageous for an individual due to the existing differences between social security systems.[10] Nevertheless, Union law, in principle, ensures that the rights of persons who move within EU borders are not violated and that workers are not treated unequally.

As the CJEU has reiterated, Regulation 883/2004 – previously 1408/71 – does not establish a common (single, European) social security system, but allows for separate systems to coexist. Independent claims from the national systems might arise and can be submitted against independent institutions. A beneficiary can raise direct claims against a state's competent institution, either exclusively under domestic law or under domestic law supplemented, if necessary, by Community law.[11]

---

[9] See E. Pataut, Chronique citoyenneté de l'Union Européenne – Quelle solidarité?, RTDEur., 2015, 640.
[10] CJEU, 23.1.2019, Zyla, C-272/17.
[11] CJEU, 28.11.1991, Durighello, C-186/90, thought 15.

The foregoing starting point for coordination is no longer compatible with the evolution of EU law. It no longer suffices to link coordination with the free movement of workers – which is a rather instrumental approach – but is instead essential to integrate coordination into the logic of fundamental rights and in particular in the EU Charter of Fundamental Rights. The Union, as proclaimed in Article 25 of the Charter, recognises and respects the right of the elderly to live a dignified and independent life and to participate in social and cultural life. More generally, the coordination of social security systems should not be limited to a purely technical role. On the contrary, coordination should become a mechanism for organising citizens' mutual solidarity based on appropriate articulation of national social security systems to facilitate the free movement of European citizens.

The EU ceased to be an exclusively single market a long time ago and has been transformed into a civil society. In the case of insured persons, EU citizenship tends to be the "statut fondamental" (fundamental status), which ensures equal legal treatment for those who are in the same situation, regardless of their nationality.[12] As *Prodromos Mavridis* aptly notes, the EU should be awarded the Nobel Prize on the ground of its social protection of third-country nationals.[13] In this context, a new role for coordination should be sought in addition to the protection of acquired rights.

The ghost of "social tourism"[14] is hovering over Europe. National legislators' fears of wandering hordes of poor have materialised. The search for social protection in another Member State is the expression of European solidarity under the aegis of European citizens' social status[15] and cannot be perceived as a threat to the social (welfare) nation state. It is not an export of national social policy, but an expression of solidarity with European citizens who need to be protected, regardless of where within the EU borders they actually reside. On the other hand, rather than closing the borders to national social pro-

---

[12] CJEU, 20.9.2001, Grzelczyk, C-184/99.
[13] See Prodromos Mavridis, Union européenne: un prix Nobel de protection sociale des ressortissants des pays tiers?, Revue de Droit du Travail 2012, 719.
[14] See Prodromos Mavridis, Arrêt Vatsouras: fin du cauchemar du «tourisme social» dans l'Union européenne?, Revue de droit du travail 2009, 671.
[15] See Frans Pennings and Martin Seeleib-Kaiser, EU citizenship and social rights, 2018.

tection, it would be better to raise the level of protection in *all* Member States on the basis of European solidarity.

Although the purpose of coordination has shifted its focus from the free movement of workers towards the free movement of persons, and the fact that the personal scope of coordination currently covers all insured persons in general, the expected promotion of European citizenship has not yet occurred. Instead, we have observed that the promotion of European citizenship is folding. Directive 2004/38/EC on the right of Union citizens and of their families to freely move and reside in Member States' territory now threatens to seriously invalidate Regulation 883/2004 and to annul the compromise reached on the issue of special non-contributory benefits to which "lex loci domicilii" applies. The borders are closed for those who do not have sufficient resources to ensure that the national social state is not overburdened. Discussions have already begun on a possible amendment of Regulation 883/2004. The European Commission presented a proposal on access to social benefits on 13 December 2016, incorporating recent case law.[16] Each Member State must bear responsibility for its poor. When the freedom of citizens who depend on social assistance is limited[17], European solidarity itself is perceived in a restrictive way.

Coordination is characterised by a dynamic that reflects the European course itself. The more the idea of Europe is promoted, the more coordination develops in a positive way. The more it recedes, the more it is entangled in national interests. The new European economic governance calls on Member States to pursue a tight fiscal policy. This "race to the bottom" will also have an impact on coordination. The "golden fiscal rule" for the eurozone, an obsession of some Member States, will also have a detrimental effect on coordination.

---

[16] CJUE, 18.12.2014, Dano, C-133/13.
[17] See Cecilia Bruzelius, Catherine Jacqueson and Martin Seeleib-Kaiser, "(Dis)united in diversity? Social policy and social rights in the EU", in Frans Pennings and Martin Seeleib-Kaiser (eds), EU citizenship and social rights, 2018.

References

Bruzelius, Cecilia/Jacqueson, Catherine/Seeleib-Kaiser, Martin, (Dis)united in diversity? Social policy and social rights in the EU, in Pennings, Frans/Seeleib-Kaiser, Martin (eds), EU citizenship and social rights, Cheltenham, 2018.

Mavridis, Prodromos, Union européenne: un prix Nobel de protection sociale des ressortissants des pays tiers?, Revue de Droit du Travail 2012, pp. 719-729.

Mavridis, Prodromos, Arrêt Vatsouras: fin du cauchemar du «tourisme social» dans l'Union européenne?, Revue de Droit du travail 2009, pp. 671-678.

Pataut, Etienne, Chronique citoyenneté de l'Union Européenne – Quelle solidarité?, RTDEur., 2015, p. 640.

Pennings, Frans, European Social Security Law, 6th ed., Cambridge, UK, 2015.

Pennings, Frans/Seeleib-Kaiser, Martin, EU citizenship and social rights, Cheltenham, 2018.

Stergiou, Angelos, The community judge and the coordination of social security systems, Athens/Thessaloniki, 1997.

List of Contributors

Effrosyni Bakirtzi, LL.M, studied law in Thessaloniki (Greece), Rome (Italy) and Frankfurt (Germany). Since 2020, she is the Coordinator of the academic research project "Social Security Coordination and Migration: A German-Greek Perspective (2020-2022)" at the University of Applied Sciences Fulda in Germany. Previously, Bakirtzi held a fellowship at the collaborative Doctoral Programme on Social Human Rights of the University of Kassel and the University of Applied Sciences Fulda (Germany). Bakirtzi is a member of the Academic Network on the European Social Charter and Social Rights (ANESC), the Greek Association for Labour Law and Social Security Law (EDEKA), the European Institute for Social Security (EISS) and the Serres Bar Association (Greece). Her previous books include *Civil Status Certificates with Foreign Elements* (2009) (with Eirini Tsifopoulou in Greek) and *Case Studies in Merging the Administrations of Social Security Contribution and Taxation* (2011) (with Danny Pieters and Paul Schoukens). Her papers have been published by, among other outlets, the *Hellenic Review of European Law*, the (Greek) *Social Security Law Review*, the *VSSAR – Vierteljahresschrift für Sozial- und Arbeitsrecht*, the *ZESAR – Zeitschrift für europäisches Sozial- und Arbeitsrecht* and the *Online Journal of the Greek Association of Labour and Social Security Law* (edeka.gr).

Linda Bojanowski, LL.M., studied Social Law and Social Economy in Fulda and Kassel. Since 2019 she is Senior Administration Expert at the National Association Health Insurance Funds – German Liaison Agency Heath Insurance – International (GKV-Spitzenverband, DVKA) in Bonn and lecturer for the module "European Social (Insurance) Law" at the University of Applied Sciences Fulda.

Stamatia Devetzi is Professor of Social Security Law at the University of Applied Sciences in Fulda, Germany. She studied law in Athens, Rome and Osnabrück, has a diploma in law from the Law Faculty of University of Athens

(1994) and a PhD from Osnabrück University (1998). After working as a legal expert with the German Pensions Insurance Institution (1998-2003), in 2003 she became professor in Fulda. From 2011-2016 she was delegated as professor for Public Law and European Social Security Law at Osnabrück University, Faculty of Law. She is member of the advisory board of FNA (Research Institute of the German Pensions Insurance) and of FIS (Network for Interdisciplinary Research on Social Policy, funded by the German Ministry of Labour. Her previous books include *Die Kollisionsnormen des Europäischen Sozialrechts* (Duncker & Humblot, 2000), *Die offene Methode der Koordinierung und das Europäische Sozialmodell* (Ibidem, 2009, editor with Hans Platzer), *Too Sick to Work?* (Kluwer, 2011, editor with Sara Stendahl) and *Social Security in Times of Corona* (Sakkoulas, 2021, with Angelos Stergiou). Her papers have been published by, among other outlets, the *European Journal of Social Security*, the *European Journal of Migration and Law*, and *ZESAR – Zeitschrift für europäisches Sozial- und Arbeitsrecht*.

Eberhard Eichenhofer was born 1950; after studies at the universities of Tübingen and Saarbrücken he received 1979 a doctoral degree by the Universität des Saarlandes, Saarbrücken. Between 1980 and 1982 he worked as law clerk at the Federal Court for Social Law. From 1982 till 1989 he was researcher at the Max-Planck-Institut für ausländisches und internationales Sozialrecht Munich. 1987 he received the degree of a facultas docendi (= Habilitation) by the Universität des Saarlandes Saarbrücken with an inquiry on the topic: international social security and social welfare law and private international law. 1989 he became Professor for civil law and social security law at the universities Osnabrück (till 1997) und Jena (1997-2016). His recent books include: *Werner Maihofer, Vordenker des Sozialliberalismus* (Grimma, 2022); *Sozialrecht*, 2021 (12th edition), translated in Mandarin 2019 and Korean 2021; *Sozialrecht der Europäischen Union*, 2022 (8th edition); *The Law of the Activating Welfare State*, 2015; *Soziale Menschenrechte im Völker-, Europa- und deutschen Recht* (Social human rights in international public, European and German Law), 2012.

Daniel Hlava is Professor of Health and Social Security Law at the Frankfurt University of Applied Sciences in Germany since October 2021. He studied Social Law in Fulda and Kassel. From July 2014 to March 2022, Hlava was an expert for Social Law and European Labour Law at the Hugo Sinzheimer Institute for Labour and Social Security Law (HSI) of the Hans Böckler Foundation in Frankfurt. He is co-editor of the HSI REPORT ON EUROPEAN LABOUR AND SOCIAL SECURITY LAW. His papers have been published by, among other outlets, in NEUE ZEITSCHRIFT FÜR SOZIALRECHT, NEUE ZEITSCHRIFT FÜR ARBEITSRECHT, ARBEIT UND RECHT and on the website www.hugo-sinzheimer-institut.de.

Moira Kettner studied law in Passau, Cracow and Bonn. In 2015 she joined the Division "Coordination of Social Security Systems" at the German Federal Ministry of Labour and Social Affairs, since 2021 she is head of that Division. Previously, Moira Kettner held positions as desk officer at the Ministry's Directorate-General for Matters Concerning Persons with Disabilities and as labour attachee at the German Embassy in Ankara.

Stefanie Klein, LL.M., is Head of the Liaison Body of the Social Accident Insurance in Duisburg. From 2011-2016 she served as a lawyer and general counsel at SOKA-BAU's European Department in Wiesbaden, preceded by a period from 2004-2011 as a Lawyer at the National Association of Statutory Health Insurance Funds, Liaison Body Health Insurance, in Bonn. Before, she had worked in London followed by studies of law at the universities of Jena, Tilburg (NL) and Cologne. She holds a Master in European Social Security of the University of Leuven, passed the Cours de Civilisation Française de la Sorbonne and the Certificat de Français Juridique de la Chambre de Commerce et d'Industrie, Paris. Since 2017, she serves as Judge of Honour at the German Federal Social Court, Kassel.

Anna Rizou is a social security expert and is the Director of the Directorate for Special Insurance and benefits at the Ministry of Labor and Social Affairs of Greece. She is the representative of Greece in the Administrative Committee and the Advisory Committee for the coordination of the social security systems of the European Commission. For many years, she has been dealing with the implementation of the provisions of European Regulations 883/04 and 987/09 on the coordination of social security systems in the Member States, as well as the preparation, negotiation and conclusion of Bilateral Social Security Agreements with third countries.

Dr. Anna Tsetoura studied Law in Thessaloniki (Greece) and European Social Security Law in Leuven (Belgium). Since 2018, she is member of the teaching staff of social sciences faculty at the Hellenic Open University in Greece. Previously Tsetoura held Associate of the Greek journal REVIEW OF SOCIAL SECURITY LAW (EDKA). Tsetoura is a member of the Scientific Committee of the Journal Social Security Law (DtKA), of the "Social Administration Research Lab – SARL", Social Policy Unit (University of West Attica) and Member of Alexandroupolis Legal Bar Association. Her previous books include THE EUROPEAN PENSIONER, Sakkoulas publications, 2017 and THE FREE MOVEMENT OF PERSONS IN THE EUROPEAN SOCIAL MODEL, Papazisi, 2019. Her papers have been published by, among other outlets EUROPEAN JOURNAL OF SOCIAL SECURITY, SOCIAL SECURITY LAW (Greek review) and SOCIAL COHESION AND DEVELOPMENT.

**AN INTERDISCIPLINARY SERIES
OF THE CENTRE FOR INTERCULTURAL AND EUROPEAN STUDIES**

**INTERDISZIPLINÄRE SCHRIFTENREIHE
DES CENTRUMS FÜR INTERKULTURELLE UND EUROPÄISCHE STUDIEN**

CINTEUS • Fulda University of Applied Sciences • Hochschule Fulda
ISSN 1865-2255

1 *Julia Neumeyer*
Malta and the European Union
A small island state and its way into a powerful community
ISBN 978-3-89821-814-6

2 *Beste İşleyen*
The European Union in the Middle East Peace Process
A Civilian Power?
ISBN 978-3-89821-896-2

3 *Pia Tamke*
Die Europäisierung des deutschen Apothekenrechts
Europarechtliche Notwendigkeit und nationalrechtliche Vertretbarkeit einer Liberalisierung
ISBN 978-3-89821-964-8

4 *Stamatia Devetzi und Hans-Wolfgang Platzer (Hrsg.)*
Offene Methode der Koordinierung und Europäisches Sozialmodell
Interdisziplinäre Perspektiven
ISBN 978-3-89821-994-5

5 *Andrea Rudolf*
Biokraftstoffpolitik und Ernährungssicherheit
Die Auswirkungen der EU-Politik auf die Nahrungsmittelproduktion am Beispiel Brasilien
ISBN 978-3-8382-0099-6

6 *Gudrun Hentges / Justyna Staszczak*
Geduldet, nicht erwünscht
Auswirkungen der Bleiberechtsregelung auf die Lebenssituation geduldeter Flüchtlinge in Deutschland
ISBN 978-3-8382-0080-4

7 *Barbara Lewandowska-Tomaszczyk / Hanna Pułaczewska (ed. / Hrsg.)*
Intercultural Europe
Arenas of Difference, Communication and Mediation
ISBN 978-3-8382-0198-6

8 *Janina Henning*
In Dubio Pro Europa?
An Analysis of the European External Action Structures after the Treaty of Lisbon
ISBN 978-3-8382-0298-1

9 *Claas Oehlmann*
Europa auf dem Weg zur Recycling-Gesellschaft?
Die EU-Rohstoffinitiative im Kontext der Strategie Europa 2020
ISBN 978-3-8382-0401-7

10 *Volker Hinnenkamp / Hans-Wolfgang Platzer (ed. / Hrsg.)*
Interkulturalität und Europäische Integration
ISBN 978-3-8382-0573-1

11 *Vera Axyonova*
The European Union's Democratization Policy for Central Asia
Failed in Success or Succeeded in Failure?
ISBN 978-3-8382-0614-1

12 *Lisa Moessing*
Lobbying Uncovered?
Lobbying Registration in the European Union and the United States
ISBN 978-3-8382-0616-5

13 *Andreas Herberg-Rothe (ed.)*
Lessons from World War I for the Rise of Asia
ISBN 978-3-8382-0791-9

14 *Agnieszka Satola*
Migration und irreguläre
Pflegearbeit in Deutschland
Eine biographische Studie
ISBN 978-3-8382-0692-9

15 *Vera Axyonova (ed.)*
European Engagement under
Review
Exporting Values, Rules, and Practices
to the Post-Soviet Space
ISBN 978-3-8382-0860-2

16 *Işıl Erduyan*
Multilingual Construction of
Identity
German-Turkish Adolescents at School
ISBN 978-3-8382-1201-2

17 *Hans-Wolfgang Platzer*
Bronislaw Huberman und das
Vaterland Europa
Ein Violinvirtuose als Vordenker der
europäischen Einigungsbewegung in
den 1920er und 1930er Jahren
ISBN 978-3-8382-1354-5

18 *Aileen Heid*
Erinnerungspolitik
Nordirlands langer Weg zum Frieden
ISBN 978-3-8382-1351-4

19 *Juliana Damm, Maren Mlynek*
Die AfD und Geflüchtete
Was rechte Ideologie gesellschaftlich
bewirkt
ISBN 978-3-8382-1448-1

20 *Julian Wessendorf*
Euroskeptizismus auf dem
Vormarsch
Positionen der politischen Rechten im
Europaparlament
ISBN 978-3-8382-1557-0

21 *Kirsten Nazarkiewicz,*
Norbert Schröer (Hrsg.)
Verständigung
in pluralen Welten
ISBN 978-3-8382-1345-3

22 *Stamatia Devetzi (Ed.)*
Practical issues of European
Social Security Law: A Dialogue
between Academia and
Practitioners
ISBN 978-3-8382-1706-2

ibidem.eu